Turning
Church Members
into
Disciple Makers

A Few Words About the Book and Its Author

"Many recognize the "why" behind Christ's commission to make disciples but struggle with "how" to fulfill that vision. Tim's insight blends a solid foundation with practical application that instills confidence in those who desire to lead others to Christ. The reader will especially appreciate the diversity in approaches that open the door to sharing our faith."

– DR. JOHN DERRY, President Emeritus, Hope International University

Dr. Wallingford's excellent book, *Turning Church Members into Disciple Makers*, is especially timely as churches ramp up their efforts to reach people following the challenges caused by COVID-19. This book is one of the best books on apologetics, evangelism, and discipleship I've ever read. It is clear, direct, practical, and full of Scripture references. Plus, the writing style has the unusual strength of being both incredibly thorough yet easy to study and understand. I pray it is widely read, discussed, and applied.

– DR. KREGG HOOD, VP, Convoy of Hope, Springfield, MO

Tim Wallingford does Paul Little one better! *How To Give Away Your Faith* was the basic manual for many who desired to be more effective in reaching others for Christ. Tim's book provides deeper insights; a broader, multi-cultural context; and a more biblical approach to help live out the purpose and mission of God. I especially appreciated his "Let's Wrap it Up" and "Challenge" sections to clarify issues and move us to action. Wonderful book for the church today!

– DR. LARRY CARTER, President, Great Lakes Christian College

Jesus gave the Church a dual challenge in the great commission: evangelize the lost and edify the saved. Most churches are more effective at evangelism, the dramatic part, than they are at discipleship, the tedious part. As a result, many new converts slowly drift away or never mature. In this stimulating book, Tim Wallingford makes practical applications from the book of Acts to illustrate ways we can turn "church attending Christians" into believers who "grow up into him who is the Head, that is, Christ" (Ephesians 4:15). Emphasizing the principles of this book will deepen your church and produce disciples who make disciples.

— **BOB RUSSELL**, Retired Minister, Southeast Christian Church, Louisville, KY

Tim Wallingford has captured a new and fantastic way to view outreach and evangelism in *this* century through *first*-century conversions in the NT book of Acts. As I have heard him share these practical and Biblical nuggets of truth, I am amazed at how timely they are in a post-COVID world. I wholeheartedly recommend this book for sharpening your conversations that lead to *conversions* in the life of your church.'

— **DAVID VAUGHAN**, Senior Pastor, Whitewater Crossing Christian Church, Cincinnati, OH

I have the privilege of being Tim Wallingford's friend for a lifetime. I'm happy to endorse *Turing Church Members into Disciple Makers* because I know Tim is a practitioner and not just a theorist and academic. Tim's work reflects both academic integrity (Chapter Two is worth the price of the book!) and practical principles (Part Two). It is a useful tool for anyone interested in being a disciple who makes disciples that make disciples. I give Tim and his work my highest recommendation.

— **JEFF METZGER**, Senior Pastor, River Hills Christian Church, Loveland, OH

We are blessed, God is glorified, and the angels rejoice when we become followers of Christ. All of this is magnified when we become disciple makers. Tim Wallingford's book inspires and challenges us to actively participate in Christ's command to: "Go and make Disciples"

— **DR. GENE WIGGINTON**, Former President, *The Christian Standard* and Elder, First Christian Chuch, Johnson City, TN

"Jesus' mission was clear. Drawing from the Scriptures and from his own experiences in ministry, Tim Wallingford answers the 'Why' and the 'How' of making disciples. Now the question is 'Who'? Will we respond to the Lord's call and join the Lord in his mission to see lost people reconciled to God?"

— **DAVE FAUST**, Executive Minister, East 91st Street, Indianapolis, IN

Acknowledgments

I want to thank Larae Thompson who has assisted my ministry for nearly twenty years. Larae has helped check the manuscript for accuracy, fixed the grammar, selected the cover, and framed the book. Her assistance was invaluable! I also want to acknowledge Shawn McMullen, a friend in Christ, for proofing the document and giving helpful feedback and suggestions.

Table of Contents

Introduction

The gospel of Matthew records that as Jesus walked along the Sea of Galilee, he stopped to watch Peter and Andrew "casting a net into the sea, for they were fishermen" (Matthew 4:18). That's when Jesus called out, "Follow me, and I will make you fishers of men" (Matthew 4:19). Immediately Peter and Andrew left their nets and embarked on a disciple-making adventure that "turned the world upside down" (Acts 17:6).

Like catching fish, making disciples is not an automatic skill Christians acquire at baptism. Sharing the gospel and leading others to salvation involves educating, training, and perfecting through practice. Notice Jesus said, "I will *make* you fishers of men." The word "make" in the Greek is *poieo*. It can mean to manufacture for a specific purpose, to fashion into something useful, or to craft a harmonious poem.[1] The word is also translated in Ephesians 2:10 as God's "workmanship" (*ESV*) or "masterpiece" (*NLT*). Jesus shaped the twelve disciples into expert "master" disciple makers. So, what was his method of training?

First, the **CALL** to be his follower includes bringing the lost to Jesus. It's not exclusive to preachers or believers who claim evangelism is their gift. Jesus has the same expectation for every Christian from every nation, in every generation. The Great Commission is for you, me, each one of us: "Go, make disciples" (Matthew 28:18-20).

Second, every congregation must make disciple making a **PRIORITY** with a training process to equip believers to share the gospel. Experienced "fishers of men" teach the next generation to love and reach lost people (2 Timothy 2:2). If they do not, the church will decline and the number of people going to hell is exacerbated.

---

1. Biblehub.com/lexicon/matthew/4-19.htm

Third, for several years Jesus was a **MODEL** of the disciple-making lifestyle. He took the twelve with him into the neighborhoods of Judea, Galilee, Perea, the territory of Philippi, and "all" Syria (Matthew 4:24). It was in his DNA. The disciples observed, listened, and asked questions about presenting the good news. They watched Jesus meet the neighbors, learn their names, hear their needs, eat with, and *minister to the individual.* Jesus was a *friend to sinners* (Matthew 11:19). Jesus had compassion for people because "they were harassed and helpless, like sheep without a shepherd" (Matthew 9:36).

Finally, fishers of men **DO** fishing. As we go throughout our days we encounter friends, family members, coworkers, and acquaintances God has placed in our paths to point them to Jesus. If we don't tell them, who will? The apostle Paul asked, "How can they hear about him unless someone tells them?" (Romans 10:14, *NLT*).

The Christian life is a **MISSION** to glorify God through holy living and "saving others by snatching them out of the fire" (Jude 23). Both are important in being faithful to Jesus. Do members in our congregations understand Christ's expectations? Are church leaders equipping members to be the salt and light of the world? The apostle Paul exhorts us, "For we will all stand before Christ to be judged. We will receive whatever we deserve for the good or evil we have done in this earthly body" (2 Corinthians 5:10, *NLT*).

Let's start today and invest in what really matters; holy living and intentionally snatching our friends out of the fire. My prayer is that through this book and the accompanying video training resources we can embrace Christ's call, his love for lost people, his message, and the techniques that bring the beautiful gospel to needy, broken, and hurting people.

As we commit to a life of disciple making, the Lord promises to produce fruit in and through us (John 15:5). Imagine standing in heaven and seeing people there because God used you to lead them to Christ! This will be part of your crown and eternal reward (Philippians 4:1; I Thessalonians 2:19).

Our Approach: Turning Church Members into Disciple Makers

This book is divided into two sections: *God's Purpose for Every Christian* and *Engaging My Neighborhood with Good News.*

The first section defines God's purpose for every believer. Turning members of the church into disciple makers begins with the member understanding and embracing his or her new identity in Christ. Jesus said, "I will build my *ekklesia* (church)" (Matthew 16:18). Members are Christ's body, his "called out ones to be trained to do God's work." Christ *empowers* the members of his body with his Holy Spirit to *expand* his kingdom family by sharing the gospel. Those added to the *ekklesia* are to be *equipped* to make more disciples. We are to continue the process until Jesus returns.

The second section moves the disciple makers into the neighborhoods to fulfill their purposes and make disciples within their circles of influence. Sharing the gospel message can be a little complicated. There's more to it than just telling somebody what the gospel is and how to respond. Each person has his or her own baggage— cultural, intellectual, and emotional barriers—that need to be removed before the simple gospel can take root in the heart. Luke, the author of Acts, revealed to us *spiritual profiles*. There are different types of people that the various evangelists encounter: The religious (Acts 2), the hurting (Acts 3), the occultist (Acts 8), the seeker (Acts 8), the fanatic (Acts 9), the good person (Acts 10), the successful (Acts 16), the skeptic (Acts 17), the misinformed (Acts 19), and the hedonist (Acts 24). Actually, Luke is introducing us to his neighborhood. Every spiritual profile has a certain distortion of God that needs to be corrected before a person becomes ready to embrace the gospel. You will learn all the distortions with biblical responses.

It's amazing how relevant the Bible is today. You meet these people in your neighborhood too. God will use Luke to equip us for effective work redeeming our neighborhood with the very same gospel the Holy Spirit presented in Acts 2. The gospel never changes but we have to package the gospel differently based on the barriers that exist in different people.

Let's get started and become disciple makers!

PART ONE
Evangelism: God's Purpose for Every Christian

CHAPTER ONE
The Enlightened Church

"It is God who directs the lives of his creatures;
everyone's life is in his power"
(Job 12:10, *TEV*).

"The Lord has made everything for his own purpose,
even the wicked for punishment"
(Proverbs 16:3, *TLB*).

Your purpose in life is far greater than your happiness, your family, your career, or your wildest dreams and ambitions. If you want to know why you are here on planet earth, the best advice I can give is to listen less to people and more to God. The reason? God made you, and he created you for **his** purpose.

Finding your purpose in life is a major pursuit. As a matter of fact, many Americans are being diagnosed with "Purpose Anxiety."[2] Studies show that if a person does not live with a clear and defining purpose, it can lead to psychological illness."[3] The book of Ecclesiastes tells us about Solomon's search for purpose. After dabbling in just about everything "under the sun," he declared, "But as I looked at everything I had tried, it was all so useless, a chasing of the wind, and

---

2. Rainey, Larissa. The Search for Purpose in Life. Scholarly Commons. Page 45
    Repository.upenn.edu/cgi/viewcontent.cgi?article=1061&content=mapp_capstone. Rainey, Larissa. The Search for Purpose in Life. Scholarly Commons.
3. Ibid p. 41

there was nothing really worthwhile anywhere" (Ecclesiastes 2:11, *TLB*).

A 2012 study revealed that 72 percent of college students and nearly 60 percent of working adults stated their purpose in life was to "make a positive impact on the world."[4] That sounds good, but the million-dollar questions are what does that mean? And how is it accomplished?

This book will be your guide to discovering, embracing, enjoying, and implementing your God-given purpose in life. The goal is so that when we one day stand before God, we will hear these words, "Well done good and faithful servant, enter in the place prepared for you" (Matthew 25:21).

So, what is my God-given purpose? What is God expecting me to do? How do I find my purpose and live it out? Our journey takes us back to the beginning, to Genesis 1-3, to see God's original plan for each of us.

The Scripture depicts our former lives as "darkness" and our new lives as "light" (Ephesians 5:8). Darkness hides and light reveals. "The teaching of your word gives light, so even the simple can understand" (Psalm 119:130, *NLT*). The apostle Paul declared that the believer's "eyes" have been "enlightened" (See Ephesians 5:17-23). The Greek word is *photizo*. The idea is to make something fully known. We would say, "to shed light on the matter." God's Word will shed light on his purpose for your life.

Scripture also states that purpose is tied to identity. Knowing *who* we are "in Christ" determines *what* we do. Not being "in Christ," we find ourselves "in" something else. For example, sports fanatics find their identities in a team. What they *do* is invest huge amounts of time and money vicariously living life through their heroes. Workaholics find their identities in their jobs.

Who are you? Examine your priorities, behavior, and the content of your weekly conversations. It will reflect who you perceive "you" to be. What was God's original purpose for humanity? Adam and Eve enjoyed a face-to-face relationship with God as they managed God's world (Genesis 2, 3). All was perfect until they wanted to be "as god," ate of the forbidden fruit, and in that rebellion lost the relationship and the managerial leadership of God's creation.

What is God's *new purpose* for humanity found in the New Covenant? It is a twofold purpose: first to be *reconciled* to God through the cross of Christ. This means we recover God's image lost in sin by taking on and being transformed into

---

4. Ibid. p. 9

Christ's character. We also embrace *Christ's mission*—we make disciples (Matthew 28:18-20). Second, it means we will *reign* with God once again on the new heaven and earth (Revelation 22:5).

God's Original Purpose

Humankind was created to know God personally and partner in God's work. This includes fellowship with God and others (Genesis 3:8) and the management of God's world (Genesis 1:28). Scripture makes it clear that God desired a close, voluntary, and collaborative relationship. The friendship was rich and fulfilling.

When God saw there was no helpmate suitable for Adam among all the animals, God put Adam to sleep and from his own rib created a wife. The Lord brought her to the man, and it was Adam who named her "woman" (Genesis 2:23). God walked with Adam and Eve in the cool of the evenings (Genesis 3:8). Regarding the management of God's world Genesis 2:15 states that Adam and Eve were placed in the garden to "work it and keep it." One example of Adam's managerial leadership was to name every living animal and bird, and we are told, "Whatever the man called a living creature, that was its name (Genesis 2:19).

God also created humankind with freewill, which placed the future of the earth in the hands of Adam and Eve. They could choose to reject God's purpose for their lives, at any time, by simply eating the fruit of the tree of knowledge of good and evil (Genesis 2:17). God had commanded Adam not to eat from the tree or he would "die," translated from the Hebrew term *muwth*, meaning "worthy of death."[5] Colin Brown connects the word to Hellenistic interpretation, suggesting separation or bringing to an end.[6]

Humanity Rejecting God's Purpose

After the inauguration of the partnership, Satan introduced himself to Adam and Eve in the form of a serpent. He slandered God and presented lies about his character.

---

5. James Strong, *Hebrew and Chaldee Dictionary Accompanying the Exhaustive Concordance* (n.d.), s.v. "muwth."
6. Brown, Colin. *The New International Dictionary of New Testament Theology*. Vol. I. Zondervan Publishing. Grand Rapids, MI. 1975. P. 432

Eve believed the propaganda and rejected God's rule and purpose. It appeared as if Adam followed Eve's lead, both ate of the tree. Both desired to be their own god (Genesis 3:5) and both chose to elevate their own agenda above God's purpose.

That first sin brought catastrophic consequences: Adam and Eve were cast out of the Garden and separated from God. The relationship was broken and their managerial responsibilities removed. Sin changed everything. It brought guilt, shame, fear, irresponsibility, self-centered living, and death. Frustration and tension became the norm with both creation and relationships. The once perfect world in the Garden was marred by manipulation and deceit (Genesis 3).

Sin poisoned the earth, brought decay, and initiated the earth's eventual destruction (2 Peter 3:7). The physical universe now opposes humanity through disease, storms, earthquakes, famine, weeds, and pestilence (Romans 8: 18-21). As I write this today, the world is essentially shut down due to the COVID-19 virus, which serves to illustrate the dire consequence of sin. God made humans "king of the earth," but their rejection of God through the devil's schemes gave Satan undue influence to "steal and kill and destroy" (John 10:10). Thankfully, this is not the end of the story. God loved us enough to create a pathway to a restoration of his purpose.

God Restoring Humanity's Purpose

After the fall, Genesis 3-6 (as well as other Scriptures) illustrates how the human heart became diseased with a propensity to sin. Truly, humanity had failed as God's stewards and came under the bondage of the evil master, Satan, who rules the minds and hearts of people (John 12:31, 14:30).

As absolute ruler, God could have judged and destroyed his creation. The flood came close, but God's grace saved Noah. His family and future generations were spared. God's plan would restore the relationship and humanity's managerial position on the "new" earth (Revelation 21:1). That redemptive plan corresponds to the two aspects of God's purpose; to restore the relationship and finally to restore God's people as managerial leaders of the new earth.

PHASE 1:
Restore the Relationship

Phase 1 was first announced in Genesis 3:15. The prophecy gives little detail but in general terms the serpent will bruise the heel of the one born of a woman. The one born will then crush the serpent's head. Obviously, the bruising of the heel represents a temporary blow, and the crushing of the head is permanent!

The New Testament interprets the prophecy as the work of Christ. The bruising occurred on the cross, in a willing sacrifice that paid our sin debt. The crushing of the serpent's head represents Jesus dealing "a crushing defeat of the usurper's sin and death, with the reestablishment of Christ's rule through his resurrection."[7] Through the gospel of Jesus Christ, people can have their sins forgiven and their broken relationships with God restored.

The Gospel

The gospel of Jesus Christ is the very core of Christianity. The apostle Paul calls it of "first importance" (1 Corinthians 15:1). It appears 76 times in the New Testament as a noun and 54 times as a verb. You will also see it modified in various ways, like "the gospel of God" (Mark 1:14), "The gospel of Jesus Christ" (Mark 1:1), "The eternal gospel" (Revelation 14:6), and "The gospel of peace" (Ephesians 6:15). Each magnify an insight or benefit of the gospel.

The heart of the gospel is that Jesus died for our sins, was buried, and then rose on the third day (1 Corinthians 15:3,4; Romans 5:8-11). It was predicted throughout the Old Testament Scriptures (E.g., Psalm 16:10; Isaiah 52:7; 53: 8-10; 61:1) and then actualized in Jesus (John 5:45-47). It is anchored in our lives when we respond to the gospel in specific ways.

Accept the Gospel

Each individual must believe and trust the good news that Jesus died for their sins and make Jesus their personal Lord and Savior (Acts 2:36). Through faith, and in baptism, Christ removes the disease and deadness of the believer's heart through a spiritual surgery (Colossians 2:11, 12). God gives a new heart that seeks to know, love, and obey God (Ezekiel 11:19-21; Romans 8: 10-17; 2 Peter 2:4). The

---

7. Jack Cottrell, *What the Bible Says About God the Ruler* (Joplin, MO: College Press, 1984), 120.

indwelling of God's Spirit gives the power to overcome the temptations of the flesh (See Romans 6; 1 Corinthians 10:13).

Take on the Character of Christ

Believers daily renew their minds through Scripture (Romans 12:2) by impressing God's Word into their new, soft, receptive hearts. With time, the Holy Spirit transforms the character in conjunction with the believer's obedience. The goal of the transformation process is that every believer reflects the character of Christ (Ephesians 5:1)!

The New Testament term for this process is *sanctification* (Romans 6:19, 22; 2 Thessalonians 2:13). Christians are called "saints" hundreds of times (Romans 1:7). The term generally means the "set apart ones," or "the holy ones." God does not view believers as "sinners," but rather "saints." Every believer is to spiritually grow up into Christ's character. The New Testament compares the spiritual maturation to stages of physical growth. In baptism, a believer is categorized as "born again" (John 3:3).

The apostle Paul refers to "infants" (1 Corinthians 3:1). The apostle John identifies "little children" (John 2:12), "young men" (1 John 2:13), and finally spiritual "fathers" (1 John 2:14). *This is your first God-given purpose: to grow up by taking on Christ's character!* The function of church leaders (1 Thessalonians 2:7-12) is to provide spiritual parenting and equip God's children to grow up in the faith. Elders, teachers, and preachers do this in Christ-centered relationships that instruct, model, and mentor God's children (See Ephesians 4:11 - 6:20).

Take on the Mission of Christ

The restored identity "in Christ" includes a *new character* and a *new mission*. This is God's new purpose for you while on planet earth! It is every believer's mission and reason for existence as God's new creation (2 Corinthians 5:17). "You are a chosen race, a royal priesthood, a holy nation, a people for his own possession" (1 Peter 2:9a). The apostle Peter states the Christian's purpose is, "that you may proclaim the excellencies of him who called you out of darkness into his marvelous light" (1 Peter 2:9b). The Greek word for proclaim is *exaggello*. It defines the person as, "a messenger who speaks and acts in place of one who has sent him."[8] The word also denotes the function of "telling the message completely,

---

8. https://www.preceptaustin.org/1_peter_29-10

and to make the message widely known. The idea is to tell everyone, everywhere the message!"

Now compare the believer's mission of *"proclaiming* the excellencies of God" to the original word for *gospel.* The Greek word is *euaggelion.* Look familiar? It is a compound word derived from *eu,* which means good, and *aggello,* which means a messenger who proclaims and tells. This is the same as proclaiming, right? The gospel includes *telling* the good news of salvation in Christ. Before the time of Jesus, in the Greco-Roman culture, *euaggelion* was the technical term for "news of victory."[9] A runner was assigned by the general to race back to the city and declare the fact that their army had won the battle. Just seeing the runner coming from a distance was good news. He would raise his hand and declare "Rejoice! We are the victors"[10] Paul wrote to the Corinthians, "We preach Christ" (1 Corinthians 1:23). The Greek word for preach is *kerrusso.* Like *euaggelion, kerrusso* conveys the idea of a king's messenger running throughout the city proclaiming the latest news of the king.

PHASE 2:
Restore God's People as Managerial Leaders of the New Earth

After Judgment, Satan and his followers will be thrown into the Lake of Fire (Revelation 20:10). Christ then leads his followers to the new earth (Revelation 21). The dimensions of heavens' city given by John are 12,000 stadia in every direction (Revelation 21:16). Figured literally, that would equate to 2.7 billion cubic miles. Revelation describes gardens, beautiful lights in the sky, a sea as calm as glass, rivers, and streams, trees, mansions, banquet tables, wonderful friendships, work, worship, and much more. It is only after the Second Coming that Christians will reign with Christ as managerial leaders of the new world (Revelation 4:4).

LET'S WRAP UP

Since our relationships with God are restored, Christians have two new purposes while on planet earth: To take on *Christ's character,* and to pursue *Christ's mission.*

---

9. Ibid
10. The Correct Meaning of "Church" and "Ecclesia." aggressivechristianity.net/articles/ecclesia.htm. Accessed August 13, 2021.

PHASE 1:
Restore the Relationship

Is there a necessary order? Do Christians first take on Christ's character and then carry out Christ's mission? While there is a prescribed order, we do both simultaneously. The Greek construction of Jesus' Great Commission states, "Go into all the world" (Matthew 28:19). This may also be read, "As you go." Throughout our days we have opportunities to proclaim God's excellencies by publicly acting out Christ's character and verbally proclaiming the good news to people. We approach people the way Jesus did. We interact and treat people the way Jesus did. We talk about the gospel the way Jesus did. All this flows from putting on Christ's character daily (Ephesians 4:24). So, we take on Christ's character and do Christ's mission simultaneously.

On the other hand, our character transformation is what authenticates the good news that we verbally share. If we are choosing to live in sin, telling others that Jesus changes lives is a poor witness and can do more harm than good. A changing life is *miraculous proof* that Jesus is alive and working in us.

This is why the primary purpose of the Sunday gathering is to equip the saved. Each week, believers are taught and nurtured to grow up into Christ's character and trained to share the good news; both of which are lived out in the neighborhood during the week. We then come back the next Sunday to get our questions answered about encounters we had the past week. As we make disciples, we are discipled.

PHASE 2:
Restore God's People as Managers of the Earth

You might be thinking, "Wait a minute! Are not Christians reinstated as managerial leaders of this world? Is not that role automatically reinstated when we become a Christian? No. Again, the world is still corrupted by sin and will eventually be destroyed (2 Peter 3:7; Matthew 24:29-31). The "god of this word" is still wreaking havoc. The world is in rebellion against humanity and refuses to submit to humanity's oversight. People cannot manage the world because the earth refuses to be managed.

Purpose Confusion

Many well-intentioned believers are confused in thinking our purpose in Phase 1 includes being reinstated as managers of God's world. This faulty belief comes by misinterpreting our Lord's prayer in Matthew 6:10. "Your kingdom come, your will be done, on earth as it is in heaven." Here are three common misinterpretations:

1. Social Gospel: One component of *progressive* belief states that Christ's sacrifice on the cross universally removes sin. Therefore, the Christian's work is not gospel proclamation (everyone is saved), but the physical restoration of the local, national, and global neighborhood. This is known as the *social gospel*. It teaches that Christ removed all sin at the cross, and therefore any wicked habit that needs to be purged or paid for by the individual happens after death for a short period in hades. Once purged, the "sanctified" person is transported to heaven!

2. Restore Justice and Mercy: A belief held by more *conservative* believers is that Christians are first responsible to do works of kindness and restore the community. When *community systems* begin to reflect fairness, justice, and love, the Holy Spirit will launch a spiritual revival that opens the hearts of people for the proclamation of the gospel.

3. Corporate Worship: The Scripture commands believers to gather regularly for fellowship, edification, teaching, prayer, and the Lord's Supper (Acts 2:42). It was so important that the Hebrew writer rebuked Hebraic believers for not gathering regularly "until the day" (Hebrews 10:25). This incorrectly assumes that corporate worship is the end purpose. Faithfulness is defined as attending church, supporting church, and serving at church. Paul defined worship as living a holy life among both believers and the lost (Romans 12).

The better interpretation of Matthew 6:10 is the *coming of the kingdom* referred to the launching of the church at Pentecost (Acts 2). Jesus challenged followers to pray daily that they would see and participate in Phase 1. Praying that God's will *be done on earth as it is done in heaven* challenges believers to do (obey) God's will just as those in heaven do the will of God. With New Testament revelation, we can *know* God's will. With the indwelling of God's Spirit, believers can now *obey* God's purpose on earth: Be Christ's character and do Christ's mission of proclaiming the gospel "As we go" (Matthew 28:19).

The Appropriate Timing

Only at the second coming will believers reign with Christ as managers of the new earth in a world that is devoid of sin (Revelation 21, 22). Jesus stated faithfulness on earth will result in "authority over ten cities" (Luke 19:17), an obvious reference to the new earth.

CHALLENGE

In the next chapter, we will discuss the kind of Church Jesus promised to build (Matthew 16:18). You will see its design is perfect for Christ's followers to *be* Christ's character and *do* Christ's mission, resulting in proclaiming the gospel in the local, national, and global neighborhood.

You may be somewhat surprised by the definition Jesus and the apostles apply to the church, but it is absolutely necessary to get a clear understanding of *who* we are and *what* Christ expects us to do.

We will all give account of our service to Christ on Judgment Day (2 Corinthians 5:10).

We are saved by grace but will be judged by works. Our works will prove our faith to be genuine or declare it to be inadequate. For us to hear Jesus' words, "Well done good and faithful servant" (Matthew 25: 21), we need to understand his definition of church, his standards of faithfulness, and his purpose for our lives.

Local congregations have not always measured up to Christ's standards. Of the seven churches in Asia Minor, Christ commanded five to repent with a warning that he would otherwise remove their lampstand (Revelation 2:5), wage war against them (Revelation 2:16), throw them on a sickbed, or into the great tribulation. Christ also promised to kill their children (Revelation 2:22, 23), and spit them out of his mouth (Revelation 2:16). We must take our faith and responsibility seriously.

As we study Christ's *ekklesia*, compare your understanding of church to the biblical pattern. Ask yourself, "Is my definition of church the same as Christ's?" "Is my definition of faithfulness the same as his?" "Am I being equipped to do the work Christ commands all believers to do?" Use this study to realign your beliefs according to Christ's standards and work to be faithful.

CHAPTER TWO
The Ekklesia Church

"I will build my **church** and the gates of hell shall not prevail against it"
(Matthew 16:18)

"But you are a chosen race, a royal priesthood, a holy nation,
a people for his possession, **that you may proclaim the excellencies
of him** who called you out of darkness into a marvelous light"
(1 Peter 2: 9)

When Jesus announced that he would build his church (Matthew 16: 18), he used the word *ekklesia* to define his kingdom. It was not a Jewish, Aramaic, or even a religious term. *Ekklesia* was a well-known Greek word that had been around for about 400 years. Hearing the word, Jesus' disciples and audience immediately would have understood what he planned to do. He was king. Jesus called his followers out of the community to be trained in his own unique kingdom ways.Once trained in his kingdom values, culture, art, language, dress, and priorities; Jesus would then send them out into conquered territory, to plant a colony for him his colony, to totally assimilate the conquered people into Christ's kingdom mores.

How did the audience know this from just the word *ekklesia*? We will take a deeper dive into the word later in this chapter, but first understand that the English term *church* is not translated from the word *ekklesia*. Our English word *church* comes from the Anglo-Saxon work *kirk*, tied to the Greek word *kuriakos,* which means, "belonging to the Lord."[11] *Ekklesia* means, "the called-out ones to assemble with a purpose."[12]

Jerome, in the late fourth century, was the first to make the switch in his Greek to Latin translation, known as the Vulgate Bible. The medieval Catholic church and King James of England believed the term *ekklesia* undermined Papal and Anglican church authority.[13] By its very definition *ekklesia* entrusts and empowers God's redemptive business of making disciples to the common people.

Though it is true Christians belong to the Lord, not translating *ekklesia* in the New Testament has altered and somewhat neutralized today's understanding of church. The change has created missional ambiguity for the twenty-first century believer and contributed to missional drift for many congregations. If you ask the average church goer the question, "What is church?" The majority's answer might include a building, a program or an event."

This could explain why just nine percent of American Christians shared the gospel with one or two non-believers over a twelve-month period.[14] Their understanding of "church" did not require them to engage in personal evangelism.

In 2018, Barna found that sixty-five percent of Christians believe sharing the gospel can be done by lifestyle witnessing instead of verbal proclamation.[15] They do not understand that being *ekklesia* requires they be trained to teach people salvation through Jesus and his kingdom values and priorities. That is what ekklesia does. Thirty-six percent of Christians believe sharing the gospel with friends and family is optional. It is the church's and not the member's responsibility.[16] They do not understand they are the church.

In 2012, Lifeway Research found that eighty percent of those who attend church believe it is their responsibility to share the faith with non-believers, yet sixty-one percent had not done so in the last six months.[17] They do not understand

11. The Correct Meaning of "Church" and "Ecclesia." aggressivechristianity.net/articles/ecclesia.htm
12. Ibid
13. Simas, Greg. Ekklesia Emerging. E-Book. Gregsimas.org/wp-content/uploads/Ekklesia%20%Emerging%20 Final.pdf. p. 7.
14. Barna Research Faith & Christianity (Blog or Article on Internet). *Self-Described Christians Dominate America but wrestle with four Aspects of Spiritual Depth.* September 13, 2011. Barna.com/research/self-described-christians-dominate-america-but-wrestle-with-four-aspects-of-spiritual-depth/
15. Barna Research Faith & Christianity. *Sharing Faith is Increasingly Optional to Christians.* May 15, 2018. Barna.com/research/sharing-faith-increasingly-optional-christians/
16. Ibid
17. Lifeway Research. *Churchgoers Believe in Sharing Faith, Most Never Do.* August 13, 2012. Lifewayresearch.com/2012/08/13/churchgoers-believe-in-sharing-faith-most-never-do/

that faithfulness to Christ includes being a witness (Matthew 22: 1-14).

In 2019, Barna exposed the fact forty-seven percent of millennials believed evangelizing people of other religions was wrong.[18] They do not understand that only Jesus, the perfect, sinless sacrifice, can remove our sins. That is why Jesus is the only way to God (John 14: 6; Acts 4:12).

The New Testament defines believers as the *ekklesia*. You don't *go* to church. You *are* the church. *Ekklesia* is who you are. When we accept the definition of *ekklesia*, our faithfulness and missional expectations change. Let's dig deeper into the believer's new identity.

NEW IDENTITY

Scripture declares you are not an accident. Your birth was not a mistake (Psalm 139:13-16). God made you with a clear purpose in mind. When Jeremiah was called to proclaim God's message, his response was, "No!" God had already explained to Jeremiah, "I knew you before I formed you in your mother's womb. Before you were born, I set you apart and appointed you as my prophet to the nations" (Jeremiah 1:5, *NLT*). Jeremiah had tried to rationalize his fear of witnessing with, "I can't speak for you! I'm too young!" (Jeremiah 1:6, *NLT*).

It is true, Jeremiah was a young man, but notice his self-assessment: *Unfit* for God's purpose. Again, consider God's characterization of Jeremiah as recorded in Jeremiah 1:5. "Jeremiah, I created you, and I designed you for a specific assignment. Therefore, I will make you competent to fulfill my purpose for your life."

When it comes to God's purpose for you, do you focus on your inadequacies? Like Jeremiah, do you sigh, "I'm not fit for this mission"? God will make you competent to be his witness (2 Corinthians 3:5). Feelings of inadequacy and the failure to believe God will make you competent to be his witness have played a role in the following stats, listed by Michael Parrott:

- Ninety-five percent of believers (American) have never made one disciple.[19]

---

18. Barna. State of Evangelism.
19. Parrot, Michael. Street Evangelism, Where is the Space for the Local Evangelist. Acts Evangelism. Spokane, WA. Pp. 9-11.

- Eighty percent of believers do not consistently witness for Christ.[20]

- Seventy-one percent of believers do not give toward the financing of the Great Commission.[21]

You may have little doubt that God loves and values you. Do you realize God is also making you competent for your new mission? In Ephesians 2:10 the apostle Paul states, "For we are God's masterpiece. He has created us anew in Christ Jesus, so we can do the good things he planned for us long ago." The good works include being Christ's witness.

Jesus announced to his disciples, "You will receive power when the Holy Spirit comes upon you to be my witnesses" (Acts 1:8). Notice, God's Spirit gives the necessary power to witness. The apostle Paul said, "I can do all things through Christ who gives me strength" (Philippians 4:13). Paul clarified that his competency was "through" Christ (2 Corinthians 3:4).

Scripture cannot be clearer. In every generation, through his church, Jesus seeks to save lost people. If you call Jesus Lord, then *his* mission becomes *your* mission. His priority is your priority, "To seek and save the lost" (Luke 19:10). Sharing the gospel is obedience to Jesus, as Lord.

Think of the great privilege and responsibility from God, but also our dependency on Christ. Fear reflects self-dependency. Faith declares God is reconciling the world through us. Jude says, "Snatch people out of the fire" (Jude 23).

The Battle to Define You

Since this is the case, why does the thought of witnessing create such a struggle with fear? One reason is that there is an enemy who whispers suggestive lies to you. Satan does not want you to rescue the lost and loose these people from his grip (Ephesians 2:13). Sinners are in the domain of darkness (Colossians 1:13). So being God's ambassador automatically places you at war with the devil (2 Corinthians 5:3; Ephesians 6:12). When he attacks you, God always rescues and provides protection (1 Corinthians 10:13; Revelation 12:13-17).

Christ ultimately defeated the devil at the cross. Satan's army holds no power

---

20. Ibid
21. Ibid

over you. Demons cannot stop you (Romans 8:31-39). The devil's scheme is to stop you. His tools (like discouragement, distraction, disappointment, intimidation, lust, desires, and frustration) are designed to convince you that witnessing is simply not worth it.

The devil's troops use guerrilla warfare. The devil lies to you about God, yourself, other people, and the very purpose of life. Satan will use your peers, state policies and laws, institutions, bosses, even friends and family to take shots at you. Snipers shoot the "fiery darts" (Ephesians 6:16). The criticism is intended to intimidate and undercut you. At any encounter you can retreat. Technically, Satan doesn't stop you—you stop yourself.

At the core of his effort, the devil viciously attacks your identity in Christ. Satan is a liar (John 8:44). He attempts to use circumstance, educators, media, friends, and even family to generate fear and intimidation. He accuses you of past sins. He declares you unqualified. The devil will try and shame you into compliance and silence.

Why else would Christians escape into television six hours a day? Spend so much time in malls? Or be engrossed in sports or hobbies, or even pornography, casinos, and questionable movies? Could it be because we have believed the lies and disregarded our true identities in Christ? How many times have we ignored Jesus' voice (John 10:3, 4) urging us to witness? The apostle Paul tied the immoral behavior of the believers at Corinth to identity confusion: "Don't you realize that your body is the temple of the Holy Spirit, who lives in you and was given to you by God? You do not belong to yourself, for God bought you with a high price. So, you must honor God with your body" (1 Corinthians 6:19, 20).

Honoring God with our bodies includes being witnesses to others. Congregations can have identity confusion too, leading to little intentionality and mobilization in order to make disciples. Study the seven churches in Asia Minor. These churches were launched by the apostle Paul, along with some dynamic preaching teams. Yet, in just thirty years, five of the seven experienced missional drift! Christ rebuked all five and called them to change. To the church at Ephesus Jesus said, "Remember where you've fallen from; repent and do the works you did at first" (Revelation 2:5). The challenge was to remember their true identities in Christ and be the witnesses that were consistent with who they were!

Four Transforming Truths that Enable You to Witness

To rediscover and engage your new self and mission, it is essential to embrace four transforming truths that enable you to witness for Christ.

You are Forgiven

When you accepted Christ as your Lord and Savior, in the watery grave of baptism your sins were washed away. You were forgiven (Acts 2:38). The Greek word is *aphesis*. The meaning is to separate by cutting away, sending away, or hurling off into the distance.[22] The word suggests letting go, leaving behind, and removal. In legal terms *aphesis* means the judge cancels a debt, with the person released from any obligation to pay.[23] God gave his Son to die in your place—that's something to witness about! Here are several Scriptures that describe God's forgiveness. Share these promises:

- "And I will forgive their wickedness and I will never again remember their sins" (Jeremiah 31:34).

- "He has removed our sins as far from us as the east is from the west" (Psalm 103:12).

- "...You will trample our sins under your feet and throw them into the depths of the ocean" (Micah 7:19, *NLT*).

- "God made you alive with Christ, for he forgave all our sins. He canceled the record of the charges against us and took it away by nailing it to the cross" (Colossians 2:14).

- "In him also you were circumcised with a circumcision made without hands, by putting off the body of the flesh, by the circumcision of Christ" (Colossians 2:11).

God's forgiveness proclaims you are loved, valued, reconciled, and competent

---

22. Brown, Colin. *The New International Dictionary of New Testament Theology*. Zondervan Publishing. Vol. I. 1975. Pp. 697-702
23. Ibid. 698.

for your new mission. The debt you could never pay was paid by Christ. Your sins are sent away. God forgets. Therefore, you can forget your past and embrace God's purpose—be a witness for him. Everyone is driven by something. Without God's forgiveness, sinful forces continue to drive your life. Don't miss God's mission and eternal rewards. In *The Purpose Driven Life*, Rick Warren identifies a few of these negative driving forces:[24]

- **Envy**: Solomon said, "I observed that the basic motive for success is the driving force of envy" (Ecclesiastes 4:4, *TLB*).

- **Guilt**: Guilt-driven people run from regrets or run to hide their shame. They allow their pasts to control their futures. One of Cain's consequences of murdering his brother was to be a "wanderer on earth" (Genesis 4:12, NLT). Cain lacked a clear purpose for his life.

- **Resentment and Anger**: Instead of releasing your pain through forgiveness (Ephesians 4:32) you rehearse it over and again in your mind. Resentment will keep you stuck in your pain and will make it impossible to enjoy your life and genuinely love other people.

- **Fear**: Everyone has been burned, rejected, excluded, and devalued. Regardless of the cause, fear will stop people from embracing the God opportunities places before them.

- **Needing Approval**: Worrying about what others might think will immobilize you and be a source of great stress. Solomon said, "Fearing people is a dangerous trap, but trusting the Lord means safety" (Proverbs 29:25, *NLT*). Not receiving God's approval in Christ and not pursuing his purpose for your life can drive you to seek the approval of people.

The Holy Spirit Lives in You

Acts 2:38 states that in baptism, the Holy Spirit indwells you. You are "in Christ." God the Father, God the Son, and God the Holy Spirit are now united *with*

---

24. Warren, Rick. *Purpose Driven Life*. Zondervan Publishing. Grand Rapids, MI. P. 31-33.

you, live *in* you, and work *for* you. Think of that. God is always present! There are many benefits that come from the indwelling Holy Spirit, but one overriding truth is this: You are a new person (2 Corinthians 5:17) made competent "in Christ" to fulfill God's purpose.

The Scripture provides "the know how" to be effective. The Holy Spirit equips you with the desire and power to live out God's purposes (2 Corinthians 5:14; Philippians 2:13). Again, your new purpose is to *be like Jesus in character and mission (witness)*. This book is about effectively living out Christ's mission of proclaiming the gospel. Here are a few verses that refer to your purpose as Christ's witness.

- "For we are God's masterpiece. He has created us anew in Christ Jesus, so we can do the good things he planned for us long ago" (Ephesians 2:10, *NLT*).

- "And now the word of God is ringing from you to people everywhere" (1 Thessalonians 1:8).

- "This same good news that came to you is going out all over the world. It is bearing fruit everywhere by changing lives" (Colossians 1:6).

- "Therefore, if anyone is in Christ, he is a new creation. The old has passed away; behold, the new has come.... Therefore, we are ambassadors for Christ, God making his appeal through us" (2 Corinthians 5:17, 20).

- "But you will receive power when the Holy Spirit comes upon you, and you will my witnesses in Jerusalem, and in all Judea and Samaria, and to the end of the earth" (Acts 1:8, *ESV*).

- "Go therefore and make disciples of all nations, baptizing them in the name of the Father and of the Son and of the Holy Spirit, teaching them to observe all that I have commanded you. And behold I am with you always, to the end of the age" (Matthew 28: 19, 20, *ESV*).

God's Love Compels You

God's love "compels" (2 Corinthians 5:14) you to *embrace God's mission to be his witness.* Everyone is driven by something. The Holy Spirit uses the depths of God's love, that you now understand and experience through Christ, to *grip and drive you forward* with the task of reconciling people to God (2 Corinthians 5:14). Here are several reasons to embrace Christ's mission.[25]

- **Your mission is a continuation of Jesus' mission on earth**: What Jesus started; each Christian continues. The Great Commission is everyone's responsibility.

- **Your mission is a tremendous privilege**: Think of it as God making his appeal to lost humanity through you. Is there any greater privilege? We are partners with God, his co-laborers (2 Corinthians 6:1).

- **Your mission is the greatest humanitarian effort**: When a vaccine was developed for Covid-19, we heard about it from every news outlet around the world. As a believer, you have the cure for sin and the promise for eternal life. If a person dies from Covid-19 they still must face Judgment. Your message can save them from hell.

- **Your mission has eternal significance**: It will impact the eternal destiny of other people, so it is more important than your job, dreams, goals, or earthly achievements. Those you influence with the good news will bring you rewards in heaven.

- **Your mission gives you a legacy**: Everything in this life will end, except the people you impacted with the gospel. Build your legacy and heavenly reward (Philippians 4:1).

- **Your mission simplifies your life**: Being God's witness clarifies your priorities. It determines your calendar and the use of your money and talents. When you get up in the morning, you have a clear picture.

Only Christians Have the Responsibility of Sharing the Gospel with Lost People

"How can they hear unless you tell them" (Romans 10:14)? That is the question

---

25   Ibid. P. 279-284

the apostle Paul asked believers at Rome. Only sinners saved through the blood of Christ qualify to share the good news with lost sinners. We tend to rationalize our lack of witnessing with several statements like, "Saving people is Jesus' job, or the Holy Spirit's job." It is true that both Jesus and the Holy Spirit have an active role in salvation, but they always speak the gospel through the voice of believers. "Faith comes by hearing, and hearing through the word of God" (Romans 10:17). Other Christians excuse themselves by putting evangelism on the shoulders of angelic beings.

Let us briefly consider four conversion accounts in Acts that involve Jesus, the Holy Spirit, and angels. *Please notice the essential roles Christians played in each conversion: proclaiming the gospel!*

The Conversion of Saul

Acts 9 recounts the conversion of Saul of Tarsus. Saul was a persecutor of the early church (Acts 8:1) and was on his way to Damascus to arrest and kill more Christians. Suddenly a bright light from heaven brought Saul to his knees. A voice asked, "Saul, Saul, why are you persecuting me" (Acts 9: 4)? After Jesus identified himself, he commanded Saul to go into Damascus and wait for a messenger to tell him what to do (Acts 9: 6).

Blinded by the light, Saul's associates led him into the city. On the third day, Jesus appeared to Ananias and commanded him to share the gospel with Saul and to explain that Christ was calling him to be an apostle (Acts 9:15-18). Saul then accepted Christ and was immediately baptized (Acts 9:18).

Why didn't Jesus just share the gospel with Saul? Jesus spoke to Saul. Why send Saul to Damascus and then tell Ananias to go to Saul and explain the gospel? The reason is that proclaiming the gospel to lost people is the exclusive job of believers. Only saved sinners are qualified to share the good news with lost sinners.

The Conversions at Pentecost

I hear Christians say, "It's the job of Holy Spirit to save people." It is true, the Spirit of God has given us the gospel of Jesus Christ and he convicts sinners of their need for salvation. God can and will use any circumstance, person, memory, kindness, or pain to move sinners to see their need for salvation. Yet the primary conviction that salvation comes through faith in Jesus' work on the cross is tied with the sharing of the gospel.

Consider the day of Pentecost in Acts 2. Did conviction come before or after the apostle Peter preached the gospel? *After* Peter shared the gospel and explained the people's need for salvation, the Scriptures record, "Now when they heard this they were cut to the heart" (Acts 2:37).

The Conversion of the Ethiopian Eunuch

The conversion of the Ethiopian Eunuch is a fascinating account. In Acts 8, the Eunuch had been to Jerusalem to celebrate the Passover, probably as a Jewish proselyte. While in town, he apparently purchased a scroll containing the writings of the prophet Isaiah.

Heading home in a chariot, the Ethiopian was reading the Scripture. Notice how the Holy Spirit brought Philip and the Ethiopian together. First, the Holy Spirit *told* Philip to take the south road from Jerusalem to Gaza (Acts 8:26). Then, after a 70-mile walk (or run), Philip spotted the Ethiopian's chariot ahead.

The Holy Spirit then *told* Philip to go up to the chariot and talk to the man (Acts 8:29). Philip asked the Ethiopian if he understood what he was reading. The Ethiopian replied that he needed help and invited Philip into the chariot. "Then Philip opened his mouth and beginning with that Scripture told him the good news about Jesus" (Acts 8:35). Further down the road the Eunuch responded to the gospel and was baptized (Acts 8:39).

The Holy Spirit *spoke* to Philip several times. First, the Holy Spirit told Philip to travel the desert road. A second time the Spirit told him to run alongside the Eunuch's chariot. Clearly, the Holy Spirit spoke to Philip. So, why didn't the Holy Spirit present the gospel to the Ethiopian Eunuch and spare Philip the hardship of travelling on foot through a desert? The reason is that sharing the gospel is the exclusive responsibility of Christians.

The Conversion of Cornelius

Acts 10 records the first Gentile conversion to Christ. Scripture says that around 3:00 p.m. one afternoon, an angel appeared to Cornelius (Acts 10:3). The angel explained in great detail that God had noticed Cornelius's good deeds, alms giving, and heard his prayers (Acts 10:4). Notice, an angel *spoke* directly to Cornelius! But instead of sharing the gospel, the angel commanded Cornelius to "Send men to Joppa and bring one Simon who is called Peter" (Acts 10:5). The angel even identified Peter's location (Acts 10:6).

Peter arrived several days later and asked the reason for the invitation (Acts 10:29). After Cornelius explained his conversation with the angel, Peter understood his assignment—proclaim the gospel. Upon hearing the good news of Jesus, Cornelius and his entire family were baptized (Acts 10: 48). As you see, it is not the job of Jesus, the Holy Spirit, nor the duty of angels to share the gospel of salvation with lost people. That responsibility falls directly on you and me, Christ's *ekklesia*.

YOUR NEW IDENITY: EKKLESIA

About 400 B.C., the *ekklesia* was associated with people who were summoned to join the army of the Greek city-state to fight its battles.[26] By 200 B.C., *ekklesia* was used to refer to select citizens of the Greek city-state who were *called out* thirty to forty times a year to create policy and carry out the town's business. The *ekklesia* even made the decision to go to war.

Caesar's Ekklesia

By the time of Christ, the term *ekklesia* described a chosen group of people serving Caesar. The *ekklesia* helped establish Roman authority across the empire. Caesar's *Ekklesia* was composed of retired military personnel, businessmen, teachers, and leaders in various fields. They were *called out* to be trained in Roman language, laws, arts, and customs. Once thoroughly trained, the *ekklesia* were *sent into* newly conquered territories, to live among the "barbarians." The goal was to convert the barbarian to the Roman way and assimilate those who were converted into Roman society. The assimilation process was successful because the *ekklesia* would continually teach and model Roman values through relationships.

Once an *ekklesia* was established in a new location, it was called a Roman colony. These colonies were to be a carbon copy of the imperial city. Philippi, Corinth, and Thessalonica were founded by Caesar's *ekklesia*. The city of Thessalonica was a Greco-Roman colony, meaning Caesar's *ekklesia* had more freedom to incorporate Greek values as well as Roman customs into the new community. The strategic use of *ekklesia* is a well-known factor in Rome's longevity as a united empire.

---

26. Brown, Colin. Pp. 291,292

Interestingly, when you consider the apostle Paul's teams, they too were composed of a variety of personnel; teachers, a doctor, and skilled workers in various fields (Colossians 4:7-14).

Jesus' Ekklesia

Understanding this background, gives us insight into Jesus' definition of church, doesn't it? When Jesus declared, "I will build my *Ekklesia*," the disciples immediately understood five facts about ekklesia.

- Jesus was a king with an empire

- Jesus called them out of society to be equipped in his kingdom values, language, and mission

- Once trained, his *ekklesia* would be sent out to plant in new territories

- Once planted as Christ's colonies, they would convert the conquered people into Christ's kingdom

- The *ekklesia* assimilate the converted to embrace the king's beliefs and behaviors

With these "called-out-ones" Jesus would create a new race of people, composed of all ethnicities and nations, to form an eternal kingdom. We will consider in detail the disciples' modus operandi as Jesus' *ekklesia* in a later chapter. If you need a sneak preview, read Matthew 9:35 through chapter 10. You might also want to read Luke 9 and 10.

THE NEW ROLES OF EKKLESIA

Throughout the New Testament the Holy Spirit describes the unique role of Christ's *ekklesia*. Let us consider several words/ideas that describe our witness.

Apostle

The Greek word for apostle is *apostolos*. It means to be commissioned, to be sent.[27] The New Testament contains two primary usages of the word. First, it refers

---

27. Colin, Brown. Pp. 126, 127

specifically to the twelve apostles. These men were chosen by Christ, spent three years in Jesus' ministry, and witnessed the resurrected Christ (Acts 1: 21, 22). They received the outpouring of the Holy Spirit (Acts 2:3, 4), giving them miraculous powers that authenticated the gospel message that Jesus was Savior and Lord. The Holy Spirit revealed the gospel to the twelve, and through inspiration kept the writing of the New Testament true (2 Timothy 2:15). The twelve laid the foundation of the church (Ephesians 2: 20). Their names are also written on the walls of the new Jerusalem (Revelation 21: 14).

In a *general* sense Christians are apostles. One example is Titus in 2 Corinthians 8:23. "As for Titus, he is my partner and fellow worker for your benefit. And for our brothers, they are messengers (*apostolos*) of the churches." Titus and "the other brothers" were apostles of Christ, in the sense they had been sent out by local churches. We might view preachers and missionaries commissioned (set apart) by their local church, as apostles too. It also applies to the way in which every Christian is commissioned on Sunday to be Christ's witness throughout the week.

Ambassador

The Greek word for ambassador is *presbeuo*[28]. This messenger was tied to the Imperial provinces of the Roman Empire to oversee the assimilation of the newly conquered people into the Roman Empire. The ambassador worked closely with Caesar's *ekklesia*. His role was to reconcile the province to their new Lord, Caesar. The ambassador was commissioned to a foreign territory as the official representative of the king to communicate mandates, promises, and the king's will.

The apostle Paul defined all believers as ambassadors in 2 Corinthians 5:20. "Therefore, we are ambassadors for Christ, God making his appeal through us." Each morning view yourself as Christ's ambassador, sent out to represent Jesus the king! You are to share his message and will.

It is also interesting the Greek word *presbeuo* gives us the English word "elder." Elders are commissioned by the local church to witness Christ's word, ways, and mission to the members. They serve by giving spiritual oversight to Christ's family as spiritual parents (1 Thessalonians 2:7-12).

Broadcaster

Jesus spoke of his followers sharing the good news like broadcasting. The word

---

28. Brown, Colin. P. 192

30

is translated in Matthew 13 as "sower," casting seeds. Broad casting the good news is pictured as a sower scattering the seed.

Defense Attorney

The apostle Peter wrote, "Always be prepared to make a defense to anyone who asks you for a reason for the hope that is in you" (1 Peter 3:15). The Greek word for defense is *apologian*, referring to a legal defense attorney in the court of law who presents a well-reasoned, thought-out response.[29] Jesus is on trial each day. You will meet people who have doubts and are skeptical about the claims of Christ. Some might even be cynical and rude. Peter instructed us to make the case for Christ with kindness and respect (1 Peter 3:15).

Evangelist

The Greek word for evangelist is *euaggelistes*. It means a bearer of good news.[30] Picture Philip in Acts 8 going from place to place sharing the gospel with groups of people in Samaria, and with the Ethiopian man on the road to Gaza. Timothy was an evangelist (2 Timothy 4:5). The role of evangelist appears in the New Testament to be a temporary office. The writers of the four gospels were also called evangelists because they shared the life, ministry, and good news of Jesus.

Acts 8:4 states that those scattered by persecution "went about preaching the word." These folks were ordinary believers. The Greek word is the *euaggelizo*. Originally it was a military word, describing a runner who proclaimed victory. Written in the present tense, *euaggelizo* indicates how the believers continuously (without stopping) shared Jesus.

Romans 10:15 speaks of *euaggelistes* as having beautiful feet. Wherever you go, you witness for Jesus. God is so pleased when you do this, he describes your feet as "beautiful."

Herald (Proclaimer, Preacher)

The Greek word for herald is *kerusso*. A herald was a public crier.[31] In Bible days, the herald was a town official who made public proclamations for government leaders. The herald's job was to repeat and publicly proclaim news

29. Ibid. p. 51
30. Gaebelein, Frank E. *The Expositor's Bible Commentary*. Vol. 11. Zondervan Publishing. Grand Rapids, MI. 1978. P.411
31. https://www.preceptaustin.org/2_peter_24-11

from the ruler or king.

Jesus cast out demons from a man in the Gerasene's. Once whole, the man wanted to follow Jesus. Jesus commanded him to go home and "declare" how much God had done for him (8:39). The Greek word for declare is *kerusso*. The man became Jesus' official proclaimer and traveled throughout ten cities proclaiming the good news.

Lamp

Jesus said, "You are the light of the world . . . . a lamp put on a stand, and it gives light to all in the house" (Matthew 5:14). The Greek word is *phos,* which carries the idea of illumination.[32] As you go throughout your day, you illuminate the story of Jesus to everyone you meet. You shed light on the salvation story.

Witness

Jesus said, "You will be my witnesses" (Acts 1:8). The Greek word is *martusin.*[33] In Revelation 11:3 Christ sent out his two witnesses to preach (proclaim) the gospel for 1,260 days. This number is understood in symbolic prophetic language to represent the entire gospel era; from Pentecost to the second coming of Christ. Jesus' expectation is for all Christians in every generation to be his witnesses until he returns.

This Greek word is also a *judicial term* common in the court of law. A witness would take the stand and testify to what she knows or what he experienced. The goal was to get a conviction. The word is also the basis of the English word *martyr.* A witness is willing stake their very life on the truth of Jesus and the gospel. Today reports suggest nearly 100,000 Christians are killed for their faith each year![34]

LET'S WRAP UP

Were you surprised by the definition of Church (*Ekklesia*)? It is absolutely necessary to the understanding of *who* you are, because your identity determines *what* you do. Here are other reasons we must live out our mission on earth as Christ's witnesses.

---

32. https://www.preceptaustin.org/john_15_commentary
33. https://www.preceptaustin.org/acts_18_commentary
34. https://www.bbc.com/news/magazine-24864587

1. Our lives on earth are but a vapor (James 5:14). Let us not waste them.

2. Eternity is forever (Jude 1:13). Let us embrace it.

3. Judgment Day is coming (2 Corinthians 5:10). Let us prepare for it.

4. Those not faithful "in Christ" will go to hell (John 14:6; Romans 3:21-26). Let us share it.

5. It is the exclusive right and responsibility of Christians to proclaim the gospel (Matthew 28:18-20). Let us proclaim it.

6. Understanding the four realities of *ekklesia* gives us confidence. Let us fulfill it.

7. There are various roles of *ekklesia*. Let us live them.

CHALLENGE

The *ekklesia* of the later first and early second century were militaristic regarding their mission. They gave us the word *sacrament*. While not found in Scripture, *sacrament* paints a picturesque view of the early church's identity. To enter Caesar's army, one had to take the *Sacramentum*. The Latin word refers to a life-changing oath. The Sacramentum was part of an elaborate ceremony where a man pledged his allegiance to Caesar. After taking the sacramentum, all his possessions, even his life, belonged to Caesar to advance his interests.

The early *ekklesia* witnessed this ceremony and declared, "We, too, have a King, Jesus. We, too, take a life-changing oath in baptism. We pledge our lives, possessions, everything to the advancement of his kingdom." Each week at the Lord's Supper these soldiers of Christ would sup with their King reaffirming their oaths to live and die for his mission.

Christ's *ekklesia* also categorized pagans (ordinary citizens) as civilians, meaning, those who had not yet taken the life-changing oath would eventually join Jesus' army in the recruitment process. The *ekklesia* believed it was their responsibility to convince the civilian to join the force (Acts 26:28, 29).[35] Do you

---

35. Joe Ellis. *The Church on Purpose: Keys to Effective Leadership* (Cincinnati, OH: Standard Publishing, 1982), p. 47-48.

live each day with this responsibility? Are you being Christ's witness? In the next chapter, you will learn about the specific gospel message you are called to share and understand how to access God's power to obey his call and be Christ's *ekklesia*.

CHAPTER THREE
The Empowered Church

"And the gospel must first be proclaimed to all the nations"
(Mark 13:10).

"Go therefore and make disciples of all nations, baptizing them
in the name of the Father and of the Son and of the Holy Spirit,
teaching them to observe all that I have commanded you.
And behold, I am with you always, to the end of the age"
(Matthew 28:18-20).

"In the last days it shall be, God declares that I
will pour out my Spirit on all flesh" (Joel 2:28).

"And the gospel must first be proclaimed to all the nations"
(Mark 13:10).

In chapter one, we discovered our purpose: To *be* Christ's character and *do* Christ's mission. In chapter two, we discovered our true identities as Christ's *ekklesia* (Matthew 16:18). We are the body of Christ (1 Corinthians 12:27), Christ's temple (1 Corinthians 6:19), Christ's house (1 Peter 2:5), Christ's bride (Ephesians 5:32), Christ lives in us (Colossians 1:27). We have his mind (1 Corinthians 2:16). We are his hands, feet, ears, and voice (1 Corinthians 12:14-26; 1 Peter 4:11).

Knowing *who* you are determines what you *do*. God has also placed within the New Testament *identity markers* for us. Scripture says we take on the role of witnesses, ambassadors, heralds, broadcasters, proclaimers, and evangelists, to further clarify that our purpose indeed includes sharing the good news.

In chapter three, let's consider three essentials to our purpose: the Great Commission, the Holy Spirit, and the power of the gospel (good news) message that we embrace and share.

THE GREAT COMMISSION

The Great Commission is the final word of Jesus before his ascension. Jesus spent 3½ years preparing his followers to make disciples. What were Jesus' final words before he left planet earth? Interestingly, Jesus did not say, "Worship me each week," or "Pray regularly, or "Study your Bible," although each of these precepts are vital. His ultimate challenge to his disciples was to "Go and make disciples!" He had prepared them and now it was time to act.

And go they did. Quickly they spread the gospel through Jerusalem, Judea, and Samaria (Acts 2-8). Acts 13-28 records the apostle Paul's evangelistic journey throughout Asia Minor and Europe. Church tradition has Peter evangelizing in Italy and Turkey and Andrew in Russia and India. John ventured to Syria, Philip to Turkey, Bartholomew to India, and Jude to Africa.

Background

Let's dig deeper into the meaning of Christ's Great Commission. After Jesus' resurrection he instructed his disciples to meet him in Galilee. Matthew 28:16, 17 states, "Now the eleven disciples went to the mountain to which Jesus had directed them. And when they saw him they worshipped him, but some doubted." Why did some doubt?

We know after his resurrection, for a period of forty days, Jesus appeared to all eleven disciples. Even Thomas believed (John 20:28). So why would Matthew indicate that some doubted? Speculation is the eleven disciples brought along over 500 believers who had yet to see Jesus. The apostle Paul makes reference to Jesus appearing to "more than 500 brothers at one time…" (1 Corinthians 15:6). Did Jesus give his "Great Commission" to the 500 plus followers? It is possible.

Given to Every Believer

There are several reasons we can be confident the Great Commission was given to every believer in every generation. First, if the Commission were given just to the eleven disciples then the church would cease to exist after the first century, right?

Second, we read throughout the book of Acts that *every believer* made disciples. Consider Acts 8 as an example. Because of Jewish persecution, the entire church of Jerusalem was "scattered throughout the regions of Judea and Samaria, except for the apostles" (Acts 8:1). The "professionals" remained in Jerusalem.

What did these every day, ordinary believers do? "Now those who scattered went about preaching the word" (Acts 8:4). Preaching is in the present tense. That means they never stopped sharing the good news. Study Acts 8 and you will see that the first congregations established outside Jerusalem, in Judea and Samaria, were started by these every day ordinary Christians. The apostles had equipped believers to share their faith.

Jesus begins his final command with, "All authority in heaven and on earth has been given to me" (Matthew 28:18). The resurrected Christ declared himself to be God. He will soon reign from heaven. Since there is no greater authority in heaven or earth, let us make disciples!

"Go"

The Greek word is *poreuomai* (middle voice), meaning the responsibility to "go" lies with each believer. Be intentional to inject Jesus into your everyday encounters. "Go" is the prerequisite to make disciples. "Go" means be opportunistic in each conversation and honor God.

> Make the most of your chances to tell others the Good News.
> Be wise in all your contacts with them. Let your conversation
> be gracious as well as sensible, for then you will have the right
> answer for everyone (Colossians 4: 5, 6, *TLB*).

This Greek word also carries the idea of cutting forward and making progress. Leading a friend to Christ may be compared to helping your friend clean out his or her attic. There is the unpacking, the story, and finally the decision to set it aside as garbage. It may take time to walk away from the past and embrace the new life, so be patient.

In your relationships you need to intentionally plant, cultivate, nurture, and water the seeds of the gospel (Matthew 13:1-23). As Christ's ambassador, the Holy Spirit will open doors for you to share Bible answers to your friends' biggest problems. Eventually, your friends will be ready to hear the gospel and hopefully accept the good news of Jesus.

"Make Disciples"

This is the only imperative (command) among the verbs in these two verses. It is a brisk command. Jesus is charging us, "Make disciples now!" The word conveys *urgency*. Often Jesus refers to evangelism in agrarian terms. The harvest is ready to bring in. Wait too late and the harvest dies. People are ready now to come to Christ today. Their times to die may be tomorrow.

> When he saw the crowds, he had compassion for them, because they were confused and helpless, like sheep without a shepherd. He said to his disciples "The harvest is great, but the workers are few. So, pray to the Lord who is in charge of the harvest; ask him to send more workers into his fields" (Matthew 9:36-38, *NLT*).

Now consider John 4: 35-36 (*NLT*):

> You know the saying, "Four months between planting and harvest." But I say, "Wake up and look around. The fields are already ripe for harvest. The harvesters are paid good wages, and the fruit they harvest is people brought to eternal life. What joy awaits both the planter and the harvester alike!"

Jesus said, "Make disciples." The Greek word for disciple is *mathetes*, the basis of our English word, mathematics. A disciple is one who listens and studies, then "adds up" all the biblical facts in order to live out those truths in everyday life. Disciples are lifelong learners who work continually at imitating their teacher. Before Jesus' death he challenged his followers,

> If you want to be my disciple, you must hate everyone else by comparison—your father and mother, wife and children, brothers and sisters—yes, even your own life. Otherwise, you cannot be

my disciple. So, you cannot become my disciple without giving up everything you own (Luke 14: 26, 27, 33, *NLT*).

Making disciples of Jesus is much more than getting someone to "ask Jesus into his or her heart." It involves the person's total commitment to Jesus as Savior and Lord. This commitment flows from a grateful heart that understands that Jesus died for his or her sins, he or she is now alive in God's presence, and has the hope of eternal life. Why would you hesitate to share this good news with others?

"Of All Nations"

Jesus commands us not to exclude anyone from hearing the gospel. Every ethnicity, homogeneous group, and individual must have the opportunity to escape hell and have eternal life by accepting the gospel.

Clare Herbert Woolston, a preacher in the 1800s wrote the song, "Jesus Loves Me." Remember the lyrics, "Red and yellow, black and white, they are precious in his sight. Jesus loves the little children of the world?" The song was put to music during the Civil War and sung by northern soldiers as they marched into battle. In cadence, the soldiers shouted out the song. The rational was that every person, "red and yellow, black and white" was made in the image of God and dearly loved by their creator so slavery was a sin that demanded correction. The gospel's freedom was for the slaves in the south too.

In the parable of the Great Banquet, the master commanded his servants to "go out quickly to the streets and lanes to bring in the poor, the lame and the blind" (people who knew they needed God). The servants reported, "Mission accomplished. We brought them all." The master then commanded the servants to go back out "into the highways and hedges to compel people to come in that my house will be filled" (See Luke 14:21-23). The highways were outside the city. The hedges were the little nooks and crannies—dirt roads, and places with no road at all. No one was to be excluded. Jesus said, "compel them to come in" (Luke 14:23). The Greek word *compel* means to urge, beg, press, and convince. Salvation in Jesus is so wonderful we need to tell everyone, "Don't miss it. Come to the banquet." The reality of hell must be part of our conversation too. It spurs us to *compel* and motivates our friend to hear the good news.

"Baptizing Them"

The Greek word translated baptism is *baptizo*, which means to dip, plunge, or immerse. This command refers to water baptism. The New Testament explains that in a spiritual way, the believer reenacts the death, burial, and resurrection of Christ (See Romans 6:1-11). Each person is dead in sin (Ephesians 2:1). What do you do with a dead person? You bury them. Through the believer's faith, in that watery grave, the Holy Spirit enters and resurrects the person into a new life (2 Corinthians 5:17).

We'll talk more about baptism later in this chapter, but for now read James Montgomery Boyce's insight employing the secular Greek meaning of *baptizo*.

The clearest example that shows the meaning of *baptizo* is a text from the Greek poet and physician Nicander, who lived about 200 B.C. Nicander says that in order to make a pickle, the vegetable should first be *'dipped' (bapto)* into boiling water and then *'baptized' (baptizo)* in the vinegar solution. Both verbs concern the immersing of vegetables in a solution. But the first is temporary. The second, the act of *baptizing* the vegetable, produces a permanent change. When used in the New Testament, this word can refer to our union and identification with Christ. Union with Christ brings a real change, like the vegetable to the pickle!"[36]

"Into the Name of the Father...of the Son...of the Holy Spirit"

Notice the believer is baptized "into the name of the Father, and of the Son, and of the Holy Spirit." You may have heard of the Trinity, or the Godhead? The titles mean that God has three distinct personalities composed of the same God "substance." God is one (1 Timothy 2:5) with three different persons. When Jesus was baptized, God the Father spoke from heaven, while God the Spirit descended upon Jesus in his baptism (Matthew 3: 16, 17).

Each personality of the Godhead is eternal, all-powerful, and all-knowing (just to name a few of God's qualities). Each person of the Godhead performed a vital function in creation. God the Father "spoke" matter into existence (Genesis 1:3). God the Spirit "hovered over" the matter and shaped it (Genesis 1:2). God the Son holds it together (Colossians 1:17).

---

36. Preceptaustin.org/romans_61-3

Regarding the "new creation" and "being born again" (1 Corinthians 5:17; John 3:3), God the Father spoke the New Covenant plan into existence (Ephesians 1:4). God the Son became the "lamb of God that takes away the sins of the world" (John 1:29). God the Spirit revealed this salvation through Scripture (2 Peter 1:21). The Holy Spirit also convicts the world of sin (John 16:8) and provides the believer with a new heart (Ezekiel 36: 25-27). The Holy Spirit empowers the Christian to obey God's Word and transforms the character of each believer to reflect Christ's attitudes and behavior (2 Corinthians 3:18).

Baptism is added as a condition to the New Testament salvation plan because it reveals and serves as the place of contact where the believer connects with each person of the Godhead, and to their particular saving redemptive work. Jack Cottrell gives insight into the phrase, "Into the Name."

> The phrase *into the name* was a technical term used in the world of Greek business and commerce. It was used to indicate the entry of a sum of money or an item of property into the account bearing the name of its owner. Its use in Matthew 28:19 indicates that the purpose of baptism is to unite us with the Triune God in an ownership relation; we become his property in a special, intimate way.[37]

"Teaching them to observe all that I have commanded"

God's goal for our salvation is not only restored relationships with him, but also restoring our characters that we tarnished in our sins. The New Testament calls this process *sanctification*. The Holy Spirit does the transforming in conjunction with our obedience to God's Word. Bringing people into a saving relationship with Christ also involves teaching them the whole counsel of God. How can new believers obey Jesus as Lord, if they don't understand Christ's attitudes, values, priorities, and relational targets?

The transformed life gives God glory. It confirms faith is genuine and gives each believer great assurance on the Day of Judgment. Finally, the changed life is the miraculous proof that validates our testimony to friends and family that Jesus is alive and still has the power to save and change people today.

---

37. Jack Cottrell, *Baptism: A Biblical Study*. College Press Publishing. Joplin, MO. 1989. p. 17.

"And behold I am with you always, to the end of the age"
What an awesome promise. Jesus is always with us. Making disciples is a cooperative effort of both heaven and earth. Jesus brings us into contact with receptive people (See Acts 8: 26-40). He has given us his written Word to study in order to share (2 Timothy 2:15, 1 Peter 3:15). Jesus also reminds us of appropriate Scripture we've already studied as we engage others with the gospel (See Colossians 4:3-6).

Let's now discuss the role of the Holy Spirit in partnership with our purpose to make disciples of everyone we meet.

THE HOLY SPIRIT

In this section it is important to speak briefly to the Holy Spirit's nature, his indwelling in believers, his role in connecting us to people, his job as prosecuting attorney, and in regenerating and transforming people.

He Is a Divine Person
The Holy Spirit is first mentioned in Genesis 1:2, "And the Spirit of God was hovering over the face of the waters." The person of the Holy Spirit played a vital role in creation. The Holy Spirit gave us the Bible. He also does the regenerating and sanctifying in each believer. He is generally referred to as the third person of the Trinity (God the Father, God the Son, and God the Holy Spirit). Every believer is baptized into the name of all three persons, making each equal as the "Godhead."

The Holy Spirit is a person in the sense that he engages in intellectual activity (1 Corinthians 2:11), makes authoritative decisions (Acts 13:2), speaks (John 16:13), teaches (John 14:26), and expresses emotions (Romans 15:30).

He Indwells Believers
The Holy Spirit enters a believer's life in baptism (Acts 2:38). He takes up residence in each of us (John 7:38). Jesus referred to him as our "helper" (John 14:16). The word can also mean advocate, counselor, a defense attorney (Romans 8:26, 27). He pleads your case to the Father.

The Holy Spirit causes regeneration in the believer. This is the saving event in baptism. He brings a literal change. He circumcises the believer's heart (Colossians 2:12), removing the sin disease and in a sense gives the believer a "new" heart. He makes the believer alive with God at the moment of conversion (Titus 3:5). The Holy Spirit is the source and giver of life (John 6:63) and is called the Spirit of life (Romans 8:2).

He Connects You to People

Throughout the book of Acts, we see the Holy Spirit connecting believers to people in need of salvation. This is often referred to as God's providential hand. God himself transcends time and space. That means God lives in the past, present, and future all at the same time. Seeing the future, God can utilize your own free will and providentially bring you into contact with people who need to hear good news. The Holy Spirit will bring to your mind Scripture that you've studied or memorized as you interact and have God conversations with friends and family. As we pray for lost people, God will connect us with them to share their particular gospel solution with them.

Notice the story of Philip and the Ethiopian (Acts 8: 26-40). The Holy Spirit led Philip to a road going toward Gaza (Acts 8:26). On this desert road, Philip met an Ethiopian riding in his chariot, reading Isaiah 52 and 53. The Spirit told Philip to run up to the chariot (Acts 8:29). The Ethiopian invited Philip into his chariot (Acts 8:31). Philip shared the gospel and baptized the Ethiopian in a pool of water along the road (Acts 8:36). Interestingly, the Holy Spirit then led Philip to his next evangelistic assignment (Acts 8:39). The Holy Spirit was the connector.

There are no coincidences regarding the people who are our family and friends, or those we meet, and those we work with. In 1992, I went to Ukraine on a mission trip to assist in planting a church. On a "free" day I went sightseeing with a coworker. We asked one of the guides, a college student, to show us around the city. He had been with us several times and we had had several good conversations about Christ. On our sightseeing tour, I asked him, "Are you a Christian?" His response was "No." I then said, "Would you like to become a Christian?" He answered, "Yes!" Over the course of several days, my friend led our guide to Christ. Today he works for Pioneer Bible Society translating Scripture into languages of unreached people.

See God in all of life, especially your contacts and relationships. The Holy Spirit will connect you to people. Your job might be to plant the seed, or cultivate the soil, or clarify the truth, or simply encourage the person to pursue God. Whatever role you play, it is vital to the person's conversion!

He Is Prosecuting Attorney

The Holy Spirit works on the hearts and minds of non-believers with the intention of eventually bringing them to salvation. He "prepared" the Ethiopian for Philip's good news conversation, as well as my guide in Ukraine. But how?

The Scripture

Notice again, the Ethiopian had been reading the Scripture (Acts 8:28). The Spirit reveals the truth about God's holiness and love, Christ's sacrifice for sin, human beings' sin and need for salvation, all this and more through the Scripture. The heavens declare the existence of God (Psalm 19). The person of Jesus and the written Scripture reveal who God is. Quote verses and talk about the Scripture whenever you can. It is the sword of the Spirit (Ephesians 6:17).

> For the word of God is alive and powerful. It is sharper that the sharpest two-edged sword, cutting between soul and spirit, between joint and marrow. It exposes our innermost thoughts and desires (Hebrews 4:12, *TLB*)

> Remember, "Faith comes by hearing and hearing through the word of God" (Romans 10:17).

Cuts and Convicts

When the Scripture is shared, the Holy Spirit will "cut" the heart and "convict" the mind (Acts 2:37). He works as a prosecuting attorney bringing to mind sin, guilt, shame, and the need of the person to get right with God (John 16:8-11). The Holy Spirit also impresses on the heart how kind and gracious God is to give us Jesus (Romans 2:4).

In Acts 7, Stephen gave a powerful message to the Jewish leaders. He accused them of "always resisting the Holy Spirit." He explained that their resistance to the Holy Spirit was keeping him from being able to convict them and without that conviction there was no way for them to share in the gift of salvation.

Special Intervention

God monitors the events of life as he works through his natural laws. But God will also answer prayer and perform a *special intervention*. He may cause something to happen, maybe negative events like a plague, sickness, or storm. God's intention through the event is to humble and cause reflection that will lead to repentance.

God can also intervene to protect or bless, perhaps heal the sick or spare a person in a car accident. The Holy Spirit can bring forgotten experiences or an idea to influence a person toward a decision to follow Christ. The Spirit can use any circumstance to comfort, disturb, and confront, or to put the fear of God in the heart. The Holy Spirit can also remind the person of a past blessing to generate appreciation in the person's heart to remember how God has cared for and loved them. Every special intervention is designed to bring a person to repentance or salvation.

He Provides Power

The Holy Spirit provides power to the believer. He sanctifies (sets us apart for God's purpose). He then progressively transforms our mental attitudes, characters, and outward behaviors to reflect more and more of Jesus (2 Corinthians 3:18). This happens in conjunction with our learning and obeying Scripture. The Spirit provides the power to obey (Ephesians 3:16).

Your transformed life is the "miracle" of proof to non-believers that Christ is alive and still in the business of saving and changing people. Don't be afraid to share your story—mistakes and all. Everyone is a sinner. No one is perfect, but grace and forgiveness have changed you. Share it. Your friend wants forgiveness and change too.

The Holy Spirit gives you power to witness. Before his ascension, Jesus told the twelve that the Holy Spirit would give power to be his witnesses. Before you interact with a friend, family member, or coworker, ask God to give you the opportunity to share the truth of Jesus with a gracious, kind, but bold spirit.

In Acts 4:31, as the church asked God to intervene in their challenge, "the meeting place shook, and they were filled with the Holy Spirit. Then they preached the word of God with boldness." The Greek word translated boldness means to go public. The Holy Spirit enables believers to go public with the good news.

THE GOSPEL

"The gospel" was Paul's favorite term for his message. The Greek word is *euaggelion*, which means, good news. In chapter two, we gave a brief history to the background behind this word. In times of war after a battle, a runner would be sent from a military campaign back to the city. His job was to shout to the waiting people the "good news" of victory. The word also was used for the public heralds who called the towns people together to announce good news from the king. Again, this is the favorite word for the apostle's message in the New Testament. The good news of Christ must be shared and carried by you.

Paul calls the gospel the *dunamis* (dynamite, power) of God that works salvation (Romans 1:16). It is compared to a supernatural seed that is constantly bearing fruit (1 Peter 1:23). It is also called the light that opens up eyes to turn people from darkness and the power of Satan (Acts 26:18). The gospel saves people from their sins and reconciles them to God through Jesus (Romans 5:10). What is the gospel? The apostle Paul clarifies the gospel in a nutshell:

> Let me remind you, dear brothers and sisters of the Good News I preached to you before. You welcomed it then, and you still stand firm in it. It is the Good News that saves you if you continue to believe the message. . . . I passed on to you what was most important and what had also been passed onto me. Christ died for our sins, just as the Scriptures said. He was buried, and he was raised from the dead on the third day, just as the Scriptures said (1 Corinthians 15: 1, 2, *NLT*).

We will discuss the gospel message presentation that you and I share in the next chapter. For now, the gospel of Christ is the only power to change our destinies from hell to heaven. Nothing on earth can save us from hell and bring us into heaven but the gospel of Jesus Christ. Below are several reasons why only the gospel has this kind of power.

God Is Holy

To say God is holy means that God is separate from everything that is sinful or evil. God is moral perfection. Since God is spirit (John 4:24), how can we know what his holiness is? The commandments in Scripture are the written expression of God's attributes and mirror God's holiness.

To have a relationship with God requires one to be holy too. "Be holy to me for I am holy" (Leviticus 20:26). Only the blameless and the pure of heart can stand in God's presence (Psalm 24:3, 4). This means a person must obey every commandment in Scripture to be holy. To break one command automatically places the person in the category of lawbreaker (James 2:10). The wages of one sin is death (Romans 6:23).

Many people wrongfully believe Judgment Day will include the "good deeds" teeter-totter. God will place our good deeds on one side and our bad deeds on the other. If the good outweighs the bad, we make it into heaven.

Because God is holy, the "good deeds" teeter-totter is an impossibility. Why? When God's holiness comes in contact with sin, it turns to wrath. God's justice demands sin be punished, making it impossible for God to overlook sin without exacting a penalty.

God's Holy Wrath

Not explaining God's wrath is a major reason people do not accept Christ. God speaks of his wrath nearly 200 times and his judgment another 235 times in Scripture (*NASV*). Both terms appear in the Old and New Testaments. Think with me, if all religious people go to heaven, then why should they shift their trust in traditions and rituals to a relationship with Jesus Christ?

What is God's wrath? Again, it is God's holiness coming in contact with sin. When the sun rises, the light dispels the darkness. It is impossible for darkness and light to coexist. The same is true for God's holiness and any person who has sinned. In his "Doctrine of Grace" course, Professor Jack Cottrell compared this truth with drops of water falling on a hot stove. Hitting the stove, the drop boils, evaporates, and is gone. When God's holiness comes into contact with sin, the result is death. Those under God's wrath (sinners) are called God's enemies (Romans 5:10). This includes sincere, faithful, religious people who practice their rituals regularly but do not place faith in Jesus' saving work on the cross.

Remember what happened to the seventy men who looked into the ark of the Lord? "The Lord killed them" (1 Samuel 6:19). The people cried out, "Who is able to stand in the presence of the Lord, this holy God" (1 Samuel 6:20)? When Uzzah tried to stabilize the ark when the oxen pulling the cart stumbled, "God struck him dead" (2 Samuel 6:7). Remember when God descended on Mt. Sinai to give Moses God's Law? God warned Israel's leadership to put up boundaries and not to allow the people to touch the mountain after he had descended, or they would die (Exodus 19:21).

God's wrath in the New Testament is expressed in two Greek words, *orge* (Romans 1:18) and *thumos* (Romans 2:8). *Orge* is the constant, continuous indignation of God toward sin. We see this in physical death, disease, suffering, famines, droughts, severe storms, earthquakes, and plagues (Romans 1:18; Revelation 6). Much of *orge* wrath is the consequence of sin in the fallen world (Genesis 3:14-24). *Thumos* is the sudden explosion of God's wrath poured out on specific and isolated rebellion. Some examples are Sodom and Gomorrah (Genesis 19), the plagues in Egypt (Exodus 7-10), Ananias and Saphira (Acts 5), as well as the final judgement of the wicked (Revelation 14:10, 19).

Here's a question we must ask our religious friends, "How many sins does it take to become an object of God's wrath?" The answer is one. "Whoever keeps the whole law and yet stumbles in one point, has become guilty of all" (James 2:10).

God's Love

God expresses his goodness to us through his love. "God is love" (1 John 4:16). In the Old Testament it was obvious that God loved Israel. He saved them from the tyranny of the Egyptian Pharaohs who had enslaved Jacob's children for over 400 years. God had told Moses that he heard the cries of his people because of "their harsh slave drivers" (Exodus 3:7). God's mercy, compassion, and pity on his people were and are expressions of his love.

Through the Mosaic covenant, God provided a temporary "covering" for Israel's sins. The person, family, and nation would present a specified animal, sacrificed on God's altar, that would serve as their substitute and pay the penalty. The animal sacrifice temporarily satisfied God's holiness and love.

The blood substitute "delayed" God's wrath and allowed God's love to work out a permanent solution through the sacrifice of Jesus Christ on the cross. The Old Testament animal sacrificial system foreshadowed Jesus as God's "lamb who takes away the sins of the world" (John 1:29). The New Testament reiterates that God is love. "For God so loved the world that he gave his one and only Son that whoever believes in him should not perish but have eternal life. For God did not send his Son to condemn the world but through his Son the world might be saved" (John 3:16, 17).

Again, God's holiness and God's love are two separate, distinct qualities of God. The love of God states, "I don't want people to be separated from me for eternity and live in hell." God yearns to show people compassion and mercy, yet God's holiness abhors sin and requires lawlessness in every form to be punished.

The Cross Satisfies God's Love and Holiness

The holiness of God demands that sin be punished, but the love of God longs to be in relationship with us. On the cross, Jesus satisfied both the holiness and love of God by taking God's wrath for our sin. Jesus took our place. He was mocked, spit upon, beaten, and nailed to the cross for us. He voluntarily became our substitute and paid the penalty of our sin. God's holiness is satisfied in the fact our sins fell on Jesus. With sin's penalty paid, God's love is satisfied, and we are reconciled to him.

Salvation is by God's grace. We deserve hell, but through faith in Jesus we have forgiveness of sins and eternal life. Jesus is God's kindness toward us (Titus 3:4). To reject Jesus is to reject God's love. Without a saving faith in Jesus' work on the cross, people will pay the penalty for their sins in the eternal lake of fire (Revelation 20:15).

Jesus said, "I am the way, and the truth and the life. No one comes to the Father except through me" (John 14:6). The apostle Peter reiterated Jesus' statement, "Salvation is found in no one else, for there is no other name under heaven given to mankind by which we must be saved" (Acts 4:12).

The Gospel of Christ Saves Us from Hell

Few talk about hell, but hell is a real place where sinners will spend eternity. Sinners who have broken God's laws get what they deserve because hell is the penalty for sin. Paul wrote, "the wages (penalty) of sin is death" (Romans 6:23). Hell is a place of darkness (Matthew 25:30), severe punishment (Hebrews 10:28, 29), pain (Matthew 13:42 NIV), intense fear (Hebrews 10:31), burning fire (Matthew 13:30), humiliation, shame (Revelation 16:15), torture, no physical sleep (Revelation 14:11), a pit (Revelation 20:3), a prison (Proverbs 7:27), and a place where the flesh is eaten by worms (Mark 9:44).

Most significantly, hell is a place of eternal separation from God (2 Thessalonians 1:9). Hell is a place without hope. It involves pain, remorse, anguish, desperation—the worst that we have ever faced in life—but without the possibility of relief. This accurate description of hell should motivate us to want to share the news of salvation with others.

God did not create hell for people, but for the angels that followed Lucifer's rebellion against the God of heaven (2 Peter 2:4ff). Second Peter 2:9 explains that God rescues the righteous through faith in Jesus Christ, but those who remain in their sin and rebellion go to hell. Our friends and family must understand the terrible state sin creates. We are obligated to tell them. The love of God compels us to tell the truth (2 Corinthians 5:11-21).

You and I will never win anyone to Christ if we skirt the truth about hell or avoid telling the shocking news that without Jesus we are lost. Why would people accept Christ if they believe they can go to heaven by being good? If they do not see themselves in danger of eternal hell, why need a Savior? When we accurately describe the eternal suffering, it serves as a significant motivation for those who are not in Christ to receive salvation.

In Rob Bell's book, *God Wins*, the author cannot fathom God's love allowing anyone to spend eternity in hell. He's right on that point. That's why God sent his only Son to earth to die for our sins. "The righteousness of God through faith in Jesus Christ" (Romans 3:22). Jesus is the loving kindness of God (Titus 3:4).

The Gospel of Christ Saves Us for Heaven

Jesus promised that his exit from earth was to "prepare" a place for his followers in heaven (John 14:2). He also promised to return to take his faithful back to live with him forever (14:3). Scripture paints heaven as a paradise, a restored Garden of Eden, with gorgeous streams, a sea that appears as glass, palm trees, lush gardens with every kind of plant, flower, shrub, and tree (Revelation 22:1, 2). Mansions line streets of gold (Revelation 21:21). Rainbow colors jet through the sky from God's throne (Revelation 4). heaven is a city 2.7 cubic miles.There is a wall "protecting" those inside the city and keeping out the "cowards and unbelievers" (Revelation 21:8). There are twelve gates made of pure pearls (Revelation 21:21). In heaven there are worship services in Christ's presence (Revelation 5: 8). Believers are assigned work without the pain or setback we experience on earth (Revelation 7: 15). There are animals in heaven, and none are wild, not even the wolves and lions (Isaiah 65: 25). We maintain our ethnicity (Revelation 7:9). There are museums in heaven with humankind's greatest achievements that glorify God (Revelation 21: 24, 26). I believe God will take us on tours of the universe.

Why would anyone not long to live in this perfect, new, heaven and earth

(Revelation 22)? But remember, there is only one way to avoid hell and spend eternity in heaven; receive forgiveness of sin through the blood of Jesus shed on the cross (John 14: 6; Romans 5: 1-11). Believers have the awesome privilege of sharing this good news, so let's share it!

> But how can they call on him to save them unless they believe in him? And how can they believe in him if they have never heard about him? And how can they hear about him unless someone tells them? And how will anyone go and tell them without being sent? This is why the Scripture says, "How beautiful are the feet of messengers who bring good news" (Romans 10: 14, 15, *NLT*).

LET'S WRAP UP

Why Don't Christians Regularly Witness?

The empowered church is compelled by the *Great Commission* to make disciples. The *Holy Spirit* has revealed the gospel in the New Testament and gives each believer the necessary power to share the good news. The Holy Spirit also connects us to people in need of hearing the message of Jesus. The Gospel is the only power to remove our sins, save us from hell, and bring us into heaven to be with God and our brothers and sisters in Christ forever.

If we have the Great Commission, the gospel message, and power from the Holy Spirit, if we understand the never-ending consequences of eternity, then why do we Christians not witness? Here are five key reasons:

1. I don't know enough about the gospel
    There is no shame in not knowing or totally understanding Scripture. There will always be verses in the Bible we struggle to understand, but Peter challenged us to, "grow in the grace and knowledge of our Lord Jesus Christ" (2 Peter 3:18). Peter also challenged us to "Always be prepared to give the reason for the hope that you have" (1 Peter 3:15). Every believer is to make it their passion to learn and grow into Christlikeness. We are also to be learning, studying, and training so we are prepared to actively share the gospel message.
    We need to remember that each of us will face Christ on Judgment Day.

We will have to tell Jesus why we thought we had other priorities and never shared the good news with the neighbors around us.

2. I don't need to; that's why we have a preacher

I have often heard people say, "It's not my job to witness; that's why we pay for a preacher." It's true every preacher is called to preach the gospel (Romans 10:14, 15). The privilege of all preachers, full or part time, is to be paid to devote themselves to God's work including sharing the good news. However, we must remember Christ himself commanded each of us to make disciples. Consider again Matthew 28:18-20.

Then Jesus came to them and said "All authority in heaven and on earth has been given to me. Therefore, go and make disciples of all nations, baptizing them in the name of the Father and the Son and of the Holy Spirit, and teaching them to obey everything that I have commanded you. And surely I am with you always, to the very end of the age."

There are some who feel that the Great Commission was spoken to the twelve apostles and not applicable to anyone else. However, there possibly were more than 500 believers present at the time Jesus spoke those words. The Great Commission is the call to every Christian throughout time.

The New Testament gives us many examples of the gospel message being shared by people who weren't apostles. For example, in Acts 8, it says the believers in Jerusalem were forced to leave their homes due to persecution—*except* the apostles. "Those who had been scattered preached the word wherever they went" (Acts 8:4 NIV). Those preaching were not the apostles but every day, ordinary Christians. God scattered them and used their witness to start churches throughout Samaria.

3. If people want to find Jesus, they can go to church

Church buildings can be found almost anywhere. We live in a free country and people can come and go as they please. But it is also true that people far from God do not desire Jesus as Lord. Their sinful nature is in control. The Scripture says, "the flesh" (another name for the sinful nature) is "hostile to God. It does not submit to God's law, nor can it do so" (Romans 8:7). The apostle Paul also said, "I know that nothing good lives in me, that is, in my sinful nature" (Romans 7:18, *NLT*). It is natural for people who live according to their own desires to not want to go to church.

A CNN opinion poll (December 16, 2011) quoted David Kinnaman's recent book, *You Lost Me: Why Young Christians Are Leaving Church and Rethinking Faith*.[38] Kinnaman says 18- to 29-year old's have fallen into a "black hole" of church attendance. Kinnaman says "These young dropouts. . . are tired of being told how they should live their lives. They don't appreciate being condemned for living with a partner, straight or gay, outside of marriage or opting for abortion to terminate an unplanned pregnancy."

One of our responsibilities as Christians is to allow God to connect us to people outside of his will. Through authentic friendships, we get to know our neighbors, coworkers, and family, and more importantly, they get to know us. Eventually God will give us the opportunity to share our story and explain that they are facing the fearful expectation of eternity without a relationship with Jesus and the love of God that provides salvation for them. *When they know us, they will be willing to listen to us.* Genuine and sincere relationships build trust and allow God conversations.

4. I'm afraid

Fear of ridicule may be the leading reason people don't witness. How sad to be afraid of identifying our lives with Jesus Christ. We find ourselves wanting the praise and acceptance of friends more than that of Christ, which is what Scripture calls idolatry. Consider Jesus' words in Matthew 10:32, 33 (*NKJV*).

Therefore, whoever confesses me before men, him I will also confess before my Father who is in heaven. But whoever denies me before men, him I will also deny before my Father who is in heaven.

We need to remember that we were headed to hell before Christ saved us. Every day we need to recommit to Jesus' mission of sharing the gospel. We need to fear God more then we fear people and realize Satan will use criticism, mockery, and exclusion to put pressure on us not to share the good news. If we don't encounter opposition and criticism for our faith, then we are not being effective for Christ and need to reassess, reprioritize, and redirect our lives.

---

38. CNN Opinion Poll

Fear of failure is another reason people don't witness. We need to remember that God is with us and we cannot fail. All we have to do is share the simple gospel presentation Peter uses in Acts 2. It explains the gospel and how people should respond. It's clear, simple, and easy.

5. I don't think God will let good people go to hell

It's hard to visualize a family member, friend, or neighbor who we love to be lost and separated from God. Nearly half of Americans, Christian or not, believe all religions are equal paths to God and that good people earn their way to heaven. Fifty-nine percent believe the Bible, the Quran and the Book of Mormon all teach the same thing.[39]

Scripture clearly teaches that without a personal, saving relationship with Christ a person is lost (John 14:6; Acts 4:12). We need to be sure that our neighbors hear how serious the consequences are if they ignore the gospel message.

CHALLENGE

If we are empowered to share the gospel, our challenge is to explore approaches or types of witnessing. Different people and encounters demand different approaches.

1. Confrontation

Peter confronted Simon the spiritualist in Acts 8 with his wickedness. Paul confronted Felix with his sinful lifestyle. In Acts 2, Peter's conversation with his Jewish neighbors eventually led him to confront them by saying "You, with the help of wicked men, put him to death by nailing him to the cross" (Acts 2:23). Peter, Paul, and the apostles didn't skirt the issue of personal sin. As Peter so clearly stated, every person's sin has nailed Jesus to the cross. The writer of Acts described Peter closing out a teaching session: "With many other words he warned them; and he pleaded with them, "Save yourselves from this corrupt generation"" (Acts 2:40).

When it comes to pointing out personal sin, there is a good biblical precedent for direct confrontation. We need to be loving, open, and honest as

---

39. Barna, George, *Poll Shows Protestant Collapse,* June 2001. http://www.adherents.com/misc/BarnaPoll.html. Accessed October 2016.

we confront our neighbors remembering that if they don't accept salvation, they will spend eternity in hell.

2. Logic and syllogism

Logic is reasoning. We build the case with evidence. Syllogism is a form of reasoning that brings an obvious conclusion. For example, the *Cosmological Argument* shows the probability of a creator is logical. The syllogism for the argument would be: Earth is a creation. A creation demands a creator. Therefore, earth is made by a creator. The apostle Paul used this method of reasoning while in Athens.

If we are having this conversation with our neighbors, once they admit it seems obvious, the next step is for us to say, "If God created the earth, doesn't it make sense that such a powerful God could communicate with us?" If our neighbors agree that this seems logical, we can tell them how God reveals himself in Jesus. Each statement leads conversation from the general to the more specific details of Christ and his gospel.

Perhaps our neighbor is an atheistic evolutionist who says that all forms of life came from matter and matter is eternal. Using this logic-oriented strategy we can respond with, "Nothing plus nothing equals nothing. It does not equal matter. Nothing can only create itself. Creation demands a creator." Again, each statement is leading to the more specific details and the opportunity for evangelism.

General revelation is God's creation. Psalm 19:1 says, "The heavens declare the glory (character) of God." We can see God's characteristics in what he has created. We see God is all-powerful, all-wise, all-benevolent, all-righteous, and so on. *Specific Revelation* is God's word as expressed through Scripture, Jesus' life, and the apostles' teachings. General revelation tells us there is a God. Specific revelation tells us what he expects from us and how to have a relationship with him.

3. Testimonials

A testimony is simply telling about an instance when God blessed your life. A testimony shows God's involvement and intervention in a problem or crisis. Answered prayer can also provide testimonies.

The man who was born blind in John 9 is a great example of using a testimony to share about God. The Pharisees were questioning Jesus' claim to be the Son of God. Jesus had given this man sight. The man declared,

We know that God does not listen to sinners. He listens to the godly person who does his will. Nobody has ever heard of opening the eyes of a man born blind. If this man were not from God, he could do nothing (John 9:31-33).

4. Service

Caring for others by meeting their needs is a wonderful door to personal evangelism. Jesus went about doing good (Acts 10:38). God gave the apostles the supernatural ability to perform miracles of healing. God opens the hearts of our friends through genuine kindness.

Again, service is a door to personal evangelism. So many see serving their community as the end in itself, but it is so much more. What good does it do to meet a temporary need like feeding the hungry but never getting around to feeding their soul with heavenly manna, Jesus Christ, the Bread of Life?

5. Story telling

Story telling was a primary way Jesus introduced people to the gospel. In the New Testament, these stories are called parables. Jesus' stories involved birds, banquets, hunting for buried treasure, tiny seeds, mustard trees, fishing, wayward sons, lost sheep, lost coins, ranch owners holding their workers accountable, and many, many more. You can use these stories to open doors to evangelism.

6. Intentional gatherings

Today most churches use their worship gathering as their main door to evangelism. The classic example of an intentional gathering to share the gospel is given by Levi in Matthew 9:9-12. It appears that Levi threw a dinner in honor of Jesus. He invited all his old buddies and fellow tax collectors to this dinner in order to meet Jesus. Jesus endorsed this strategy when criticized by the religious Pharisees. "It is not the healthy who need a doctor, but the sick. . . . For I have not come to call the righteous, but sinners" (Matthew 9:12-13).

CHAPTER FOUR
The Expansion of Church: You Will Be My Witness

"But you will receive power when the Holy Spirit has
come upon you, and you will be my witnesses in
Jerusalem, Judea, Samaria, and to the end of the earth"
(Acts 1:8)

In this chapter, we will discover that both church history and today's research confirm Jesus' teachings that relationships are the best method to bring people to salvation and ultimately to expand Christ's kingdom. Obviously, God will use books, conferences, seminars, radio, social media, TV, church services, and evangelistic events to preach and teach the gospel. However, the most effective tool for getting people to the point where they will listen to and receive the gospel message is a personal relationship. Modern communication such as the cell phone, email, and social media venues all fall in the relational category too. Jesus, the apostles, the early church, the middle ages and today's research show that the relational strategy was and is the best evangelistic strategy.

EXPANSION OF CHURCH THROUGH PERSONAL EVANGELISM

Throughout the New Testament we see Jesus and the apostles preaching to crowds, with people making decisions to follow Jesus. Scripture however highlights their interactions with individuals in the local neighborhoods, small groups, and personal encounters along the way.

Interestingly, there seems to be only one reference in the New Testament to evangelism taking place during a church service (1 Corinthians 14:24, 25). Most evangelistic encounters in the New Testament occurred outside the synagogue/ church service by way of personal relationships. Some examples of this include all the apostles, Nicodemus, Mary, Martha, Lazarus, Zacchaeus, Simon, the Ethiopian, the jailor, Cornelius, Saul of Tarsus, Lydia, Apollos, Simon the Tanner, Timothy, Titus and many more.

Jesus as Personal Evangelist

The gospel of John described Jesus' life and ministry this way: "The Word became flesh and blood and moved into the neighborhood" (John 1:14, *The Message*). So, where did Jesus live? Where did Jesus work? In the neighborhood. He met the neighbors, learned their names, heard their needs, ate with them, and ministered to them individually. Jesus was a friend to sinners (Matthew 11:19). He went into Peter's house and healed his mother-in-law (Matthew 8:14). Jesus had dinner at Levi's house where we met tax collectors and sinners (Matthew 9:10), Jesus went into a synagogue leader's home and raised his daughter from the dead (Matthew 9:23).

Jesus went through towns, villages, and synagogues getting to know the neighbors (Matthew 9: 35). He healed individuals of sickness and proclaimed the good news of his kingdom (Matthew 9:35). Living in the neighborhood, Jesus saw and heard the brokenness. The people were like sheep without a shepherd, "harassed and helpless" (Matthew 9:36). The Greek words are revealing. *Harassed* carries the idea of flaying a fish. Life had sliced and diced the people's hearts, dreams, and families. The word for *helpless* shows a people defeated, lying prostrate on the ground with life's foot pressing their face into the dirt. It was then Jesus proclaimed to his disciples, "The harvest is plentiful, but the workers are few. Ask the Lord of the harvest, therefore, to send out workers into his harvest field" (Matthew 9:37, 38).

Do you see how Jesus lived? He loved his neighbors strategically to bring them to salvation. He wasn't afraid or repulsed by people's depraved spiritual conditions or obnoxious habits. He loved the neighborhood so much he died to fix it (John 3:16).

Apostles as Personal Evangelists

As apprentices, the disciples watched Jesus proclaim the good news to individuals and groups for about fourteen months. They observed and then assisted Jesus in his ministry. In Matthew 9 and 10 Jesus called them to be evangelists.

> When he saw the crowds, he had compassion on them, because they were harassed and helpless, like sheep without a shepherd. He said to his disciples, "The harvest is great, but the workers are few. Ask the Lord of the harvest, therefore, to *send out* workers into his harvest field" (Matthew 9:36, 37 *emphasis added*).

As Jesus made personal relationships his priority, he developed trust by listening, caring, and demonstrating love in meeting peoples' needs. Notice Jesus' compassion for the people. His heart broke as he heard their stories and saw their physical and spiritual pain. The people were without a shepherd to guide them on the journey to God.

Ask God

Jesus commanded his followers to "Ask the Lord" to "send out" workers who would witness. The Greek word for *ask* carries the idea of a passionate, gut wrenching, pleading with the Lord to send out more witnesses. We often pray for the lost, but how often do we beg the Lord to send out more witnesses to go the lost?

To Send Out Witnesses

The Greek word translated "send out" carries the idea of casting or throwing out violently. It is used to describe the final Judgment when Jesus "throws out" his enemies into the Lake of Fire (Matthew 8:12). It is used when the Holy Spirit "drove" Jesus into the wilderness to be tested (Mark 1:12). The idea is that when you intentionally listen to people who are lost in sin, their pain and confusion become obvious. The Holy Spirit stirs in believers "a gut-wrenching urgency" that compels us to witness the good news. The apostle Paul explained that God's love in Christ Jesus, which removes all sin, "compels" us to witness (2 Corinthians 5:14).

Notice the prayer again: *Send out* laboring witnesses. The prayer is not "Lord have my neighbors come to my Sunday school class or small group or to the church service," even though that would be a wonderful praise. The Great Commission strategy is to go to them.

After being implored to send out more witnesses, notice who God sent out; the 12 disciples (Matthew 10). Be careful what you pray for.

The Apostles Follow Jesus' Evangelistic Method

In Matthew 10, Jesus called the twelve to be his apostles (or "sent out ones"). "Jesus sent out the twelve with these instructions" (verse 5). This particular evangelistic campaign targeted Jewish neighborhoods (verse 6). The reason was the Jews knew the Old Testament prophesies and were waiting for the Messiah. Jesus promised that God would provide food, clothing, and protection so they should not fear any threat (verses 9, 10, 26).

In Luke 10, Jesus sent out 70 followers into Gentile neighborhoods. They went "two by two" (verse 1). Read the section and you will see Jesus followed the same evangelistic method for his Gentile campaign as the Jewish campaign.

The Apostles go into the Neighborhoods

After entering the Jewish neighborhood, they were to find a "worthy person" (verse 11). This is the person who believed Jesus was the Messiah. This new Jesus follower would open his home as the neighborhood headquarters (verse 11).

The disciples would then establish relationships with neighbors. Over the course of the next days and weeks, the followers of Christ would love the neighbors by ministering to their needs and witnessing the gospel of Jesus.

If the town had no "worthy" person, or the neighbors were cold to the good news, as a sign of condemnation, the apostles were to "shake the dust of their feet and leave" (verse 14). They were also to warn the neighbors that on Judgment Day, Sodom and Gomorrah would be treated better by the Lord then those who heard and rejected the good news of Jesus (verse 15).

Household Evangelism: The *Oikos* Effect

The Greek word *Oikos* is translated in the Bible as "house," or "household." In the New Testament the household included more than immediate biological family members. It included friends, relatives, workers, and slaves (Roman slavery could be compared to employment). Household evangelism occurred throughout the New Testament. Consider some passages that suggest this.

- "Go home (*oikos*) to your own people and tell them" (Mark 5:19)

- "Today salvation has come to this house (*oikos*)" (Luke 19:9)

- "Cornelius friends and family were baptized" (Acts 10:48)

- "[Lydia] and the members of her household (*oikos*) were baptized" (Acts 16:15)

- "Immediately [the jailer] and his family (*oikos*) were baptized" (Acts 16:33)

THE FIRST 300 YEARS: BELIEVERS AS EVANGELISTS

Christianity was considered an illegal religion for most of the first 300 years of its existence. Romans believed Caesar was god. They participated in daily emperor worship which involved burning incense in public squares and at their workplaces. Christians, of course, refused to worship Caesar as god. The Romans began to believe the Christians were members of a secret kingdom which would rise and attempt to overthrow the Empire.

Persecuted

Believing Christians would eventually rebel against Rome, acknowledging only one king, Jesus, Because of this, the Caesars persecuted the followers of Christ. In its first three hundred years, Christianity endured 10 major seasons of persecution. Christians were not permitted to own property. They could lose their jobs, be put on racks, be burned at the stake, or be thrown to lions.

Secret Worship Services in Catacombs

The *ekklesia* met in homes (Romans 16:5), Christian-owned businesses or halls (Acts 19:9), and in catacombs. Throughout the second and third centuries in times of severe persecution, secret worship services were held underground in caves and catacombs. Christians gathered to worship the living Christ among the buried bodies of many who were martyred for the faith.

Worship services were held in hiding, for fear of execution. Non-believers were prohibited from participating in worship for fear they were spies who would report the church's location to authorities. Yet there was phenomenal evangelistic growth during this period.

Using the church building to attract the neighborhood to a church service was not the strategy. Church buildings were not used until AD 250 and early 300. So how did people come to the Lord?

Unbelievable Expansion through Personal Witnessing

In spite of persecution and secret worship services, conservative estimates indicate that the church grew by 40% annually.[40] How did this happen? Personal evangelism. Christians were so grateful for their salvation through their Savior and Lord, Jesus, it was an honor to suffer for their living king in this life.

Believers returned good for evil, loved their enemies, and cared for the sick and orphaned. They were willing to allow the confiscation of their property and even die for their witness. Their lives were marked by radical love. Around AD 150, Justin Martyr wrote to Emperor Pius to explain that Christians were not a threat to the Empire. Notice his emphasis on the lifestyle of believers and their goal to witness.

> Formerly we rejoiced in uncleanness of life. Now we only rejoice in chastity. Before we used magic arts. Now we dedicate ourselves to the true God. Before we loved money and possessions more than anything. Now we share what we have, to everyone in need. Before we hated and killed one another and would not eat with those of another race. But now since the manifestation of Christ, we have come to a common life and pray for our enemies to *win over* those who hate us with unjust cause (emphasis added).[41]

---

40. Rodney, Starks, *Rise of Christianity: A Sociologist Reconsiders History*. (Princeton University Press). 1997. p. 161
41. Justin Martyr, *The First Apology*. http://www.newadvent.org/fathers/0126.htm. Accessed October 2017.

Notice the end goal of these early believers; to "win over" their enemies. Rodney Stark gives insight into the early Christians' emphasis upon being a personal witness for Christ.

> Believers worshipped in their homes. They had no institutions. Evangelism was done person to person. The practice of the clergy being responsible for evangelism did not exist. These early believers lived missionally, incarnationally, which opened doors for organic evangelism through relationships.[42]

Believers Evangelize in Teams (AD 400 – 800)

St. Patrick's evangelism reflected many elements of Jesus' and the apostles' method found in Matthew 9-10 and Luke 10. The date cannot be confirmed, but in the 400s or early 500s, Patrick began to evangelize his homeland, Ireland. The church had become "organized" in the third and fourth centuries and with the institutional church, evangelism waned beyond the Roman borders. The Church believed that before a pagan people could be evangelized, they first needed to be civilized in the Roman language and ways.

Patrick learned from Jesus' method. He put together a team of about 12 people that included preachers, teachers, and experts in carpentry and agriculture. Patrick would approach the tribal king and ask permission to set up camp near the town.[43]

While establishing relationships, the *ekklesia* team members would pray for the sick, teach new gardening techniques, clothing production, and engage the pagans in everyday life. The team would return to their camp in the evening and invite their new friends to witness singing and teaching about Christ. When a church was established, Patrick would leave a few team members behind and move to the next neighborhood. New converts were trained to replace any team member who stayed behind.[44] Over 30 to 40 years, Patrick's *ekklesia* teams planted about 700 new churches and ordained over 1,000 priests (preachers).[45]

---

42. Rodney, Stark, *Rise of Christianity*. P. 38
43. George G. Hunter. *The Celtic Way of Evangelism: How Christianity Can Reach the West... Again.* (Abington Press, Nashville TN. 2000). P. 21
44. Ibid. p. 22
45. Ibid. p. 23

Believers Evangelize through Monastic Outposts (AD 1200 – 1600)

No doubt Patrick and Columba in Ireland, as well as Boniface in England, had a monumental evangelistic impact. Following the evangelistic method of Jesus and the apostles, Francis of Assisi (AD 1200) would pray for a missionary outpost to grow to seventy (Luke 10). Once at seventy, Assisi would send these missionaries out in the pagan neighborhoods two by two. Through loving service in the neighborhood, these missionaries preached repentance and salvation through Jesus.

Once again, it is the planting of these *ekklesia* type communities in pagan or conquered territories that enabled personal relationships to develop in the neighborhoods. Through love and witness the gospel message spread. Once baptized, the missionary team would disciple and assimilate the new believers into the values and behaviors of Christ's kingdom.

Historian Williston Walker wrote, "From Francis of Assisi on, missionary outreach was the primary endeavor of the monastic order. To the work of these orders the Christianity of the Southern, Central and large parts of North America is due."[46] Historian Kenneth Scott Latourette writes, "Monastic outposts carried the gospel to the major countries of Asia, such as Japan, China, and India. They were found as well in Africa. Of the major continents, only Australia was untouched by missionaries of the monastic orders.[47]

EFFECTIVE PERSONAL EVANGELISM TODAY

Donald McGavran (*The Bridges of God*, 1955)

In 1955, Donald McGavran wrote *The Bridges of God* with the goal of giving insight to how people come to Christ. McGavran was a Christian Church missionary in India, tied to the Restoration Movement. In his research, McGavran discovered the vast majority of people who came to Christ did not do so because of revivals or mass events but through family members and friends. McGavran called these relationships *The Bridges of God.*[48]

---

46. Williston Walker. *A History of the Christian Church.*, rev. ed (New York: Charles Scribner's Sons, 1959). P. 379.
47. Kenneth Scott Latourette. *A History of Christianity.*, rev. ed (New York: Harper & Row, 1975). P. 927.
48. Donald McGavran. *The Bridges of God* (London: World Dominion Press, 1955), 4.

Institute of American Church Growth National Survey, 1985)

Then in the 1980s more research was done by the Institute of American Church Growth of Pasadena, California, who asked 14,000 believers, "How did you come to church and eventually to accept Christ?"[49] These were the responses that were given most often:

Special need 1-2%

Walk-In. 2-3%

Visitation. 5-6%

Sunday school 4-5%

Evangelistic Crusade 1%

Church Program 2-3%

Friend/Relative 75-90%

Church growth expert Win Arn gives seven reasons why personal relationships rather than impersonal church services provide the most effective method:[50]

1. Friendships provide a natural network for sharing God's love.

2. Family members are receptive because trust has been established.

3. Friendships allow for unhurried dialogue and demonstrating love in action.

4. Friendships provide a natural support system when others come to Christ.

5. Friendships provide a natural bridge into the church fellowship.

6. Friendship evangelism tends to eventually win entire families because they witness life-change over a period of time.

7. Friendship evangelism provides an ever-increasing number of contacts and relationships.

Research conducted by The Institute for American Church Growth shows that ninety-seven out of every one hundred decisions for Christ, at an isolated event

---

49. *The Master's Plan of Evangelism*, p. 43
50. Ibid. p. 45-52

or that happen independently from the new believer's social network, are never incorporated into a church.[51] Seventy-five to ninety-seven percent who join a local church say that a friend or relative influenced their decision.[52]

Gary Mcintosh (Talbot School of Theology Survey, 2005)

In the early 2000s, Gary McIntosh, professor at Talbot School of Theology surveyed over 1,000 Christians across forty states asking the question, "How did you come to faith in Christ?"[53] McIntosh's research revealed around seventy-one percent came to Christ through family and friends. Seventeen percent through the professional staff of a church.

The research stated that the impact of the professional staff was smaller with millennials, suggesting a lack of connection to the local church.[54] In the future, for millennials to be reached, Christian relationships will be the key.

Barna (Revitalizing Evangelism Report, 2019)

In 2019, the Barna group released a comprehensive study of evangelism in America called *Revitalizing Evangelism*. In surveying non-Christians, fifty-three percent of millennials and thirty-two percent of all older non-Christians prefer a *one-on-one conversation* with a Christian when exploring the Christian faith over other evangelistic methods.[55] A total of eighty-five percent prefer a casual conversation with a Christian. Atheists and agnostics have a higher opinion of Christians then they do of Christian Institutions.[56] And one out of five expressed an interest in exploring the Christian faith.[57] Another benefit of the personal evangelism method is a natural network of relationships containing a level of trust. These relationships are never ending and can lead in multiple directions offering a multitude of ways to share the Gospel.

---

51. J. Hampton Keathley, III, "The Stewardship of God's Truth Through Evangelism," n.d., http://bible.org/seriespage/stewardship-god%E2%80%99s-truth-through-evangelism-part-2.
52. Ibid. 152.
53. Gary McIntosh. What Person Led You to Faith in Christ? Biola University Blogs. The Good Book Blogs. October 29, 2014. Biola.edu/good-book-blog/2014/what-person-led-you-to-faith-in-Christ
54. Ibid
55. Barna Group. *Revitalizing Evangelism*. Produced in Partnership with Alpha USA. 2019. P. 69.
56. Ibid. Pg 66.
57. Ibid.

CHAPTER FIVE
The Expansion of Church: Discipleship is Imperative

"Therefore go, and make disciples of all nations,
baptizing them in the name of the Father, and
of the Son and of the Holy Spirit..."
(Acts 28:19)

Obviously, God will use books, conferences, seminars, radio, social media, TV, church services and evangelistic events to preach and teach the gospel. The most effective tool for getting people to the point where they will listen and receive the gospel message is through personal relationships. Modern communication such as the cell phone, email, and social media venues all fall in the relational category too.

THE GOSPEL MESSAGE WE SHARE (Acts Chapter 2)

Before we go into the neighborhood and begin sketching the spiritual profile of every neighbor (this information is found in the second part of this book), we need to first understand the gospel, the good news Christ wants us to share.

The book of Acts reports the "acts" of the apostles as they established Christ's Church. During their ministries, the Holy Spirit revealed and confirmed the gospel preached by the apostles with signs, miracles and wonders. If we can learn the gospel message the apostles presented and the prescribed means of accepting the gospel, we can be confident that what we share is the authentic good news. Our friends and neighbors can also possess the assurance they are right with God.

The Gospel Message Introduced at Pentecost

Let's discover the gospel we are to share. Acts 2 begins with these words in verses 1-4:

> When the day of Pentecost came, they were all together in one place. Suddenly a sound like the blowing of a violent wind came from heaven and filled the whole house where they were sitting. They saw what seemed to be tongues of fire that separated and came to rest on each of them. All of them were filled with the Holy Spirit and began to speak in other tongues as the Spirit enabled them.

For Jews, Pentecost (fifty days after Passover) was a harvest celebration. Each Jew brought the best crops of the first harvest to the Lord (Exodus 23:16; 34:22). Giving their best brought God's promise for a bumper crop, the rest of the harvesting season.

For similar reasons, God launched the church fifty days after Jesus' crucifixion and resurrection. It is the *first spiritual harvest* (people saved through the gospel proclamation). Pentecost also suggested an overflowing crop for the rest of this spiritual planting and harvesting season. The time frame is from Pentecost to the Second Coming.

The Gospel Message Revealed through the Holy Spirit

Acts 2:2 says a loud, tornado-like wind descended from Heaven and filled the house where the one hundred and twenty believers were praying (Acts 1:15). The wind took on the appearance of tongues of fire that rested on each apostle, which then penetrated each heart (Acts 2:3, 4). Meanwhile, the loud wind drew thousands of Jewish spectators (v. 6) still in town from the Passover/Pentecost celebrations. Acts 2:7-11 suggests at least sixteen different dialects/languages are represented by the onlookers, a diverse audience, indeed.

The twelve *disciples* (ones taught) now called *apostles* (ones sent) did something amazing. The text of Acts 2:4 suggests each apostle mingled with the crowd, greeting and talking to the different people groups in their own native language (v. 6). The crowds were excited but perplexed. How could these Galileans speak "our language" (v.7)?

The Outpouring of the Holy Spirit

There is one Holy Spirit but in Scripture he manifests (expresses) himself in two different ways; through the *outpouring* and *indwelling*. The twelve apostles received the *outpouring* of the Holy Spirit. He "rested on" (Acts 2:3) them. Throughout the book of Acts the phrase, "the Holy Spirit *came upon"* is used (Acts 1:8; 8:16; 10:44, 45; 19:6). The purpose of the *outpouring* was threefold.

1. The Holy Spirit *supernaturally revealed* the gospel message to the apostles (revelation)

2. The Holy Spirit gave *miraculous gifts* as proof their gospel message was from God

3. The Holy Spirit *gave miraculous gifts* to the infant church through the laying on of apostles' hands

The New Testament was not completed until approximately sixty years after Pentecost (A.D. 90). How could the infant church know the mission, morality, and mandates of Christ that you and I read in our New Testament today during that sixty-year gap?

It is because the Holy Spirit revealed Christ's word to the infant church through supernatural gifts. The letters to the Corinthians identify *prophecy* as "proclaiming." With this gift, church leaders were able to preach, and the Holy Spirit would supernaturally reveal and deliver God's New Testament message. The gift of *wisdom* was the supernatural ability to apply God's word to everyday life. For instance, the person with this gift could counsel a couple struggling with their marriage using principles found in Ephesians 5, even though Ephesians 5 was not written for another thirty years. The gift of *teaching* was the supernatural ability to reveal Jesus as the Messiah from the Old Testament. The gift of *miracles* involved supernatural acts that authenticated the gospel message. After hearing that Jesus died and rose from the grave, people wanted proof. Miracles confirmed the supernatural claims of the gospel. Speaking in a *tongue* was the supernatural ability to speak a foreign language without prior training. The purpose was for cross-cultural evangelism. The miraculous gifts ceased with the death of the apostles (Acts 8:14-18). They were no longer needed since the written Scripture, now completed, replaced the miraculous revelatory gifts (I Corinthians 13: 8-10).

The Indwelling of the Holy Spirit

The *outpouring* came by the laying of the apostles' hands on believers (Acts 8: 14-18), manifesting in miraculous gifts that communicated and confirmed the gospel message. The *indwelling* of the Holy Spirit comes in water baptism (Acts 2:38) and manifests through the believer with their character transformation called the fruit of the Holy Spirit (Galatians 5: 22, 23).

The *indwelling* Spirit also provides the believer with power to obey God's word, witness the gospel, and endure trials and persecutions (Acts 4: 31; Philippians 2:12, 13). He "seals" the believer for eternal life (Ephesians 4:30).

The Gospel Message Foretold in the Old Testament

In Acts 2:14-21, Peter explained to the Jewish crowd that what they heard the apostles teaching and what they saw the apostles doing (the supernatural acts) had been predicted 800 years earlier through the prophet Joel. Joel had predicted that in the last days, also known as the Messianic period, God would pour out his Spirit on all people (Joel 2:28). We conclude from Joel's prophecy and Pentecost (Acts 2) that the last days began when Jesus ascended into Heaven.

In verse 21, Peter, who quoted Joel in Acts 2:16-21, told the crowd that the message they were about to hear would be the message that brings salvation to anyone *who calls on the name of the Lord.*

The Gospel Message Presents Jesus as Lord & Savior

Peter's presentation is *apologetic*, meaning to give a defense. It's courtroom jargon used by a lawyer presenting the proofs or the evidence for a case. That's exactly what Peter does, and what we need to do too. You might be wondering, "Evidence for what?" Look at Acts 2:36: "Therefore let all Israel be assured of this: God has made this Jesus, whom you crucified, both Lord and Christ." Sharing the good news means we learn how to convince our friends that Jesus is both *Lord* (Master) and *Christ* (Savior).

THE FOUR PROOFS JESUS IS SAVIOR AND LORD

How do we convince people that Jesus is both Lord and Savior? We present the four proofs Peter shared with his audience. We then give the invitation and challenge them to accept Jesus as their *personal* Lord and Savior. We are to use persuasion and show them how to "accept" Christ as seen with Peter's audience in Acts 2:38-40. We must become familiar with these proofs so we can interject them throughout conversations with friends and acquaintances.

Proof #1: Jesus Performed Miracles

Men of Israel, listen to this: Jesus of Nazareth was a man accredited [proved] by God to you by miracles, wonders and signs, which God did among you through him, as you yourselves know (Acts 2:22, insertion mine).

The first proof that Jesus is both Lord and Savior is found in his miracles. Study the Gospels (Matthew, Mark, Luke, and John), study the miracles of Jesus. He healed the sick; cast out demons; raised the dead; calmed the storm; walked on water; fed 5,000 men, women and children with a few loaves and fishes; and so many more.

The miracles of Jesus prove his claim to be the Lord and Savior of the world. For example, Jesus walked on the Sea of Galilee, through hurricane force winds, to reach the disciples, struggling to stay afloat in a boat As Jesus got into their boat, the winds died down. "Then those who were in the boat *worshiped* him, saying,

'Truly you are the Son of God'" (Matthew 14:33, emphasis mine). You never see a good, sane, or righteous person accepting worship. Only God is to be worshiped. Mohammed, Confucius, and Buddha would not accept worship, but Jesus did. As C.S. Lewis said, Jesus is either a liar, a lunatic or the one he claimed to be, the Son of God.[58]

I had the privilege of baptizing a Muslim friend into Christ. One day I casually mentioned that Muslims teach that Mohammad did three miracles, yet the gospels record Jesus performed many. Most Muslims read and believe Matthew, Mark, and Luke (the life of Christ), to be true. I asked my friend, "Does that suggest Jesus has greater authority than Mohammad?" My friend responded, "I've never looked at the miracles of Jesus that way." It was the *many* miracles of Jesus that enabled my friend to draw the line between Mohammad and Christ. Eventually he was baptized.

Proof #2: Jesus Fulfilled OT Prophesy

The second proof is Jesus fulfilled Old Testament prophecy. We tell our friends that Jesus fulfilled messianic prophecy. In Acts 2:25-28, Peter quoted Psalm 16:8-11. This is one of many descriptions of the coming Messiah, revealed by God, through OT prophets, hundreds of years before Jesus was born. Why prophesy? To ensure the Jewish nation would recognize and receive the Messiah when he arrived.

Through his prophets, God revealed that Jesus would be born of a virgin (Isaiah 7:14), be called the Son of God (Psalm 2:7), be born in Bethlehem (Micah 5:2), begin his ministry in Galilee (Isaiah 9:1), perform miracles (Isaiah 32:3, 4), teach in parables (Psalm 78:2), and fall under a cross (Psalm 109:24, 25). Old Testament prophesy predicted his body would be pierced (Zechariah 12:10). He would be crucified between two thieves (Isaiah 53:12) and have a physical resurrection (Psalm 16:10). There are hundreds more messianic prophecies in scripture. Learn 20-30 of these prophesies from the easy-to-read book, Josh McDowell's *The New Evidence That Demands a Verdict*.[59]

Remember, these prophecies were given 400 to 1,500 years before Jesus was born. The final week of Jesus' life was almost completely mapped out in prophecy

---

58. Lewis, C.S., *Mere Christianity*, revised edition, New York, Macmillan/Collier, 1952. P 55 ff.
59. Josh McDowell, *The New Evidence That Demands a Verdict* ([Rev., updated, and expanded]. Nashville: T. Nelson, 1999), 168-192.

with fifty-four prophesies being fulfilled in that week alone! The probability of one person fulfilling all the messianic prophecies recorded in the Old Testament would be the same as covering the state of Texas knee deep in quarters, then having a friend fly over in a helicopter and try to pick out the specific quarter you have in mind. The chance of picking the right one is 1 in 100, 000,000,000,000,000.[60]

The Dead Sea Scrolls validate all the Old Testament prophesies about Jesus. Discovered in the 1940s – 50's, the scrolls include all of the Old Testament books except Esther. Carbon dating has put the copies at least two hundred years before the birth of Christ. That is significant because it proves the prophecies from the Old Testament could not have been written after the life of Christ.

Proof #3: Jesus' Bodily Resurrection

The third proof that Jesus is both Lord and Savior is found in his bodily resurrection. In Acts 2:29-32, Peter compared King David's tomb to Jesus' grave. Peter said the Old Testament king was still in his grave but "God has raised this Jesus to life, and we are *all witnesses* of the fact" (v. 32 *added italics*). There are many proofs for Christ's resurrection. We need to familiarize ourselves with them so we can share them with our friends. I will list several.

Jesus' Dead Body Could Not Have Been Stolen

Jesus predicted his resurrection. Many people—from his followers to the religious leaders, to the Roman officials—knew it. The Jewish leaders feared the disciples would steal the body then proclaim that Jesus was alive. They went to the Roman officials to ask that the tomb be sealed. The tomb was not only closed with a huge boulder that required the strength of many men to move, but it was also closed with the governor's seal. Anyone who dared to break this seal would be executed. Finally, a contingent of Roman guards was placed at the tomb; they would have been executed if the body of Jesus were stolen. (Matthew 27:62-66).

Dead People were Resurrected in Jerusalem

Matthew 27:51-53 records that after Jesus' death, the curtain in the temple that divided the Most Holy Place from the Holy Place split in two. An earthquake broke open tombs, "…the bodies of many holy people who had died were raised to life.

---

60. Peter Stoner, *Science Speaks* (Rev. ed.; [S.l.]: Moody Press, 1976), 100-107.

They came out of the tombs after Jesus' resurrection, went into the holy city and appeared to many people" (v 52, 53). This incredible fact demonstrated the power of Jesus' death and resurrection. It foreshadowed the day when every grave will open (1 Corinthians 15:50-56).

Roman Authorities Confirmed Jesus' Death on the Cross

Muslims believe that Jesus was miraculously caught up into heaven and that someone surreptitiously took his place on the cross (Quran 4:157). There are also those who suggest Jesus was not dead when taken from the cross. They maintain he revived in the tomb, pushed aside the stone, and came forth as if he had experienced a resurrection. This claim is ludicrous when one understands the brutality of a Roman flogging and crucifixion (Matthew 27:26). Many prisoners died from the flogging alone.[61]

Furthermore, it was the duty of those who presided over the crucifixion to make sure that each prisoner was dead. When the Roman soldiers ran a spear through Jesus' side, both water and blood flowed out separately, proving that Jesus' heart had stopped (John 19:34). People who loved Jesus took his body down from the cross and carried him into the tomb. If there had been any doubt Jesus was dead, they would not have left him alone in a tomb.

Jesus Appeared to 500 People at One Time

Yet, on the third day after his death, Jesus appeared first to a group of women (Matthew 28:4), next to two men traveling to Emmaus (Luke 24:13-35), then to a group of disciples gathered in an upper room (Luke 24:36-45). A week later, Thomas was with the disciples when Jesus appeared to them again, coming in "… though the doors were locked…" (John 20:26). He later had breakfast with some disciples, including Peter, on the shore of the Sea of Tiberius (John 21:1-14). John writes, "This was now the third time Jesus appeared to his disciples after he was raised from the dead" (John 21:14). Jesus did not show himself only to those who were close to him. He also appeared to a huge crowd, so when Paul was writing to the church at Corinth he was able to say, "…he appeared to more than five hundred of the brothers and sisters at the same time, most of whom are still living…" (1 Corinthians 15:6). These are all convincing arguments.

---

61. Bible History Online, *The Roman Scourge,* http://www.bible-history.com/past/flagrum.html. Accessed 8/19/15.

Doubters became Believers

The disciples did not believe the testimony of the women who saw Jesus alive at the tomb (Mark 16:11, 14; Luke 24:9-11). Their shattered dreams of a political messiah sent them into a tailspin. Peter turned into a temporary recluse (Luke 22:62). Two disciples walked away to search for another dream (Luke 24:13-35). Afraid of the Jewish leaders who were hostile to Jesus, the remainder went into hiding behind locked doors (John 20:19). However, after these doubters touched, saw, interacted, and ate with Jesus over a period of forty days, they were convinced that he was alive.

Christ commissioned them to take the gospel to the world. They were *transformed into bold preachers* proclaiming, "Christ is alive." Notice Peter's courage as he testified before the same Jewish Sanhedrin that sentenced Christ to death (Acts 4:1-22).

> "Salvation is found in no one else, for there is no other name under heaven given to mankind by which we must be saved.' When they saw the courage of Peter and John and realized that they were unschooled, ordinary men, they were astonished and they took note that these men had been with Jesus" (Acts 4:12, 13).

Cynics suggest the disciples hallucinated, but the group of Jesus' chosen eleven, the other disciples, the women at the tomb, and hundreds of others who saw Jesus alive, cannot have shared the same hallucination. It is impossible for more than five hundred people to have the same hallucination.

The Apostles Exhibited Miraculous Powers

Study the book of Acts. See how the apostles' gospel presentation was confirmed with hundreds of miracles. Even the shadow of Peter heals the sick lying on the street (Acts 5:12-16).

The Apostles Accept Suffering and Death for Their Message

Throughout Acts, the apostles were persecuted by religious and government leaders for their testimony that salvation is found only through Jesus (5:17-42). Perhaps the apostle Paul suffered more than any other (2 Corinthians 11:16-29), yet he was able to boast about Christ's power in him. No one submits to torture for what he knows to be a lie or hoax. No one goes around doing things that result in being beaten and ostracized unless he believes one hundred percent in his cause. The apostles staked their lives on their testimony that Jesus, the Son of God, had been raised from the dead and salvation was found only in him.

Saul the Persecutor Became Paul the Preacher

Saul's transformation into Paul is further proof of Jesus' resurrection (Acts 9). The great persecutor of Christians (Acts 8) became the greatest Christian and evangelist who ever lived. Paul started churches across the known world, wrote thirteen of the New Testament books and shared the gospel with Roman aristocracy—from senators to Caesar himself (Acts 23-28). Paul's life is a testimony to the transforming power of the resurrected Christ working in a person.

The Church Continues to Exist 2,000 Years Later

Jesus said the "…the gates of Hades will not overcome" the church (Matthew 16:18). Jesus' resurrection split time (BC to AD). Our calendar is set by Jesus' life. God's written word and its physical manifestation in Jesus have shaped Western Civilization for more than twenty centuries.

God Answers Prayer in the Name of Jesus

We need to share answered prayers with our friends. We can sketch our spiritual journeys and show Christ's hand working all the events in our lives together for good (Romans 8:28). We need to share how Christ's hand guides our lives. We also need to share the fact that only Jesus' death and resurrection make our access to God via prayer possible and they can have the same access once Jesus is Lord of their lives (John 14:13; Hebrews 4: 14-16).

Lives are Changed

People have set out to disprove the divinity of Jesus but have become believers. The evidence is overwhelming. Consider the testimony of men like Josh McDowell and Lee Strobel.[62]

We need to personalize our message. We need to share how Christ has changed our lives. We need to share our testimonies. We must tell friends that Christ removes

---

62. To learn about the investigative journey that led both Josh McDowell and Lee Strobel to give their lives to Jesus, visit the "About" section of their websites: www.josh.org and www.leestrobel.com.

the fear of death, helps deal with anxiety in life and gives power to conquer bad habits. God is transforming our personalities to reflect Jesus' character. We need to talk about the change from selfishness to service or share Christ's impact on our families. Christians are Jesus' hands and feet. Christ lives inside each of us doing his work on earth (See 2 Corinthians 3:18; Colossians 1:27; 1 Corinthians 12:12-31; Ephesians 2:10; 1 Peter 4:8-11). We are living miracles attesting that Jesus is alive.

Proof #4: Jesus is Exalted (Rules) at the Right Hand of God

The fourth proof that Jesus is both Lord and Savior is his exaltation. He rules today at the right hand of God. In Acts 2:32, Peter proclaimed that all twelve disciples witnessed Jesus ascend to heaven. Others suggest the five hundred believers mentioned by Paul in 1 Corinthians 15 were also present at the ascension.

Peter further stated that the living Jesus was orchestrating the outpouring of the Holy Spirit that the crowd witnessed on Pentecost. The ascension of Christ means Jesus rules the universe, sitting next to God the Father. He intercedes as our Great High Priest (Hebrews 4:14-16). Jesus has the authority to return and judge both the wicked and righteous (See Acts 17:31; 2 Timothy 4:8; Revelation 20:4). His Second Coming could come at any moment. Sharing salvation is an urgent responsibility of Christians. God wants no person to perish (II Peter 3:9).

Becoming a Christian is about understanding and accepting Jesus as Lord and Savior. Peter's message included four proofs that validated the person, role, function, and position of Jesus Christ. Familiarize yourself with this evidence. Be able to walk a friend through Acts 2. Take time to focus on specific miracles of Jesus in the gospels. Take time to open the Bible to various prophesies that predict, hundreds of years before the fact, different aspects of Christ's life.

Remember, the Dead Sea Scrolls prove these prophesies could not have been written after the life of Jesus because they are dated at least two hundred years before his birth. The literal, physical resurrection of Christ is essential to our salvation. If Christ did not rise from the dead, we are still in our sins. There will be no resurrection of the human race. Christianity is a hoax. There is no life after the grave (See I Corinthians 15: 12-20).

However, more questions remain. What process or plan does God reveal for a person to accept Christ, be forgiven of sins, and obtain hope of eternal life?

THE GOSPEL MESSAGE MUST BE ACCEPTED

Looking again at Acts 2 and Peter's testimony to the crowd we can see that so far, the audience has heard the four proofs that Jesus is Lord and Savior. Peter has explained that Jesus' death on the cross was substitutionary (2:3), Jesus died to remove people's sin. The audience has come under the Spirit's conviction. Many in the crowd realized they could not save themselves by keeping the Mosaic Law. Peter then gave the conclusion to his message:

> Therefore, let all Israel be assured of this: God has made this Jesus, whom you crucified, both Lord and Christ [Messiah]. When the people heard this, they were cut to the heart and said to Peter and the other apostles, "Brothers, what shall we do?" (Acts 2:36, 37)

The realization they were not in right standing with God cut their hearts. The Spirit pierced their consciences with the truth that they needed a Savior. In essence, the people cried out, "What shall we do since we've killed the Messiah? How can we be saved?" Peter replied:

> Repent and be baptized, every one of you, in the name of Jesus Christ for the forgiveness of your sins. And you will receive the gift of the Holy Spirit. The promise is for you and your children and for all who are far off—for all whom the Lord our God will call (Acts 2:38, 39).

People must Repent

Peter replied, "Repent…" (Acts 2:38). The Greek word is *metanoeo*. To repent means *to turn away* from one thing and *turn to* something else. Repentance is changing directions. What attitudes and activities need to change? To be saved, our unsaved neighbors must first *change their view* of Jesus. They must stop thinking Jesus is just a great prophet, miracle worker, humanitarian, or teacher. They must *accept Jesus as their personal Savior*. They must see Jesus as their *substitute*, suffering and dying on the cross in their place.

No one on earth will ever live a sinless life. *Repentance means our lives take a new direction*. With a new future, we change our attitude from despair to hope, from negative to positive. As the Spirit reveals our new purpose on earth through

Scripture, he also provides the power to live it (Ephesians 4-6).

The other act of repentance is *to accept Jesus as Lord.* To be Lord is to be boss, CEO, president, king, or master. "You are not your own; you were bought at a price. Therefore, honor God with your bodies." (I Corinthians 6: 19). With his blood, Jesus paid the price to free us from the bondage of sin. He now owns us. We must entrust our lives to Jesus as Lord. This means that we must seek to obey him.

People must be Baptized

Peter said: "Repent and be baptized..." (Acts 2:38). After our neighbors have responded with repentance, then we must baptize them into Christ. The Greek is *baptizo.* It means to immerse. To accept the gospel, we must now re-enact the gospel.

What gospel? "...that Christ *died* for our sins according to the Scriptures, that he was *buried,* that he was *raised* on the third day according to the Scriptures" (1 Corinthians 15:3, 4). Sin killed our spirits (Ephesians 2:1). What do you do to a dead person? You bury him. Through the repentant sinner's faith, and in the grave of baptism the Holy Spirit enters the sinner's heart, removes the sin, and resurrects his or her spirit to arise and walk a new life (see Romans 6:4). The water does not save. It is not magical or holy water. It is faith in the blood of Christ that washes away sin.

In Acts 2:38, notice the conjunction "and" after the word "repent." This conjunction means that *both* repentance and baptism are conditions to receive Jesus as Lord and Savior. We are saved by God's grace, through faith in the blood of Christ, in baptism. We are not saved by God's grace *plus* baptism or through faith *plus* baptism. We are saved by God's grace through faith in Jesus Christ, but the point of transfer from deadness to life is in baptism. Colossians 2:11-12 states:

> In him you were also circumcised with a circumcision not performed by human hands. Your whole self-ruled by the flesh was put off when you were circumcised by Christ, having been buried with him in baptism, in which you were also raised with him through your faith in the working of God, who raised him from the dead.

Paul used the Old Testament ritual of *circumcision* to describe what happens to the person in baptism. Circumcision is the act that validates the Jewish child as a member of God's covenant with Israel. It also involves cutting away impurities. Paul said Christ himself cuts away the impurities (sin) around the heart. When does Christ perform this spiritual surgery? Paul said it happens in baptism. The person comes out of the water a new person "...having been buried with him in baptism" (v. 12). Did we do anything to make this cleansing possible? Paul said it is accomplished *through* our faith.

It is this cutting away of the old that allows room for the new. Our old person is buried in Christ, and we are free to live a new life in his salvation. This moment starts a new process in our lives of growth and restoration which is referred to as regeneration. How did this miracle of regeneration occur? Paul said the *power of God* raised the person out of the watery grave, as if he were resurrected to live a new life. Jesus called this experience being *"born again"* and *"born of water and Spirit"* (John 3:3, 5).

Every single conversion recorded in Acts included baptism: Acts 2:41; 8:12, 13, 389; 9:18; 10:48; 16:15; 33; 19:5; 22:16. Peter stated:

> ...God waited patiently in the days of Noah while the ark was being built. In it only a few people, eight in all, were saved through water, and this water symbolizes baptism that now saves you also—not the removal of dirt from the body but the pledge of a good conscience toward God... (1 Peter 3:20, 21).

Peter's reference to Noah helps explain the importance of baptism. God saved Noah from disaster. The world was completely wicked except for Noah and his family. Noah built the ark, but Peter said the *floodwaters saved Noah.* Most people think the ark saved Noah, not the water. How did the water save Noah and his family? The *flood washed away* all the wickedness on the earth. Peter said the flood symbolizes baptism washing away our wickedness, our sin.

LET'S WRAP UP

The apostle Peter says, "Always be prepared to give an answer to everyone who asks you to give the reason for the hope that you have" (1 Peter 3:15 NIV).

1. Be prepared—the Greek word for "prepared" has a rich background.

It carries the idea of being fit, fully trained, ready for anything.[63] Peter challenged us as Christ followers to do our daily workout and become fit and fully trained in giving answers to questions that non-believers have about Jesus and salvation.

2. Give an answer—this Greek phrase has leadership connotations. It literally means to go before as guide, a forerunner, or herald.[64] Peter called us to guide people who might be confused about salvation with the light and clarity that comes from truth.

3. Give the reason—this Greek phrase means we learn to speak intelligently regarding the issues. We not only know the answer, but we become skilled in speaking the answer convincingly and with tact.[65] If you rehearse the answers found throughout the training manual, they will help you so that you can be obedient to the command in 1 Peter 3:15 and bring many to Christ.

If you can give short, pithy answers that make sense, that's all most people want. Being able to present the answers with confidence communicates conviction and accuracy. The Holy Spirit will use you to convict others of their need for Christ.

1. View yourself as God's herald bringing the good news. Make a list of friends and family you will run to with the good news. Now, pray for these people.

2. Realize that the job of introducing others to Christ involves presenting the evidence for his death, burial, and resurrection. Salvation comes through a personal relationship with the living Christ. We can help our friends deal with their skepticism presenting the proofs for Christ's death, burial, and resurrection.

3. Study and discuss some of your favorite miracles that prove Christ to be God's Son. Be ready to "wow" your friends with Jesus' miracles (See Matthew, Mark, Luke, John).

63. Zodhiates, Spiros, *The Complete Word Study Dictionary: New Testament.* Chattanooga: TN, AMG Publishers. 1994. P 667,
64. Ibid. p 1225.
65. Ibid. p 925.

4. List several fulfilled prophecies. What are the top ten that impress you most? Remember, fulfilled prophesy demonstrates God's well-orchestrated plan preparing the Jewish nation to recognize and receive the Messiah.

5. Memorize the incredible statistic found on page 42 in this chapter that shows the probability of Jesus fulfilling all prophesies given by different prophets in different times and on different continents.

6. Study the final week of Christ's life (Matthew 21-28; Luke 19-24 NIV). Select the basic arguments that prove the resurrection.

7. Realize that your changed life and answered prayers are great proofs that Christ is alive. You are God's miracle and proof that Jesus is alive. Work through your life journey so you can show God's involvement in your life to your friends.

How can we know the Bible is accurate?
There are three good arguments for the accuracy of the Bible.

1. The documents of the early church fathers
   The early church fathers wrote commentaries on different books in the Bible as well as letters to other Christians, congregations, and peoples. These men quoted the Scripture 86,000 times. Their quotations allow experts to construct 99.86% of the New Testament; only eleven verses of the New Testament are not quoted.[66]

2. Manuscripts of the New Testament
   We possess over five thousand Greek manuscripts from the New Testament, more than any other piece of ancient literature. To put this figure into perspective, consider that the runner-up in this respect is Homer's *Iliad* of which only 650 Greek manuscripts are known to us.[67]

3. Archaeology
   It has proved the existence of hundreds of cities mentioned in the

---

66. Charlie H. Campbell, *One Minute Answers to Skeptics* (Eugene, OR: Harvest Publishing House, 2010), 22-23.
67. Lee Strobel, *The Case for Christ: A Journalist's Personal Investigation of the Evidence for Jesus* (Grand Rapids, MI: Zondervan, 1998), 78.

Bible including Bethel, Jericho, Joppa, Ephesus, Capernaum, to name a few.[68]

How can we know Jesus really existed and performed miracles?

We've already mentioned four arguments for biblical accuracy. There are also thirty-nine sources outside of the Bible that speak of Jesus' life, teaching, death, and resurrection.[69] Charlie Campbell mentions the Babylonian Talmud, which is a collection of ancient Jewish writings that talk about Jesus being killed on the eve of the Passover.[70] The fifteenth edition of the *Encyclopedia Britannica* devotes 20,000 words to Jesus. Charlie Campbell says the encyclopedia authors "never once hint that He didn't exist."[71]

Secular historians such as Tacitus (Roman) documented the miracles of Jesus. Tacitus also recounted how the wicked Herod, who beheaded John the Baptist, wanted to have an audience with Jesus in order to witness a miracle (Luke 23:8 NIV).

Read the words of Flavius Josephus, a Jewish historian (c. 37-100 AD):

> At this time there was a wise man that was called Jesus. And His conduct was good, and He was known to be virtuous. And many people from among the Jews and the other nations became His disciples. Pilate condemned Him to be crucified to die. And those who had become His disciples did not abandon His discipleship. They reported that He had appeared to them three days after His crucifixion and that He was alive.[72]

Is Baptism Necessary?

1. The Thief on the Cross wasn't baptized, and he went to paradise?

   The thief hanging on the cross next to Jesus was still under the Old Testament dispensation. Jesus had not yet died on the cross or been raised from the grave, so there was no blood shed to cleanse the thief of sin. The New Testament church is launched 50 days later on Pentecost (Acts 2).

---

68. "Archaeological Evidence Verifying Biblical Cities", n.d., http://carm.org/questions/archaeological-evidence-verifying-biblical-cities.
69. Strobel, *The Case for Christ*, 351.
70. Campbell, 29.
71. Ibid, 30.
72. Ibid, 30.

2. Why do some churches baptize by immersion and others baptize by sprinkling?

Baptism by immersion was the method used during the first 200-250 years of the church's existence. Then a heresy developed that baptism washed away on past sins, not the sins committed after baptism. In the second century, some began postponing baptism until they were on their death bed. It was impossible to immerse a person dying in bed, so sprinkling was introduced as a new mode of baptism.[73]

The Greek word for sprinkling is *rhantizo* and for immersion is baptizo. *Baptizo* is used in the New Testament for water baptism. Sprinkling does not portray the gospel, which is the death, burial, and resurrection of Jesus.

3. Why do some churches baptize infants?

Another incorrect practice is infant baptism. It came about after Origen (c. AD 250) explored the idea of original sin. Augustine (c. AD 400) developed and introduced it as a church doctrine. Basically, the doctrine of original sin states Adam and Eve's sin is passed down through the sexual act of procreation. This means a child is born with the sin of Adam. This false teaching says baptism washes away the original sin, so it follows that babies must be baptized. You can't immerse a baby; he or she might drown. Therefore, sprinkling became the acceptable mode of baptizing infants.

Eventually the Catholic Church introduced the idea of water regeneration. When the priest blessed the water, it became holy. It was believed that sprinkling the child with the holy water removed the original sin of the child. Aquinas (c. AD 1250) later called this holy baptism.

With the Catholic Church introducing the practice of infant baptism, Catholicism negated the necessity of belief, confession,

---

73. Mitchell Carl, "The History of How Sprinkling Replaced Immersion as a Baptismal Form". Search for Biblical Truth.http://searchforbiblicaltruth.com/library.tex.carl/ HowSprinklingReplacedImmersionAsBaptismForm.pdf.Accessed 8/21/2015.

repentance and faith in Christ prior to baptism.

4. When was baptism removed as the response to accepting Christ as Lord and Savior?

Reformers like Martin Luther believed, as did the Catholic Church that the Holy Spirit came in baptism. Most Reformers accepted this belief except for Zwingli (c. AD 1500). He began to teach that baptism was only an outward sign of an inward grace. His teaching was in response to the Catholic doctrine of water regeneration.

CHAPTER SIX
Equipping the Church

"The student is not above the teacher, but everyone
who is fully trained will like their teacher"
(Luke 6:40)

"So, Christ himself gave the apostles, the prophets, the evangelists,
the pastors and teachers to equip his people for works of service"
(Ephesians 4:11, 12)

"Come, follow me and I will make you fishers of men"
(Matthew 4:19).

Several years ago, I was in a boat on the Sea of Galilee watching a demonstration of casting nets. The net was circular with heavy weights around the perimeter. The fisherman bundled the net in one hand and slung it over his shoulder. He held the weights with both hands as he cast the net out into the water. While in the air, the net opened completely, before gently descending across the water and slowly sinking. The fisherman waited several minutes and then pulled hard to see if he had caught any fish. The skills involved had to be taught and practiced in order to be performed successfully.

TRAINING COMMANDED

Jesus commanded his followers to be taught and trained to witness (Matthew 4:19; Luke 6:40; Ephesians 4:11, 12). It is the purpose of all believers to witness the grace of God through Jesus Christ to every person we meet. That is the most important task Christians should be doing.

Surgeons can heal the physical body but eventually people die and will stand before a holy God. Did our friends or family members receive the cure for sin that God provided through the gospel of Jesus Christ? That is the most important question Christians should be asking.

Individuals who aspire to be a doctor spend years in training and apprenticeships in order to be effective in saving lives. Should not we as Christians approach our call with the same tenacity and thoroughness? We want to get it right. We want to be effective. We want God to be pleased with our witness, right?

Jesus Required Training for His Followers

Jesus said to Peter and Andrew, "Come, follow me and I will make you fishers of men" (Matthew 4:19). The Greek word for "make" is *poieo*. The word means to manufacture or construct. Study Jesus' relationships with his disciples and you quickly observe a culture of disciple making. Jesus manufactured and constructed disciples who made disciples. Love and devotion were at the core, but the relationships were strategic and intentional. Jesus modeled and mentored disciple making. It defined the nature of their relationships. The disciples listened, watched, practiced, and obeyed.

"The student is not above the teacher, but everyone who is fully trained will be like their teacher" (Luke 6:40). What was Jesus saying? As a leader, he shared the vision with his followers to imitate his character and do his mission. The mission is to evangelize neighborhoods across the known world. He also provided the training to do the job effectively.

Notice the word Jesus used to describe his followers: *students*. Keep in mind that Jesus' disciples had little education and were judged by the Jewish leaders to be "uneducated and untrained" (Acts 4:13). In the ancient world, the teacher-pupil relationship was a personal, one-on-one relationship. The student lived alongside the teacher. The point is this, if uneducated fishermen could be trained to make disciples, how much more can Christ's followers be trained as disciples today?

Jesus also said his followers should be "fully trained," from the Greek word *katartizo*. It conveys the idea of restoring a person to function efficiently. The Christian's priority is to become proficient in disciple making. Are you doing this? Church leaders should make evangelistic training the expectation for all members. Jesus concluded his statement in Luke 6:40 with the goal, "My followers will make disciples just like me."

Training Programs Fall Short

The American church growth movement was launched in the 1970s. The call was to reach and save America. The window of opportunity was "now" and "urgent," since church attendance had experienced a decline. To curb the drift into secularism, the experts shifted the evangelism strategy from reaching the "individual" to reaching the "masses." To reach the masses, the church paradigm also had to reposition from "family" to "organization."

To accommodate this new church model, hundreds of books on church leadership hit the market to train ministers and elders to be "organizational" leaders. Bigger was now better. Church growth books began defining Sunday worship as the place to reach the lost. Training the members as disciple makers became secondary. Church leaders like Robert Schuller used "the power of positive thinking" to package Christianity to attract lost people to church services. In the 1980s Bill Hybels created the seeker service.

The 1970s also gave birth to the church "program." Church seminars introduced the latest and best programs to move the masses through the conversion and maturation process. The formula: Program + Participation = Conversion and Christian maturity. After more than forty years of members participating in church programming, the Reveal Study (Willow Creek), along with reports by Ed Stetzer and Thom Rainer, have demonstrated that programs have little to do with transforming people.

James Kennedy's *Evangelism Explosion* was another packaged program. The program included a "canned" script that believers could walk their non-believing friends through. Like all programs, *Evangelism Explosion* ran its course and today is considered ineffective.

CREATE A DISCIPLE-MAKING CHURCH CULTURE

What is effective and never faddish is the transformed believer trained to love people by witnessing the grace and truth of Jesus. Sharing Christ happens best in relationships and natural conversations. The truth and application of the gospel is shared but better yet modeled.

Training members to make disciples begins by creating a disciple-making culture. Church as "family" takes precedent over church as "organization." We organize to create Christ-centered relationships, but our identity is not an "organization." We are Christ's family. The task of organizational leadership is to approve the latest church program. Leaders as "spiritual parents" (1 Thessalonians 2:7-12) focus on relational oversight by modeling and mentoring disciples who make disciples.

Church Culture as an Organized Production

During the COVID-19 pandemic (2020), church research projected that 30 to 40 percent of church attenders would not return to the weekly gathering when the pandemic ended. More research is needed to pinpoint causes, but speculation has identified two reasons.

First, the elderly are waiting for a COVID-19 vaccine. Second, the "drop-outs" see church as an organizational production. In our post-modern society churches have substituted shared New Testament doctrine for a shared worship experience. To "feel" trumps to "know." One person expressed it this way, "Why go back? I can watch the show online and in my pajamas." Preachers have made corporate worship optional and primarily an event. The missing gem is authentic, Christ-centered culture that disciples believers who make disciples.

The Power of Church Culture

When we talk about church culture, we are referring to the unspoken values that dominate church relationships. Unspoken values define culture. You must understand that core values are tied to the perceived purposes of the church by the members and will grip their focus. Evangelism is the first half of Christ's Great Commission. A New Testament core value of evangelism might read, "Lost people matter to Christ, therefore lost people matter to me." When that value is baked thoroughly into the church, you see an evangelistic culture emerge that generates passion. Members become burdened for lost people and gladly engage the training to assist in the rescue. Without an evangelistic culture, your mission statement is only ink on paper.

The church culture holds immense power. The culture will either hold you back or propel you forward. For now, understand that every church has a culture (unspoken values). How would you describe yours? Is it a consumer culture, a legalistic culture, a knowledge-based culture, a committee culture, a scattered culture, or a mobilized Christ-centered culture that makes disciples who make disciples?

The Unhealthy Church Culture

The term "culture" originated as an agrarian (farming) term. It meant to cultivate, plant, and nurture the soil. If you're a weekend gardener, you get down on your knees each Saturday and pull weeds, till the soil, water and fertilize plants. After hours of backbreaking work, you stand up and admire your healthy beautiful garden, right? But neglect your garden Monday through Friday and Saturday morning what do you see? New weeds are choking, and new bugs are eating the plants. That once churned fluffy soil has now turned hard. You must work the garden regularly to maintain its healthy culture. If you don't, the bugs and varmints will destroy it.

The same is true of church culture. Culture is dynamic, not static. That means your church culture can shift or change at any time. It takes work to ensure that the staff, elders and members all share the same beliefs and evangelistic values. Neglect the culture and weeds will grow and varmints will eat away at mission and relationships. If church leaders do not define church culture (values), someone else will. Consider the parable of the weeds in Matthew 13.

> A man sowed good seed in his field. But while his men were sleeping, his enemy came and sowed weeds among the wheat and went away. So, when the plants came up and bore grain, then the weeds appeared also. And the servants of the master of the house came and said to the master, "Did you not sow good seed in your field? How then does it have weeds?" He said to them, "An enemy has done this" (Matthew 13:24-28)

The weed is probably the darnel. It looks similar to wheat but is definitely a counterfeit. As church leaders guide and parent God's children, they should listen for beliefs and values to surface. They then need to clarify and work through any distortions.

"Preach the word; be ready in season and out of season; reprove, rebuke and encourage with complete patience and teaching" (2 Timothy 4:2). Enable members to recognize the difference between weeds and wheat. There is the biblical pattern for marriage, parenting, priorities, money, relationships, handling conflict—a pattern for everything that God deems essential. Satan has a counterfeit (weed) for every biblical pattern. When weeds (distorted values) appear, pull them up with grace, truth, and gentleness (Galatians 6:1). If the weeds are not pulled, they can spread quickly and choke out the mission.

Now consider Matthew 13:10-17 which is the parable of the sower. A sower went out to sow. And as he sowed, some seeds fell along the path...Other seeds fell on rocky ground, where they did not have much soil, other seeds fell among the thorns, and other seed fell on good soil (Matthew 13:3, 5, 7, 8).

Preachers can proclaim God's Word yet see little results. The problem is not with the seed or the farmer, but with the soil, the hearts of the people. If the Word falls on hard, shallow, or thorny soil (individuals who make up the unhealthy church culture), the seed will struggle to grow. This is a major frustration for preachers.

What is the solution? Continue to preach the Word with clarity and boldness, but also till the soil. Have healthy honest conversations with leaders and members about biblical values. These interactions might be one-on-one, or in small groups. Nurture their hearts. Love them. Listen to their concerns but keep sharing the biblical values of evangelism. Another solution is the leadership must model evangelism. Members imitate leaders. If you want members to be evangelistic, then church leaders must set the standard.

Watch out for busyness. Maintenance and dying churches can be busy doing many good things, but they do not do the right things. Busyness actually becomes a strategy to keep members in church. Faithfulness is redefined as coming to church instead of being church. Evangelism is relegated to passing out water on street corners once a month (while wearing the church T-shirt), instead of developing relationships that model and share the good news of Christ.

Watch out for the tyranny of the urgent. Years ago, Charles E. Hummel wrote a little booklet titled, *The Tyranny of the Urgent*. His point was that we can miss the important priorities by allowing the urgent things of everyday life to distract us from investing in the most important. We are all guilty, right?

Define the Healthy Church Culture

The purpose of the church is to be like Jesus in character and mission. It's that simple. Again, church has two components. First, members are transformed into the image of Christ (2 Corinthians 3:18, Colossians 1:28, 29). Second, members are equipped to make disciples: "Each One Reach One" (Matthew 28:18-20; Acts 8:4, 5). That's it. You have to teach and clarify those two purposes over and again with the leaders and members. You teach and clarify one-on-one, in groups, from the pulpit, in meetings and gatherings, you clarify, clarify, and clarify. Your ministry plan develops a multiple-year process that enables members to be and do those two priorities. All activities must align within those two categories or you're confusing and cluttering your ministry.

The early church was attractional. The world was fascinated with their imitation of Christ. Christians are different from the world. We are sanctified (1 Corinthians 1:12; 6:11). The word can mean set apart, different, unique, or cut away. The godly behavior and radical love of the early believers caught the eye of the Roman world. One writer noted, "See how they love one another." The Jews and Romans held Christians in "high esteem" (Acts 5:13).

Again, the early church's attraction was not the outstanding Sunday morning event, but the transformed lives and radical love within the community of believers. Study church history and you will see Christianity was illegal for most of the first 300 years of its existence. The Roman Caesars were intimidated by King Jesus. Yet, the annual growth of the church during this time is estimated at 40 percent.[74]

Also, to avoid being killed, Christians often worshipped underground in catacombs (among the tombs). Worship services were held in secret and obviously not marketed in the papers. Yet the church grew exponentially. How? Through "one-on-one" disciple making encounters. The non-believing friends could see that the power of the gospel transformed lives. They wanted this salvation and transformation too.

Christians generally understood their purpose and were thoroughly trained to make disciples. Acts 2:42 says the first church was "devoted" to training (apostles

---

74. Stark, Rodney, The Rise of Christianity: How the Obscure, Marginal Jesus Movement Became the Dominant Religious Force in the Western World in a Few Centuries. Princeton: Princeton University Press, p. 3.

teaching). After the apostles died, the catechumenate was a well-known, three-year intensive training process for believers in the second and third centuries.[75] The disciple-making culture permeated the early fellowship (Acts 2:46, 47).

The New Testament calls the authentic church culture *koinonia*. We translate the word "fellowship." *Koinonia* appears in several different contexts throughout the New Testament. Each setting will help us understand what the authentic church culture looks like in relationship to evangelism.

Shared Partnership in Christ's Fishing Business

Today when Christians use the word fellowship, eating a meal together usually comes to mind. Christians might also say, "We need a little fellowship" implying they'd like to go to a ballgame or spend some time catching up on life.

The Greek word *koinonia* carries the idea of having things in common, a communion. It means a shared position, possession, or purpose. Being baptized into Christ, believers are automatically connected to God the Father, God the Son, and God the Holy Spirit. Christians share the same Father, Lord, faith, hope, love, future, and blessings. Christians are also connected to other members who are in Christ. We are united, joined together, grafted in, and glued together (Colossians 2:19). The church is now commanded to exemplify this spiritual union by loving and serving one another in the community of faith. Our goal is to reflect the oneness of the Trinity.

God is love (1 John 4:7). His love must permeate our relationships. But God is also strategic, goal oriented, and mission driven. After Adam sinned, God announced the *protoevangelium* (Genesis 3:15). A big name for God's redemptive plan through Jesus. All Bible history was God preparing the world for Jesus. Throughout the Old Testament there are hundreds of prophecies describing and defining the Messiah so that the Jews would not miss him. God is the original strategic planner.

Jesus loved people. His love made him the most intentional missional person who ever lived. He came to "seek and save the lost" (Luke 19:10). When the people of Capernaum begged Jesus to stay longer, his response was, "I must preach the good news of the kingdom in other towns as well; for I was sent for this purpose" (Luke 4:43). When the Pharisees tried to intimidate Jesus with the threat that Herod was pursuing him. Jesus responded with, "Go tell that fox, today I will cast out

---

75. Clinton E. Arnold, *JETS* 47/1 (March 2004) p. 39-54.

demons, tomorrow perform miracles and on the third day I will reach my goal" (Luke 13:32).

Fellowship in Christ is strategic and missional. Jesus called his disciples into a fishing for men fellowship/partnership. "Follow me, and I will make you become fishers of men" (Mark 1:17). The Greek word "become" suggests the disciples would begin a new partnership with Jesus. The fishing for men enterprise. We've already studied the Great Commission in depth. Jesus declared this fishing fellowship/ partnership would last "till the end of the age" (Matthew 28:20).

The apostle Peter used this fellowship/partnership scenario when describing how elders function in relationship to Jesus (1 Peter 5:1). What is the believer's role in this fellowship/partnership? We are Christ's body. His Spirit literally lives within us (1 Corinthians 6:19). As Christians submit to Jesus as Lord, we naturally function as his hands, feet, and mouth (Romans 12:4-8).

Christ's Spirit directs us to lost people and we share the Word of Christ with them (Acts 8:26-39). It truly is a fellowship/partnership. When believers are disobedient and do not share the gospel, we neutralize the expansion of Christ's enterprise. The apostle Paul challenged the Roman believers to witness for Christ. He asks them, "And how will they hear without someone proclaiming" (Romans 10:14). Paul told the Philippians that he prayed for them daily "because of your partnership in the gospel from the first day until now" (Philippians 1:5, 19). Again, Paul used the Greek word *koinonia* to describe their fishing fellowship/partnership.

The healthy church culture lives and breathes fishing for men. It's what our fellowship does. When fellow fishermen get together, they ask, "How's the fishing business?" We talk fishing, discuss fishing techniques, lament fishing challenges, and share fishing stories. When we fish, we develop fishing skills and eventually catch fish.

Shared Responsibility to Fish

Not only are we fishing business partners with Jesus, but every believer is to invest their time, talent, and treasure to make the fishing business a success (Philippians 4:2,3; Matthew 25:14-30; 2 Corinthians 8:4,5). We are called to share (koinonia) our resources (stewardship) to advance the fishing business. Image how frustrated you'd be if your fishing partners never took responsibility but placed all the fishing duties on you.

Christians who don't share the gospel often use the excuse, "I don't have the gift of evangelism." Study the New Testament and you'll discover there is no gift of evangelism. Ephesians 4:11 mentions "the apostles, the prophets and the evangelists." The three are not gifts but rather temporary positions in the first-century church prior to the completion of the New Testament Scripture.

The apostles, the prophets, and the evangelists received the outpouring of the Holy Spirit, which gave them the ability to do miracles and receive direct "scriptural" information from the Holy Spirit to pass on to the people. Philip was such an evangelist. He performed miracles that confirmed his gospel message (Acts 8:6). After the apostles died, these temporary positions ceased. Paul stated, "When the perfect comes the partial will pass away" (1 Corinthians 13:10). "The perfect" is the New Testament Scripture we now study to share.

In the parable of the talents (Matthew 25:14-30), the owner of the enterprise entrusted three servants with talents. A talent was a lot of money. Each servant was to advance the enterprise and each servant's work was judged with fair compensation. All the servants were responsible to contribute. In the parable, Jesus was probably talking directly to the religious leaders (Pharisees and Scribes). He had already pronounced seven woes upon their leadership (Matthew 21). Jesus probably continued to give a series of parables that denounced their stewardship of God's Word.

The religious leaders and teachers of the Jewish nation were called to embrace Jesus as the Messiah and promote salvation through him, to both Jew and Gentile (Isaiah 42:6-9). Their job was to be Christ's greatest ambassadors and evangelists. Their assignment was to reconcile the nation to Jesus. They were called of God to reveal the Messianic prophecies to the Jewish people, demonstrating that Jesus fulfilled them all. They were poor stewards of Scripture. They discarded Christ's miracles, his character, and his teachings. In the parable, the owner, who represented Christ, challenged his workers to use their resources for the expansion of his kingdom. In due time he would return, and they would receive their reward. When the master returned, he found two faithful and one unfaithful.

As you study the parable, notice that the unproductive worker did not appear to be a bad employee (the Pharisees were highly respected as God's servants). He appeared to be God's business partner. He interacted with his coworkers. He attended the business meetings and talked the business goals. But he never promoted the master's product (salvation through Jesus) and he did not expand the master's enterprise (winning souls to Christ). The master called him "lazy and wicked" and threw him into the "outer darkness where there is weeping and gnashing of teeth" (Matthew 25:30).

Now notice the rewards for the two effective workers. He declared them "faithful," and acknowledged "a job well done" (Matthew 25:21, 23). He also made them official partners in the enterprise and sharers of the master's wealth (Matthew 25:21, 23). The apostle Paul also declared that "it is required of stewards that they be found faithful" (1 Corinthians 4:2). Every believer is responsible to use their time, talent, and treasure to make disciples.

Shared Suffering from Our Competition

Every member is in the fishing fellowship/partnership with Christ. Being in the fishing business we talk fishing, discuss fishing methods, share fishing stories, and lament together the ones that "got away." Members in the authentic church culture have a shared responsibility to make disciples. We are to use our time, talent, and treasure to advance the mission of Christ. We suffer together as we take "hits" from our rival fishing business (Philippians 1:29, 30; 2 Timothy 1:8).

That's right, Satan is fishing for men too. I call his fishing business the "Devil's Crab." He slanders our fishing company. He lies and distorts our product. He tries to sabotage our ships and recruit our workers. Most of the apostle Paul's suffering throughout the book of Acts stems from the lies promoted by Jewish authorities. Jesus said, "They say they are Jews and are not. They are of the synagogue of Satan" (Revelation 3:9).

The apostle Paul said that he shared in Christ's sufferings, and so do we (Philippians 3:10). The word share, again, is *koinonia.* Christians understand there's a battle for the souls of people. Our competition is brutal, wicked, evil, and cutthroat. At times, together, we suffer with Christ but never give up. We persevere in the mission.

Shared Yoke of Christ

Christ's authority permeates the authentic church culture. He is the owner and boss of every believer and of the fishing business. Jesus is Lord and every member submits and obeys. We wear his yoke. Jesus said, "Take my yoke upon you and learn from me" (Matthew 11:29). The yoke is a wooden cross piece that is fastened over the necks of two animals and attached to a plow or cart they are to pull. The authentic church culture acknowledges Jesus as Lord. We all wear his yoke, and we remind one another that we all wear his yoke.

The yoke of Christ defines our church culture. Suppose a married couple is divided and they come to you for intervention. You listen but eventually say to the husband, "Christ says you are to love your wife just as he loves you." In frustration the husband might say "I don't want to love her. She hurt me." Your response can be "Brother, have you taken off the yoke? Loving your wife has nothing to do with how we feel; it's a command. Put on the yoke and love your wife."

There must be authority in the church. Christ must define the mission and values. Preachers and elders are not the authority, but they have the obligation to remind the members that Christ is Lord. Put on the yoke. Submit to Christ's definition of church. Obey his command to be equipped to make disciples. Like the shoe commercial states, "Just do it."

Maintenance churches are full of members who attend Sunday services and hear Bible preaching. They know what Scripture says but they choose not to obey. Maintenance churches can claim Jesus as Savior but ignore Jesus as Lord. Let's put on the yoke.

LET'S WRAP UP

Jesus commanded his followers to become trained to make disciples (Mark 1:17; Ephesians 4:11-17). Leadership is Christ's gift to the church (Ephesians 4:8, 11). Leaders are to equip *katartismos* the members to take on Christ's character and to make disciples. Leaders give members the needed equipment necessary to be effective.

As a verb, the term *equip* is a dynamic, purpose-oriented concept. It means to furnish or prepare someone for service or action. It also carries the idea of adjusting things out of order, readjusting priorities, and adding to what is lacking. Other expressions for the word *equip* include mending nets, resetting a broken bone, and restoring what is useless to being useful. New Testament leaders function as "spiritual parents" (1 Thessalonians 2:7-12) and focus on relational oversight by modeling and mentoring disciples who make disciples.

CHALLENGE

Jesus' Process of Training to Witness

First: Take Responsibility

Jesus called the twelve to take responsibility and make disciples.

> Follow me and I will make you fishers of men. Immediately they left their nets and followed him. And going on from there he saw two other brothers, James the son of Zebedee and John his brother, in the boat with Zebedee their father, mending their nets, and he called them. Immediately they left the boat and their father and followed him (Matthew 4:19-22).

Second: Learn the Gospel Story

The disciples had to learn the gospel message. Jesus shaped the twelve into his team with on-the-job teaching and training. The original word for *team* is associated with journey. It is seen in a group of animals who are harnessed together and driven by a teamster for the purpose of moving or transporting something heavy from one place to another.[76] The idea is that of bringing together two oxen under one yoke. The apostle Paul referred to the church at Philippi as his "yokefellow" (Philippians 4:3). Christians had placed the yoke of Christ (Lordship) around their neck, uniting them together as Christ's team, to be taught, trained, and then share, side by side, the gospel story.

During the first 14 months of Jesus' ministry, the disciples were probably part-time followers. They would accompany Jesus for certain periods of time (Mark 1:38, 2:23) but would later return to their jobs and homes (John 1:40-42, Luke 5:1-11). They were able to observe, watch, listen, and learn what Jesus meant by fishing for men.[77] After fourteen months, Jesus went up on the mountainside and prayed for the twelve all night. The next day Jesus called them to "be with him" (Mark 3:14). The twelve spent a total of three years with Jesus in training.

The Acts 8 believers who spread the gospel throughout Samaria were trained in the "apostles' teaching" (Acts 2:42). That teaching also involved on-the-job training

---

76. Ibid. pg 111.
77. Coleman, Robert, *The Master Plan of Evangelism*. Fleming H. Revell Company, Old Tappan: NJ, 1964. pg 54.

for three-plus years. "And day by day, attending the temple together, and breaking bread in their homes" (Acts 2:46). There is overwhelming evidence that these believers were not worshipping in the Jewish temple but rather witnessing as teams in the temple courts. These evangelistic teams would take interested prospects back to their homes for a meal and further study. The point is training is an on-the-job process. Church leaders must teach but also provide mentoring opportunities. The perfect setting is yokefellow witnessing teams. They must see it done in action by you and other leaders.

Third: Hear Their Stories

Engage friends to hear their story. Everyone has experienced periods of broken-ness. Jesus took the disciples with him into the neighborhoods. "The word became flesh and moved into the neighborhoods" (John 1:14, *The Message*). Throughout Jesus' three- and one-half-year ministry, he and his disciples visited the neighbor-hoods in Galilee, Samaria, Judea, the territory of Philip, Perea, Phoenicia, and all of Syria (Matthew 4:24). According to Arthur Blessitt who literally has traced the steps of Jesus, he and his disciples walked 3,125 miles in the three and one-half years.[78]

What did Jesus do in the neighborhoods? He met the neighbors, learned their names, heard their needs, ate with, and ministered to the individual people. Jesus was a friend to sinners (Matthew 11:19). He went into Peter's house and healed his mother-in-law (Matthew 8:14). Jesus had dinner at Levi's house and met many tax-collectors and sinners (Matthew 9:10). Jesus went into the synagogue leader's house and raised his daughter from the dead (Matthew 9:23). Jesus went through all the towns and neighborhoods proclaiming the good news of the kingdom and healing every disease and sickness (Matthew 9:35). When Jesus met each individual, "he had compassion on them, because they were harassed and helpless, like sheep without a shepherd" (Matthew 9:36).

Fourth: Share Jesus' Story

The disciples were called to multiply their efforts through duplication. Jesus challenged them to pray, "The harvest is plentiful, but the workers are few. Ask the Lord of the harvest, therefore, to send out workers into his harvest field" (Matthew 9:37, 38).

---

78. The Official Website of Arthur Blessitt, http://www.blessitt.com/index.html. Accessed November, 2015.

We are to beseech God in prayer, asking him to send out workers into the neighborhoods, because the harvest is plentiful. In Luke 9 Jesus commissioned the twelve to go to Jewish neighborhoods. In Luke 10 Jesus, commissioned the 70 to go to Gentile neighborhoods. Possibly the 70 were recruited and trained by the twelve.

This is New Testament discipleship. Members of the church must be taught their new mission in life is to make disciples in their neighborhoods. This mission must shape how we do church. Believers actually grow up in the faith as they interact with neighbors and come back to church full of questions. Learning the answers gives them biblical knowledge and living it out makes them Christlike. The harvest field is the neighborhoods. The duplication process never ended from that point and today two billion people claim Jesus as Lord and Savior.

PART TWO
<u>The Effective Church</u>

CHAPTER SEVEN
Engaging People With the Gospel

I began to practice personal evangelism living in Ft. Lauderdale in the 1990s. My subdivision literally allowed me to take Christ to a global neighborhood. South Florida is international. The community where we lived was not yet a year old so everyone moving in was new to the area. Many of them were from a different part of the world. Homes with zero lot lines meant one's property extended right up to the neighbor's house. Our front yards were small and connected by sidewalks. There was a community pool used year round. All these factors provided the perfect environment to make new friends. It was not uncommon to be working in the front yard and a couple taking an evening stroll would stop and introduce themselves. At some point, another neighbor might walk over too. After general introductions, the question usually surfaced, "What country are you from?"

Most Everyone is Interested in Talking About God

When the conversation turned to professions, they would discover I was a minister. I was pleasantly surprised at the optimism and desire people showed to talk about religion. It seemed everyone was interested in God or comparing and exchanging religious beliefs and practices. Adam, the son of a Jewish family nearby, would play in the streets with my two boys. Our families became friends. Knowing us well, Adam's mom and dad allowed him to visit a Christian worship service. I'll never forget driving home and Adam kept asking, "Why do you call us Israelites? We are Israelis."

Barna's 2020 research revealed sixty-eight percent of people who consider themselves religious but non-Christian are on a spiritual quest, and fifty-eight percent of atheists/agnostics are searching for spiritual truth.[79] Eighty-four percent of religious non-Christians and atheists/agnostics state they are curious about God and that something feels missing from their life.[80]

Most Everyone Struggles to Articulate Their Spiritual Beliefs

Living in a global neighborhood caused me to grow exponentially in understanding Islam, Judaism, spiritualism, and atheism. It helped me to learn how to share the Biblical truths of God and his New Testament Church. I discovered that most neighbors could not clearly articulate or defend their beliefs. I also discovered my neighbors' syncretic presupposition regarding religion sparked a lot of inquiry. Disheartening as it seems, my neighbors approached God as a smorgasbord of ideas to select or throw away based on their spiritual appetites. Sometimes they held conflicting views. One friend claimed to be a Christian but liked the idea of reincarnation. Religious conversations were often like walking into Baskin Robins with thirty-one kinds of religion and hundreds of potential combinations. Sometimes as I listened, I would ponder, "Okay, they're Christian, Buddhist, New Age and they have a little bit of Secularism."

Often, we don't speak up for Christ because we feel we are not as proficient as we'd like. Barna asked lapsed Christians, Religious non-Christians, and atheists/agnostics what would make them more interested in Christianity. At the bottom of the list was Christians being more articulate about their faith. It hovered around ten percent.[81] So don't worry if you're not as polished as you'd like.

Most Everyone's Religious Affiliations are Tied to Family Tradition

I discovered that our neighbors' religious allegiances and affiliations were often tied to family traditions. Rarely did they attend a house of worship and seldom did

79. Barna. *Revitalizing Evangelism*. 2019. P. 33.
80. Ibid
81. Ibid. p. 23

their faith impact their daily lives. For example, my wife and I were in a grocery store around Christmas time. A Jewish mother and her son were standing in front of a Christmas tree admiring the decorations and lights. We overheard the little boy ask, "Mother, when are we going to put a Christmas tree in our house?" The Jewish mother responded, "Whenever your grandmother dies." We couldn't believe what we had just heard. It was as if their Jewish faith was simply a tradition to discard when the matriarch died.

Most Everyone Is Open to God Solutions

From my vantage point, most of my neighbors either viewed me as their minister or as a man of God to serve all faiths and religions. When a Jewish neighbor had marital problems, the husband came and talked with me. When neighbors saw Middle East issues on TV, they would ask for a quick, CliffsNotes explanation of the religious beliefs involved with both groups.

Religious pluralism permeated my global neighborhood. You may know religious pluralism as "all religious paths lead to God." When you think about it, religious pluralism can't be true. How can all religions with mutually exclusive truth claim to be equally valid? However, I used my knowledge of their beliefs to my advantage by injecting the gospel when I could.

I'll never forget the night before Hurricane Andrew hit South Dade County. Ft. Lauderdale is in Broward County, just twenty minutes north of where it hit. Those were the days before mandatory evacuation. Several neighbors knocked on my front door and ask if I would lead the neighborhood in prayer. Outside, I noticed all sorts of folks standing in the street, waiting to see if I would pray for and with them. We organized into a giant circle, held hands, and I prayed for protection and God's oversight.

Barna's 2020 research showed that more than half (fifty-four percent) of religious non-Christians, and forty percent of atheists/agnostics are interested in exploring solutions in different faiths.[82] So be bold and ready to share God's solutions from the Bible. People will listen.

---

82. Ibid. p. 22

Most Everyone Wants Acceptance and Friendship

Jesus said, "Love your neighbor has yourself" (Mark 12:31). I worked hard to love them as myself. I also sensed at times my neighbors had to work to love me. As we accepted each other, laughed together, and ate together, our friendships grew. I began to see that loving my neighborhood was the precursor to deeper conversations about life, God, and the gospel. Love enables God to cultivate the heart. They were seeing the benefits of being a Christian. Love enabled my neighbor to trust me. It removed the emotional barriers of suspicion and doubt. They first had to trust me before they would trust the gospel that I hoped to share.

Barna's research showed non-Christians are skeptical and hostile to organized, institutional church and ministries it is involved in. They were unfavorable of every institutional church category from hospital visitation, welcoming committees, the church actually caring about them as people, and felt that institutional church is not where you look to find reasonable or intelligent practical life solutions. Yet, in every one of those same categories, non-Christians give individual believers high positive marks.[83]

Everyone Needs Salvation

I soon realized that loving my neighbors was not enough to get them into heaven. God began to lay on my heart an urgency to take the next step by presenting the gospel to my eclectic community. My response to God was not enthusiastic. "Yes, but it's so complex. They're from all sorts of places. They have such different cultures. Who knows what their religious beliefs might be?"

After nearly a years' worth of research on the state of evangelism in America, David Kinnaman concluded that Christians must develop a deeper conviction than, "Evangelizing others is good and worthy of our time, energy, and investment."[84] Christians must rediscover the teaching in Scripture that without a saving relationship with Jesus Christ people will spend eternity in hell. Christ's love for lost people must compel us to share the good news.

---

83 Ibid. 66, 67
84 Ibid. 94.

EVERYONE HAS A SPIRITUAL PROFILE

Again, persuading (witnessing) people to accept the gospel message involves helping our neighbors to understand who the God of the Bible is, as seen through his Son, Jesus Christ. Now, let's move on to conversations about God and spiritual profiling.

Build Genuine Relationships

As I've already shared, building relationships is the first step. I became friends with many of my neighbors. I loved and accepted them. We talked and had fun. We ate together. Barna 2019 research revealed that 41 percent of religious non-Christians and atheists/agnostics preferred to explore Christianity one-on-one with someone who is a Christian.[85]

Sketch Out Their Spiritual Profiles

I began to have conversations about their spiritual backgrounds. This was easy. I asked questions like "Tell me about your childhood," and, "What about your religious life?" One question usually led to another. Asking my neighbors to talk about themselves communicated that I valued them as people and friends. Most people like to tell their stories.

As I listened, I began to sketch out in my mind their spiritual profiles. Everyone has one. It began as a child with a family model of beliefs and patterns that created an imprint of God, Christianity, life, and eternity into their impressionable minds. Did they have a church experience or a religious affiliation? Who were the important people in their lives that influenced their perspectives? What traumas, losses, and painful experiences (which play a big part in shaping beliefs) did they have? People will readily share their stories if they trust you.

Life contributes to the development of everyone's spiritual profile. Education and teachers also play a role. Each profile has its own package of intellectual barriers and distortions of God. A key identifier of the correct profile is the type of questions they ask about God.

---

85. Ibid. 67.

Questions and Statements About God Help Identify Spiritual Profiles

As I listened to my neighbors talk, I began to make mental notes. Work from the general to the specific. First, get the big picture. Determine the ballpark. Are they atheists, agnostics (not sure there is a God), humanists, deists (impersonal God), Muslim, Hindu, or do they play in the Christian ballpark? To be sure I was hearing them correctly, I would give a summary statement to my neighbor. I might say, "Ah, so you're a Hindu," or, "You were raised in a Catholic home, but you haven't attended in years?" If they answered the latter question in the affirmative, I'd think, this person might be profiled as the religious.

If I asked a question like, "So, your biology professor convinced you that with scientific evidence our universe is eternal and without a creator? So, there is no God?" I would think this person is probably best profiled as a skeptic.

"I see the loss of your mother impacted you greatly." This person's profile is the hurting. "You believe you will go to heaven based on your good works?" This profile is the good person. I wanted to see how life had shaped them. I worked to identify their spiritual profiles.

God will give you more conversations, so continue to ask genuine, caring questions about their stories until you have a basic understanding of their beliefs regarding God. Those beliefs determine how they see salvation, eternity, and what they live for in this life.

Spiritual Profiles Identified in the Book of Acts

The apostle Peter said, "Always be prepared to give an answer to everyone who asks you to give the reason for the hope that you have" (1 Peter 3:15). I began to ask God for insights in identifying my friends' basic beliefs in order to respond appropriately from Scripture. As I read through the Scriptures, God answered my prayers. I began to see that my global neighborhood was actually in the book of Acts.

The Religious

Acts 2 lays out the simple gospel presentation clearly and succinctly. It was also presented to the religious.

The Hurting

In Acts 3, Peter presented the gospel to the hurting. A lame man was sitting outside the temple. Immediately Peter engaged the man and saw the man's problem. Once the problem had been identified, Peter showed compassion by meeting the need. All this attention to the man's physical problem opened the door for Peter to address his spiritual dilemma through the gospel presentation. I realized that I had a neighbor just like Peter's friend. My neighbor was burdened with physical pain. I thought that perhaps I should try Peter's strategy for connecting more deeply with my neighbor. It worked.

The Occultist

In Acts 8, Peter encountered Simon the occultist. Simon was heavily involved in the occult and what many now call *New Age* beliefs. Simon was attempting to tap into the universal powers, much like *wicca.* My neighbor across the street was from Trinidad. I noticed one day she had strange figurines dangling from her clothesline, clanging against one another in the South Florida breeze. It turned out these figurines were tied to a voodoo exercise. The incredibly happy and kind Janice, who shared recipes with my wife, was involved in the occult. Janice was a lot like Simon. I decided to see if the Acts strategy would work as effectively in this situation, and it did just as it had with Simon.

The Seeker

In Acts 8, Philip met the Ethiopian seeker who was searching for God. This man had traveled 800 or so miles one way to worship at the temple in Jerusalem. As he returned, Phillip found him reading Isaiah the prophet. He had many questions about God. Philip answered his questions and then immediately baptized him into Christ. I thought of my neighbor, Jose, who lived several houses down from us. He was seeking God, too, and had questions. I learned some basic steps in approaching seeker Jose from Philip's approach to the Ethiopian seeker.

The Fanatic

In Acts 9, a fanatic appears. Radical religious groups are not unfamiliar today. Millions of people around the world are terrorized by fanatical terrorist organizations. Saul was a religious fanatic. He might pass today as a radical terrorist. His goal was to remove Christianity from the face of the earth. He was arresting Christians and confiscating their property. Then Saul the fanatic encountered Jesus. I didn't have any fanatics in my neighborhood, but they are all around us today. I know that if we apply the principles found in Acts 9, they can understand and obtain salvation.

The Good Person

In Acts 10, I met the good person. Cornelius believed heaven could be earned by doing good works. And what a good person Cornelius was! An angel came to visit Cornelius stating, "Your prayers and gifts to the poor have come up as a memorial offering before God" (Acts 10:4). Cornelius was a good person, but he was not saved. God went to extraordinary measures to connect the apostle Peter with Cornelius. I also had good people in my neighborhood. Living nearby was Dave. Dave was all about humanitarian causes, kindness, helping the less fortunate. Unfortunately, Dave placed his trust for salvation in being good. Once again, I could use the Acts account and apply the strategies Peter used to effectively reach Dave.

The Successful

In Acts 16, I met the successful. Lydia was a wealthy owner of a manufacturing company that produced fine clothing. She arrived in Philippi from Thyatira probably to open up a new clothing store in the city. She was in a prayer meeting outside the city. Paul joined the gathering and introduced the group to Christ. Successful people without a biblical perspective can believe their success is rooted in their gifts, talents, and skills but seldom acknowledge God. Other successful people believe God has blessed them because of their goodness/virtues versus the poor who deserve their fate.

The Abuser

In Acts 16, I met the Abuser, the Philippian jailor. Abuse is rampant in our society. I've counseled men, women, and children who have been abused by friends or family members. Many of these abusers are not Christian. Paul was severely beaten and became a victim of abuse. In Acts 16, he shows us how to witness to the abuser, hopefully leading them to salvation in Jesus Christ.

The Skeptic

In Acts 17, Luke introduced me to the intellectual. Paul traveled to Athens and debated with philosophers, the intellectual elite of the city, about the existence of God. In my neighborhood, I too encountered skeptics and intellectuals who tried to argue away the gospel as a myth. My next door neighbors were from Greece. They loved nature, flowers, and art. They were very nice. One day my youngest son came home and described a full-size statue of a nude lady in their living room. After getting to know them better, I surmised they were secular humanists. They deified humankind and believed if the world would unite, we could create a heaven on earth. I realized as I studied Acts 17 that this was a great outline to reach my skeptic neighbors.

The Misinformed

In Acts 19, I met the misinformed. The apostle Paul attended a Bible study in Ephesus. After listening to the teacher, Paul interrupted with a question, "Did you receive the Holy Spirit when you believed" (Acts 19:2)? From the answer, Paul realized, not only did they mistakenly believe they were saved, but they were misinformed on many other points of Christian doctrine. The conversation resulted in Paul baptizing all of them into Christ. I thought of my close neighbors, Karen and Mike. They had a church background but had a little understanding of their Christian faith. They were members of a church, but I wasn't not sure they knew Jesus so Acts 19 was helpful in witnessing to them.

The Hedonist (Pleasure Seeker)

In Acts 24, I found King Felix, the hedonist or the pleasure seeker. For two years, he had Paul brought out from prison to speak with him. Paul would talk about the need for repentance and righteous living. Each time Paul began to talk about Judgment Day, Felix would get scared and end the conversation. Scripture never tells us if Felix came to Christ but Acts 24 is full of practical ways to share the gospel message with hedonists. I had pleasure seekers living in my neighborhood too, so I knew this was the insight I needed to approach them.

SPIRITUAL DISTORTIONS

What I discovered as I worked more with the spiritual profiles as shown in Acts, is that every spiritual profile is built around a spiritual distortion of God. This distortion holds people captive and can block the person from embracing and trusting Christ as Lord and Savior.

Satan's Strategy Is to Distort God's Attributes (Character)

In Genesis 3, how did the serpent convince Eve to resist God's authority and reject his command? Satan distorted God's character. Satan, the father of lies, labeled God the liar. God had told Adam and Eve they would die if they ate from the tree of knowledge of good and evil. Satan emphatically declared to Eve, "You surely (absolutely) will not die" (Genesis 3:4). He continued, "God knows that if you eat from it your eyes will open, and you will be like God" (Genesis 3:5). In other words, "God wants no rival. He is depriving you of wisdom. God is not for you, Eve; he is actually holding you back." At this point Eve believed the serpent and placed her trust in him. *Obedience follows trust.*

Satan has used this strategy throughout time. Again, every person has a spiritual profile with its own unique distortion of God. You can pick up these distortions in the statements and questions your friends ask about God, life, salvation, and eternal life.

Spiritual Distortions of God Create Barriers to Trust Christ

Why are people God haters (Romans 1:30) and how has God hurt them? God loves them. He provides for their needs and gives them joy (Acts 17:25, 26). He sent his Son to die for their sins to restore their broken relationship with their Creator. It is true that the arrogant see disappointment as God blocking their path to happiness, but isn't that, in and of itself, a distortion of God?

Talk to the *hurting person* about trusting God and she might ask, "How can I trust God when he allows me to suffer like this?" Or a mother whose child was molested. She might say, "If God is God, then why did he not stop this evil before it was done to my child? If God is all powerful, then he is not all loving. If God is all loving, then he is not all powerful, for a loving and all-powerful God would not allow this to happen."

The *seeker's* questions and distortion of God are different from the hurting. Seekers want to know, "How can God know me? How can God have a plan for me? How can God communicate with me?" Every profile has its unique set of questions that reflect a particular distortion of God. Before the person will trust Christ, often these distortions must be corrected.

To Correct the Distortions, Present the True God

Throughout the Bible, the names of God describe the many facets of his character. God revealed himself in pivotal times in Israel's history by intervening to solve an individual or national problem. The recipient of God's grace would often declare God's name as the solution to their particular problem. For example, Hagar and Ishmael had been cast out of Abraham's home by Sarah. In the desert she wept, expecting they would die. God spoke to Hagar and told her where to find water. She then spoke of God as "the One who sees me" (Genesis 16:13).

When Israel went to battle against the Amalekites, as long as Moses held up his staff toward the heavens, God fought for Israel. Moses then spoke of God as "our banner" (Exodus 17:15).

In an act of obedience to God, Abraham was about to kill his son Isaac on the altar. God stopped Abraham and provided a ram for the sacrifice. Abraham then declared, "God will provide" (Genesis 22:14).

Other names of God are "almighty" (Genesis 1), "the all-sufficient God" (Genesis 17), "the God who heals" (Exodus 15), "the God who purifies"(Leviticus 20), "the God of peace" (Judges 6), "the God who shepherds his people" (Psalm 23), "the God who is present" (Ezekiel 48), "the everlasting God" (Psalm 90), "the self-existent God" (Exodus 3), and many more.

You and I interpret our challenges, victories. and life events through the lens of Scripture. God meets our every need. We stay optimistic and faithful. We all have experienced the many names of God. However most people in the world define God through a human lens. They experience injustice, rejection, suffering, and then project incorrect characteristics onto God. God is distant, uncaring, aloof, impotent, a kill joy, a policeman, and a grumpy old man.

As we interact with friends, our goal is help them to see the God of the Bible in their situations. We defend God's personhood. We help people who struggle with God to see him through Jesus (John 14:9).

Like the atheist Richard Dawkins, others read the Old Testament and misinterpreted God's character. Dawkins interpreted God's justice on the wicked Canaanites like this:

> The God of the Old Testament is arguably the most unpleasant character in all fiction: jealous and proud of it; a petty, unjust, unforgiving control-freak; a vindictive, bloodthirsty ethnic cleanser; a misogynistic, homophobic, racist, infanticidal, genocidal, filicidal, pestilential, megalomaniacal, sadomasochistic, capriciously malevolent bully.

Notice the names by which Dawkins defined God. Obviously, he is the extreme God hater. Scripture explains that someone like Dawkins knows there is a God, but vehemently rejects his authority. When Dawkins stands before his creator and judge, he will be "without excuse" (Romans 1:20). Who will help people shape an accurate understanding of God? That's the job of every Christian. Consider 2 Corinthians 10:3-5 (*NASB*).

> For though we walk in the flesh, we do not war according to the flesh, for the weapons of our warfare are not of the flesh, but divinely powerful for the destruction of fortresses. We are destroying speculations and every lofty thing raised up against the knowledge of God, and we are taking every thought captive to the obedience of Christ.

The weapon that destroys the distortion is truth found in Scripture. Notice we are to destroy three things: fortresses, speculations, and lofty things. The fortress is a distortion of God. The speculation is distorted belief. The lofty thing is the distorted system/practices that flow from the other two distortions. These half-truths, or overt lies about God, hold people captive. They hinder society from trusting God and his salvation through Jesus Christ. The distortions need to be destroyed so our friends can see God clearly.

Here's a brief example. Let's consider the atheist profile. He has built a *fortress* that attacks God's existence (God distortion). The lie is that there is no god. Atheist's *speculation* is evolution (a distorted belief). Atheist's *lofty thing* is the system/ practices he has created around his presupposition that there is no God. This system of "a no God-evolution" distorts biology, politics, history, philosophy, theology, and the definition of humankind. We are to bring it down thereby allowing Atheist to see God is worthy of his trust and faith.

Sound pretty complicated? Not really. We simply place the counterfeit next to the authentic. In the case with the atheist no one can prove or disprove God. Our job is to show the probability of God. If our friend acknowledges the probably that God exists, then we've successfully laid the foundation. The next step is show them Jesus, who is God in the flesh. Interestingly, we see Jesus got upset with Philip when Philip asked Jesus to show the disciples the Father (John 14:8).

Jesus said to him, "Have I been with been so long with you and yet you have not come to know me, Philip? He who has seen Me, has seen the Father; how do you say, `Show us the Father' (John 14:9)? Jesus is God in the flesh. If you see Jesus, you see God. We reveal Jesus' interactions with life and people to our friends through the gospels (Matthew, Mark, Luke, and John). We learn his stories.

Again, we see exactly what God is like in the person of Jesus (Hebrews 1:3). What do we see? Jesus conquered every obstacle of life. He walked on water, calmed storms, healed every disease, fed multitudes with a few loaves and fishes, forgave sins, and raised the dead. Jesus conquered the grave and ascended into heaven. God is the Almighty. Also consider, what were Jesus' priorities and values? How did he handle relationships? How did Jesus treat the hurting, the lost, the arrogant, the poor, and the outcast of society? Jesus will remove all the distortions people have of God. There is a Jesus story for every distortion.

Removing Distortions and Seeing God Clearly is a Process and Takes Time

Revealing Jesus removes every distortion of God. To see Jesus is to see God (John 14:10). After a healthy conversation with a friend about who Christ is, your friend might see God and salvation clearly. He or she may ask, "What must I do to be saved?" But personal experience tells us that most people require time to process truth. Their distortion(s) of God have been baked into their thinking, creating their current mindsets. Every human being is in the process of "seeing" the heavenly Father "clearly," including Christians. Paul declared this truth to the believers at Ephesus, "I pray that the eyes of your heart may be enlightened, so that you may know what is the hope of His calling, what are the riches of his glory of His inheritance in the saints and what is the surpassing greatness of His power toward us who believe" (Ephesians 1:18, 19).

If learning to know God correctly takes Christians a lifetime, why would we expect our non-Christian friends and family to accept him right away? Even Jesus used processes as shown in Mark 8:22-26.

> When they arrived at Bethsaida, some people brought a blind man to Jesus, and they begged him to touch the man and heal him. Jesus took the blind man by the hand and led him out of the village. Then spitting on the man's eyes, he laid his hands on him and asked, "Can you see anything now?" The man looked around, "Yes," he said, "I see people, but I can't see them very clearly. They look like trees walking around." Then again Jesus placed his hands on the man's eyes again, and his eyes were opened. His sight was completely restored, and he could see everything clearly.

Every other healing Jesus performed was instantaneously complete. Why was the blind man's sight restored in stages? It metaphorically describes people's grasp of who Jesus is. In the next verse, Jesus asked the disciples, "Who do people say I am?" (Mark 8:27). The disciples responded, "Some say John the Baptist, some say Elijah, others say you are one of the prophets." "Who do you say I am?" (Mark 8:29). Then Peter revealed his distorted his view of Jesus (Mark 8:31-38).

LET'S WRAP UP

1. Engaging people effectively with the gospel happens best in friend-ships. The apostle Paul told Timothy to share the gospel whether the time is favorable or not (2 Timothy 4:2).

2. The reason many do not jump at salvation through Christ is Satan has distorted their perceptions of God. As you listen to your friends describe their views of God, you might respond, "I wouldn't follow that god either." Our job is to present God through the character of Jesus. We do this by telling Jesus' stories found in the gospels (Matthew, Mark, Luke, John). There is a story that counters every God distortion.

3. There is the urgency of eternity. We don't know when a person will die and face God as his judge (2 Corinthians 5:10). Without Jesus as Lord and Savior, our friends and family are doomed (Acts 2:40; Romans 3:23-36).

4. Our motivation is God's love expressed through Jesus Christ (2 Corinthians 5:14). God loves every sinner, and he cries out, "Be reconciled through Jesus" (2 Corinthians 5:20).

CHALLENGE:
YOU ARE GOD'S GOSPEL DISTRIBUTION STRATEGY—SO DO IT

William Carr Peel and Walt Larimore wrote the helpful book, *Going Public with Your Faith*. The authors' first chapter is titled, "Spiritual Economics." They make the argument that the greatest hinderance to saving the world from the deadly sin virus is not the absence of a cure, but the paucity of a "distribution" strategy. They make the point with the polio vaccine.[86]

In 1921, Franklin Delano Roosevelt was stricken with polio. On the tenth anniversary of his death, Dr. Jonas Salk announced that the polio vaccine had been developed and was ready for use by the general public. Over thirty years later, in the late 1980s thousands of doses of oral polio vaccine were being stored in drug company refrigerators. Yet hundreds of thousands of polio cases were still being reported around the globe. The supply was plentiful. The problem was a failure of distribution. In stepped Rotary International, which set a lofty goal-to eradicate polio

86. William Carr Peel & Walt Larimore. *Going Public with Your Faith*. Zondervan Publishing Company. Grand Rapids, MI. 2003. P. 17.

from the world. The organization raised more than 200 million to buy enough vaccine to meet the entire global need. But they, too, confronted the same massive problem-distribution. Working in conjunction with the World Health Organization, Rotarians developed a strategy that called for "national vaccination days" in countries around the world. Thousands of health officials and volunteers vaccinated entire countries. By 2001, only 500 cases of polio were reported worldwide. By addressing the challenge of distribution, the Rotarians saved countless lives.

The supply of the gospel is never ending. The blood of Christ is available. Christ is waiting to cure every person on the planet from the terrible plague of death caused by sin. One reason people remain in their sickness and will die in their sins is the that the warehouses (churches) are full of the cure, but the believers fail to distribute it to their neighborhoods.

CHAPTER EIGHT
The Effective Church
SPIRITUAL PROFILING
THE RELIGIOUS

The book of Acts contains a series of spiritual profiles based on unique distortions of God. These distortions cause resistance to or rejection of the gospel. Before people can be open and receptive to God's marriage proposal (Matthew 22:1-14; Ephesians 5:21-32), their distortions must be replaced with accurate perceptions of God as seen through Jesus (John 14:8-14). Distorted views of God lead to distorted beliefs and practices. This chapter will reveal the distortions within each profile and give appropriate biblical responses.

In 2 Corinthians 10:4, 5, the apostle Paul identified "fortresses," (distortion of God), "speculations," (distorted beliefs), and "lofty things," (distorted systems/ practices). Using God's Word, the apostle commanded that we dismantle the lies. God's truth sets us free (John 8:32).

There are several key attitudes essential in the witnessing process. *First, speak the truth in love.* Kindness communicates that we genuinely care and creates a bond through the rocky process of values clarification where people must honestly confront their mistaken beliefs. *Second, humility places everyone in the same boat.* At one time we were all deceived and in bondage. We are still continuing our growth in the grace and knowledge of God. We too are saved only through faith in Christ's work on the cross. There is no room for arrogance. *Third, Christ's love "compels us"* (2

Corinthians 5:14). In Acts, the reader is introduced to Luke's neighborhood. Luke shares eleven neighbor profiles he had to confront in his neighborhood. As we read about his experience, we realize that those same profiles fit neighbors living in our twenty-first century circles of influence too. By studying Luke's methods to engage his neighbors with the gospel, we gain insight into reaching our neighbors for Christ.

THE RELIGIOUS

The first neighbor we encounter is the *religious* in Acts 2. In a sense, Christianity is a religion. The Latin word for religion is *religio*. *Re* means "back" and *ligare*, "to bind." From the Latin, religion involves reviewing over and again what is sacred then re-committing our time, talent, and treasure. At the weekly Lord's Supper, the major focus for each individual is to be the relationship with Christ and being his witness during the week. Yet, at its core, Christianity is not a religion, but a relationship—with God our creator through faith in Jesus our Savior.

Spiritual Profiling of the Religious

The religious profile stresses that tradition, heritage, and rituals make people right with God. Jesus is not *the* way (John 14:6), nor is his substitutionary death on the cross the key. To the religious, a personal relationship with God is not essential thereby making God impersonal. The religious incorrectly believe that breaking God's laws (sin) can be mended or justified by performing religious rituals. Fulfilling religious traditions brings mercy and potentially creates a good standing before God. The religious mindset creates distortions involving God's holiness, love, and justice.

Distorted God: The Impersonal Law Enforcer

The religious see God as the impersonal law enforcer primarily concerned with justice. For example, the highway patrol monitors the speed of cars with radar. When a driver is caught speeding, the officer will stop the driver and dole out the appropriate penalty or give a warning (mercy). He may be kind and polite after the encounter, but the officer does not stand around and ask about your family or your concerns and challenges. Police are about law enforcement. They uphold the law. Keep the law and the police keep their distance. Break the law and they either serve justice or overlook the crime and state, "Be more careful. A second offense will result in a ticket." Tickets and penalties can be forgiven by attending driver's school. Continue to break the law and your driver's license will be suspended for a designated period, then reinstated.

The religious distort God's holiness, love, and justice. The belief is that God's love allows people to break his holy laws to a limit. Exceed the limit and God's justice requires attending religious school, doing religious rituals, and/or fulfilling religious traditions. These obligations either keep the person in good standing or reinstate the law breaker to God. The religious can never be sure about the holy limits, or if the person's religious efforts are enough to pay the debt. Just as the speeder has no idea if the patrolman will give a ticket or warning, the religious cannot be absolutely sure if God, the impersonal law enforcer, will show mercy or administer justice. This perspective applies to everyday life and Judgment Day.

The Distortion of God in Judaism

Many within Judaism believe God is impersonal and unknowable.[87] The largest sect of Judaism is the reformed sect, which holds that a person can be an atheist, naturalist, or religious humanist and still be Jewish if they maintain Jewish tradition.[88] For Jews who believe in God, the study of the Talmud is primary. One Rabbi states, "A single day devoted to study of the Talmud outweighs 1,000 sacrifices."[89] Seeking to understand and obey God's commandments through the Talmud (traditions and rituals) gives adherents o Judaism "good standing" with God.

The Distortion of God in Islam

Islam teaches that Allah is the only true God. Muslims denounce Jesus the "God-Man," and consider Christian beliefs blasphemous. The Quran (Holy Book of Islam) states that Allah has no likeness (Sura 42:11), which means humankind is not made in his image. The Quran also states that Allah is unknowable and neither

87. Pewforum.org/2018/04/25/1-beliefs-about-the-nature-of-god/
88. Ray Comfort, *World Religions In A Nutshell*. Bridge Logos. Newberry, Florida. 2008. P. 8
89. En.wikipedia.org/wiki/Torah_study

spirit nor physical (Sura 4:171). "The Muslim God is unapproachable by sinful humans. The Muslim's desire is to submit to the point where they can hold back the judging arm of Allah and inherit eternal life in a heavenly paradise, often pictured in terms of food, wine, and sexual pleasure"[90] The term *Islam* in the Arabic means "submission."

The Distortion of God in Hinduism

The Hindu God is called Brahman, who *is* the universe and everything in it. This view of God is called pantheism. Brahman is an impersonal God, part of the rocks, streams, trees, etc. Every person also has the divine spark and the capability to reach god status. Hindus acknowledge that millions of people have "achieved" this god state, including Jesus.

Distorted Belief:
Salvation Involves Doing Religious Traditions and Rituals

The Distorted Beliefs of Judaism

Many Jews continue to claim the Old Testament promise that being the children of Abraham makes them God's chosen people. Their heritage is their free ticket to heaven. Most Jews do not believe in hell, thus removing any need for salvation. All good people go to heaven, but Jews have their special place with God.

Heritage as Abraham's children trumps religious beliefs and practices. The Jewish have many rituals that maintain a right standing with God. These include celebrating the circumcision of male newborns signifying the child is one of God's chosen. There is also the bar mitzvah (for boys), and the bat mitzvah (for girls) which signify that the teen is coming of age and has chosen to be Jewish. Most Jews also celebrate some of the holy days such as the Passover, which also reinforce good standing with God. Not only that, but forty-two percent of millennial Jews celebrate Christmas.[91] Twenty-one percent believe Jesus was God in human form.[92] But again, that does not mean they believe Jesus died for their sins. Being the children of Abraham is good enough.

---

90. Walter Martin. *The Kingdom of The Cults*. Bethany House Publishers. Bloomington, MN. 2003. P. 444.
91. Jpost/diaspora/study-one-fifth-of-Jewish-millennials-beieve-jesus-is-the-son-of-god-512015
92. Ibid

In addition, Jews also believe that those who study and practice the traditions of the Talmud will have a better seat at the heavenly banquet table. The Talmud is a record of 1,000s of Rabbinic teachings that span approximately 100 BC to AD 500. The Rabbis gave countless interpretations and applications of the commandments of the Torah (first five books of the Old Testament). Adherents of Judaism believe that with so many "interpretations" no one can actually know the truth, but through arguments and debates, individuals can determine what is right for themselves. In January 2020, over 90,000 Jews filled Met Life Stadium in New Jersey, with another 20,000 filling Barclay Center in Brooklyn, New York, and 1,000s more at satellite locations. They gathered to celebrate their 7½ year reading of the Talmud.

During Jesus' ministry, Jewish Pharisees and teachers of the religious law traveled over 100 miles from Jerusalem to Galilee in order to ask Jesus one question. "Why do your disciples disobey our age-old tradition? For they ignore our tradition of ceremonial hand washing before they eat" (Matthew 15:1). Jesus responded, "And why do you, by your traditions violate the direct commandments of God" (Matthew 15:3). Jesus then quoted Isaiah the prophet. "Their worship is a farce, for they teach man-made ideas as commands from God" (Matthew 15:9).

The Distorted Beliefs of Islam

The religion of Islam contains five pillars. It is the Muslim's duty to fulfill each one. Keeping these traditions and customs and doing their prescribed rituals define a person as Muslim and produce good standing with Allah.

- *Shahada*: Confess the faith by reciting, "There is no God but Allah, and Muhammad his messenger."

- *Salat*: Pray five times daily. Washing of hands and body prior to prayer. Face Mecca.

- *Zakat*: Give 2.5 percent of income to help the poor.

- *Sawm*: Fast from sunrise to sunset for Ramadan (30 days)

- *Hajj*: Take a pilgrimage to Mecca at least once if possible (Only Muslims can enter Mecca, the birthplace of Muhammad)

Ramadan is observed during the ninth month of the Islamic calendar. Ramadan is one of the five pillars Muslims are obligated to do in order to satisfy Allah and avoid judgment. Ramadan is allegedly the month the Quran was revealed to Muhammad (A.D. 610). Ramadan rituals include several 30-day prohibitions such as no sexual relations, no brushing the teeth, no smoking, no drinking alcohol, no gossiping, and no becoming angry. They must also give alms, pray, and read the Quran. Fasting is required from sunrise to sunset every day. If a Muslim does not fast during the allotted time, he or she must make up the unfasted hours (with good deeds) sometime in the future.

The Imam is the head of the Muslim community. The Caliph is the national political leader. Muslims (Shiite denomination) believe the chief Imam is appointed through the family lineage of Muhammad and is divinely inspired, infallible, free from sin (divine grace), and can also forgive sins. This concept is borrowed from the Roman Catholic church and its teaching on papacy and apostolic succession.

In the Hadith (sayings of Muhammad) there is an Imam called the "Guided One." He disappeared in AD 873 and is alleged to be the spiritual guide of the Imams. He is also called the Mahdi. Muhammad stated that he will return with Jesus at Armageddon. Both will fight and defeat the infidels, restore all the land to Muslims, and usher in the seven-year utopia with justice and peace. Judgement Day follows.[93] Radical jihad Muslims emerge from the Shiite denomination. To usher in the future utopia, spiritual compromise to Allah must be purged from the Muslim lands; thus, the killing of Sunni's (Muslim compromisers) and Christians. This idea is a perverted expression of the Old Testament teaching that individual sins can bring God's punishment on the nation (Joshua 7).

The Distorted Beliefs of Hinduism

Hindu society is based on a caste system that ranks individuals by their occupational class: Brahmins (priests), Kshatriyas (soldiers), Vaishyas (merchants, farmers, and laborers), and Harijans (untouchables). Even though the Indian government banned the caste system in 1948, it is still considered the proper way to order society. The higher the class, the more the person is blessed with material luxuries and benefits. A person's caste is determined by works in relationship to the laws of karma. Untouchables (lepers and outcasts) are the way they are because of their past actions. They must suffer and pay the penalty for their bad karma (sins) in

---

93. Britannica.com/topic/imam

order to transmigrate into another caste system in their next life (reincarnation).[94]

According to Hinduism, the physical world is an illusion. The individual's problem is ignorance that he or she is in fact God. Following one's desires brings consequences and will keep the individual in the karma cycle. The goal is to detach from selfish desires and get in touch with your god self. This can be done through yoga, transcendental meditation, and other exercises.

HOW TO RESPOND TO THE RELIGIOUS

The religious define God as the impersonal law enforcer, a clear distortion of God as described in the Bible. Let's consider what Scripture says about God's personhood, his justice, holiness, and love.

God is Personal

God is spirit (John 4:24). The biblical word for *spirit* can also mean "breath." God is described as "the Living God" (Isaiah 37:4). Jack Cottrell points out that God's spirituality means that he is personal.

> This is possibly the most significant thing we can say about the essence of spirit: spiritual beings are persons. Angelic and human spirits are persons; the very idea of spirit implies personhood. Thus, to think of God as impersonal or as anything else less than personal is a denial of Jesus' affirmation that God is spirit.[95]

- Cottrell states that personhood means four things:

- Rational consciousness. God thinks, has knowledge and reasons.

- Self-consciousness. God is aware of his own existence (Exodus 3:14).

- Self-determination. God makes his own decisions. No one can impose or dictate to God what to think.

94. *The Kingdom of the Cults*, p. 391
95. Jack Cottrell, *The Faith Once for All*. College Press. Joplin, MO. 2002. P. 68.

- God has relationships with other persons.[96]

Throughout Scripture God speaks to angels (Job 1:6), Satan (Job 1:6), Jesus (John 12:28), the Holy Spirit (Romans 8:27), Moses (Exodus 3:4), Adam and Eve (Genesis 3:8), Cain (Genesis 4:6), Noah (Genesis 6:13), Abraham (Genesis 12:1), Jacob (Genesis 28:13), Samuel (1 Samuel 3:4), Elijah (1 Kings 19:9), the prophets and more. God has personal names (see Genesis 16:13). God loves (Jeremiah 31:3), has emotions (Psalm 33:5), is compassionate (James 5:11), can express anger (Exodus 32:10, 11), has a will to make choices (Psalm 115:3), shows mercy (Jonah 3:10), and has intellect (Isaiah 48:17). Clearly God is a person who reveals himself to humankind and works on our behalf.

God is Three: The Trinity

There is but one God (Deuteronomy 6:4). This is called monotheism. The one true God is three persons who share the same God essence. There is God the Father, God the Son, and God the Holy Spirit. Three distinct personalities sharing the same God "substance." Before God created humankind he said, "Let us make man in our image, to be like us" (Genesis 1:26), an inference to the Trinity.

All three personalities were present at Jesus' baptism. The Spirit of God descended upon Jesus in the form of a dove, and God the Father spoke from heaven (Matthew 3:13-17). Other trinitarian passages include Romans 15:30; 1 Corinthians 6:11; Galatians 4:6; Ephesians 2:18; 1 Thessalonians 5:18,19; Titus 2:13; 1 John 4:13, 14; and Revelation 1:4, 5.

God is Holy and Love

Study carefully in chapter three the section called *The Gospel*. Understand how the cross satisfies both the holiness and love of God. This is a key part of your presentation to the religious.

---

96. Ibid.

LET'S WRAP UP

Study the interaction of the apostles with the Jewish people, especially in Acts 2-9. Peter used three primary arguments: fulfilled messianic prophecies; the miracles of Jesus, and the historical resurrection of Christ. Also use the four proofs that Jesus is Lord and Savior found in chapter 4.

Since adherents of Judaism are still waiting for the Messiah, it's important to use messianic prophecy as Peter did with the Sanhedrin and with his audience at Pentecost. Remember, the Dead Sea Scrolls (copies of all the Old Testament books except Esther) are carbon dated no later than 200 B.C., proving these prophecies were not written after the fact. Here are just a few prophecies that speak of the Messiah. Jesus fulfills them all.

Prophecy	Fulfilled
1. Born of a virgin (Isaiah 7:14)	1. Matthew 1:18, 24 25; Luke 1:26-35
2. Called Son of God (Psalm 2:7)	2. Matthew 3:7; 16:16; John 1:34, 49
3. Seed of Abraham (Genesis 22:18)	3. Matthew 1:1; Galatians 3: 16
4. Tribe of Judah (Genesis 49:10	4. Luke 3:23, 33
5. House of David (Jeremiah 23:5)	5. Luke 3:23, 31
6. Born at Bethlehem (Micah 5:2)	6. Matthew 2:4
7. Ministry begins in Galilee (Isaiah 9:1)	7. Matthew 4:12, 13, 17
8. Teacher of Parables (Psalm 78:2)	8. Matthew 13:34
9. Betrayed by a friend (Psalm 41:9)	9. Matthew 26:49, 50
10. Sold for 30 pieces of Silver (Zech. 11:12)	10. Matthew 16:15
11. Mocked (Psalm 22:7, 8)	11. Matthew 27:41-43
12. Fell under the cross (Psalm 109: 24, 25)	12. John 19:17
13. Crucified with Thieves (Isaiah 53:12)	13. Matthew 27:38
14. Buried in a Rich man's tomb (Isaiah 53:9)	14. Matthew 27:45
15. Resurrected from the dead (Psalm 16:10)	15. Matthew 28:6

The Muslim Tension

Our general responses to the religious apply to Muslims. Let me share a personal story about Zef, a Muslim I baptized into Christ. We had many talks about religion.

Islam means submission to Allah and his law. The Muslim's teach that Islamic law (sharia) was given to humanity to provide right guidance.[97] Law and justice are the major topics where we can connect with the Muslim and explain God's laws.

Zef explained that following Allah's law provides personal salvation and blesses all of creation. His struggle came as he tried to decide whose interpretation of the law should be followed. There is the tension and the battle raging within the Islam faith today over this very topic. The war between Sunni and Shiite sects is based not only in Muslim leadership but in how to interpret and apply their law to everyday life.

As a Christian, remember we need to be understanding and use the laws of God found in Scripture as a tool in witnessing to our Muslim neighbors. We can say, "Have you ever broken any of God's laws?" The honest response will be yes because lying makes us a liar. Stealing makes us a thief. Hating someone makes us a murderer (Matthew 5:21, 22), lust makes us an adulterer (Matthew 5:27, 28) and so on. Now explain why we need a savior by explaining God's holiness and love.

Zef was also in awe of how Jesus went into the neighborhoods loving and meeting needs. Jesus was so different from Muhammad who was a man of war and conquest. Islamic practices today often demand justice but lack love. Jesus is the prince of peace (Isaiah 9:6). We studied the life of Jesus in the Gospels. We studied the trials of Jesus and his crucifixion. The Gospel is clear, Jesus himself claimed to be God in the flesh, and the final Lamb of God who takes away the sins of the world (John 1:35, 4:24, 25; 8:58). It was an understanding of God's holiness and love that won Zef over to Jesus. There are more insights below as you witness to the Muslim.

CHALLENGE

There are other questions the religious may ask you as your conversations go deeper. Your challenge is to learn these doctrinal responses and "Be ready to give the reason for the hope that lies with you" (1 Peter 3:15).

1. **How is Christianity any different from the other religions, don't they all lead to God?**
   If you search "How many religions are there?" various sites will state that the number ranges between 4,200 – 5,000. But actually, there

---

97. Martinson, Ibid. p 51.

are only *two* main categories: Judeo-Christianity and Hinduism. Judeo-Christianity states that God reveals himself to humanity. Hinduism teaches that God is discovered by looking within yourself. If God has the capability to create the universe (which he does) then God is able to reveal himself to us and keep his written word pure (2 Timothy 3:16; 2 Peter 1:20, 21).

Every other religion is an off-shoot of either Judeo-Christianity or Hinduism. Under Judeo-Christianity comes for example, Islam (AD. 500). Other Christian Cults tied to Judeo-Christianity are be Mormonism and Jehovah's Witnesses. Religions that come from Hinduism are Buddhism, Confucianism Shintoism, and other eastern religions.

Judeo-Christianity teaches that the removal of sin comes through substitutionary atonement. New Testament Christianity teaches that Jesus Christ is the lamb of God. Hinduism states that atonement of sin comes through suffering and good works. When a person suffers enough and performs good deeds, he or she at death is reincarnated to a higher level. Eventually perfected, the person becomes a god, being one with the universe.

2. **How can you say the Bible is the only revelation from God for humanity?**

    The writers of Scripture spoke and wrote through the inspiration of the Holy Spirit (2 Peter 1:20, 21). The Apostle Paul wrote to Timothy, "All Scripture is God-breathed and is useful for teaching, rebuking, correcting and training in righteousness, so that the servant of God may be thoroughly equipped for every good work" (2 Timothy 3:16). There is external and internal evidence proving the Bible to be God's revelation to humanity. First, let's look at:

Internal Evidence:

*   The Bible's Unity. There are 66 individual books, written on three continents, in three different languages, over a period of 1,500 years by more than 40 authors from all walks of life. Yet the Bible is one unified message from Genesis to Revelation. No other religious book meets this standard.

- Fulfilled Prophecies. There are hundreds of prophecies describing in graphic detail the coming and qualities of the Messiah. Genesis 3:15 is the first prophecy. After Adam and Eve sinned, God declared that one born of a woman would crush the head of the serpent. From that general prophecy God gave more very detailed information so no one would miss Jesus. Here's just a few: Born of a virgin (Isaiah 7:14); called the Son of God (Psalm 2:7); to be born in Bethlehem (Micah 5:2); begin his ministry in Galilee (Isaiah 9:1); perform miracles (Isaiah 32: 3, 4); teach in parables (Psalm 78:2); fall under a cross (Psalm 109: 24, 25). His body would be pierced (Zechariah 12:10); he would be crucified between two thieves (Isaiah 53:12); he would have a physical resurrection (Psalm 16:10). There are hundreds more.

- Power and Authority of the Bible. Throughout history the Bible has transformed lives and defined western civilization.

External Evidence:

- The Dead Sea Scrolls. In 1947-1957 every book in the Old Testament was discovered except for Esther. Each book was carbon dated. The latest copy was created 200 years before the birth of Christ, proving the Old Testament prophecies of Christ were written prior to the birth and ministry of Jesus. Only God can predict the future with one hundred percent accuracy.

- Historicity. The historical data is subject to verification. Through archeological evidence and other writings, the historical facts are accurate.

- Manuscripts. We possess over 5,000 Greek manuscripts from the New Testament, more than any other piece of ancient literature. To put this figure in perspective, consider that the runner up in this respect is Homer's *Iliad* of which only 650 Greek manuscripts are known to us.[98]

The earliest fragment of the Gospel of John is dated between A.D. 80-125.

---

98. Lee Strobel, *The Case for Christ: A Journalist's Personal Investigation of the Evidence for Jesus* (Grand Rapids, MI: Zondervan, 1998), 78.

Conservative scholars suggest the gospel was written between A.D. 70-80, placing this piece very near the original.

- The documents of the early church fathers. The early church fathers wrote commentaries on different books in the Bible as well as letters to other Christians, congregations, and peoples. These men quoted the Scripture 86,000 times. Their quotations allow experts to construct 99.86 percent of the New Testament; only eleven verses of the New Testament are not quoted.[99]

- Integrity of human authors. Study the life of each writer that God used to reveal his truth and you will see integrity and sincerity. All were willing to suffer or die for their testimony and most did.

Compare the Bible to the Quran (Muslim Scripture)

The history of the **Quran** was so disputed in its early years that an official edict was established on standard Quran and the rest were ordered destroyed (Sahih Bukhari 6:61: 509-510). All of the Sirah (Various traditional Muslim bibliographies of Muhammad) rest on accounts from 150-200 years after his death. The earliest accounts of Muhammad's life have been conveyed by only one devout Muslim. He clearly communicated that what he received contained fabrications and false reports (Ibn Hisham, who edited Ibn Ishaq's Sirah Rasul Allah)[100].

Compare the Bible to the Vedas (Hindu Scripture)

It is speculated the Hindu Scripture, called the Vedas, were written between the years 1,500 to 1,000 BCE. They were transmitted orally for approximately 800 to 1,200 years and then written around 200 BCE. The authors are unknown. Hindus believe this is best so they will focus on the ideas and not the authors. There are four Vedas: Hymns of Praise; Melodies for chanting; Sacrificial formulas; and Magical formulas. The Vedas are predominately written for Hindu priests.[101]

---

99. Charles H. Campbell, *One Minute Answers to Skeptics* (Eugene, OR: Harvest Publishing House, 2010), 22,23.
100. Premier, A Blog by Nebeel Qureshi
101. Cristian Violatti, *The Ancient History Encyclopedia*. May 8, 2018.

How can you say Jesus is the only way to heaven? Isn't this being intolerant of others?

Again, Jesus' death on the cross was necessary because of God's nature. God is both holy and love. In the category of holy, we might include the words righteous, pure, and just. In the category of loving, we could include mercy, grace, compassion and benevolent. The sacrifice of Jesus on the cross satisfied both attributes of God. His holiness demands that sin be punished (hell). His love desires that no one perish but have eternal life (2 Peter 3:9). Jesus' death on the cross satisfied both, believers avoid eternal hell and experience heaven (Romans 3: 21-26).

CHAPTER NINE
The Effective Church
SPIRITUAL PROFILING
THE HURTING

The Spirit of the Lord is on me, because he has
anointed me to proclaim good news to the poor.
(Isaiah 61:1)

When Jesus landed and saw a large crowd,
he had compassion on them and healed their sick.
(Matthew 14:14)

For I was hungry and you gave me something to eat,
I was thirsty and you gave me something to drink,
I was a stranger and you invited me in, I needed clothes
and you clothed me, I was sick and you looked after me,
I was in prison and you came to visit me.
(Matthew 25:35, 36)

THE HURTING

Every day we meet hurting people. They live within our neighborhoods and circles of influence. At some point, everyone hurts through loss or pain because struggles are a part of life. What defines the people who fall into the hurting profile is the fact that their struggles have shaped their views of God, others, themselves, and life.

I'll never forget the Saturday morning I was cutting my grass in the front yard when my neighbor across the cul-de-sac burst from her front door screaming, "No, no, no, no!" She then fell on her knees in the grass and began sobbing, "No, God! No, God! No, God!" I ran to her shouting, "What's wrong?" All she could do was to point back into her house. When I reached her son's bedroom, I found him lying against the wall dead. He had shot himself through the head. Todd had always appeared happy. He had been soft spoken and friendly. His dream had been to go to college. Obviously, deep in Todd's heart there had been real hurt and pain.

Throughout our neighborhoods and circles of influence there are families and individuals who believe their situations are hopeless—unemployment, broken marriages, the death of a child, sickness—the list is never ending. With the covid-19 pandemic (2020) isolation, loneliness, and fear have escalated.

Spiritual Profiling of the Hurting

In Acts 3, Peter and John went to the synagogue for the second time in one day. It was the 3:00pm prayer time. They were about to enter the gate to the temple court when they noticed a group of men coming up the road to the temple carrying a disabled man. They positioned him outside the gate called "Beautiful." He had been paralyzed since birth. Each day, this man had gotten ready for work. His job was to beg as people went into the temple to worship. Giving alms was a part of the Jewish law, so he appealed to their mercy in hopes of a coin.

Peter told the man, "Look at us!" The man's shame kept him from looking people in the face. His pain was real. Peter said, "Silver or gold I do not have, but what I have I give you. In the name of Jesus Christ of Nazareth, walk" (Acts 3:6). Verses 7 and 8 tell us Peter took the man by the hand and helped him stand.

Instantly, the man's feet and ankles become strong. He jumped to his feet and began to walk. "He went into the temple courts walking, jumping, and praising God (Acts 3:8). Notice that even though the cure is miraculous and instantaneous, Peter still had to approach this man, feel compassion, get involved, and help him to his feet. God intervenes in people's lives through us.

In verse 11, "While the man held on to Peter and John, all the people were astonished and came running to them. Notice that the beggar held onto Peter. Helping people with unconditional kindness will create gratitude and a trust that God can use to open their hearts to the gospel. The old saying is true, "People don't care how much we know until they know how much we care." Before people will receive spiritual healing, they first may need to experience God's love through Christians. Hurting people often believe God is against them. They've experience injustice and conclude that God must be aloof or uncaring. Peter and John's example show how we can change perceptions of God by loving the hurting through acts of kindness (James 2:14-17).

God Really Cares when People are Hurting

The apostles declared to the crowd that they were witnessing the kindness of God. Addressing the crowd, Peter said, "Men of Israel, why does this surprise you? Why do you stare at us as if by our own power or godliness we had made this man walk? The God of Abraham… has glorified his servant Jesus.… By faith in the name of Jesus, this man whom you see and know was made strong" (Acts 3:12, 13, 16).

The apostles lived the priorities of Jesus. Later in the book of Acts, Peter reminded his listeners that Jesus "went around doing good" (Acts 10:38). In every town, Jesus helped hurting people. Here is another verse that describes a typical day of our Lord: "At sunset, the people brought to Jesus all who had various kinds of sickness, and laying his hands on each one, he healed them" (Luke 4:40). Notice Jesus touched each person. Jesus cared about individuals. He entered Peter's home and healed his mother-in-law (Luke 4:38, 39). Jesus encouraged Jairus as they walked together toward his home, "because his only daughter, a girl of about twelve, was dying" (Luke 8:42).

Jesus Made House Calls

Jesus made house calls. Study his ministry. Most of Jesus' work was done in the neighborhood. Only a few times does Scripture say Jesus was in the synagogue (place of worship) when people came for healing.

A key to bringing people to Christ is to show God's love in our relationships. Caring for the physical and emotional needs of people often opens the door to sharing the gospel and spiritual salvation. We must be willing to hang out with our neighbors and love them. Their hurts will surface as we spend time with them.

When I preached in Louisville, Kentucky, I shared with the congregation that I was visiting a hospice house for AIDS patients in downtown Louisville. I was excited to see members join me in my efforts and tell their friends how our church family was reaching out to AIDS victims. As a result of that kindness, I was given the opportunity to share Christ with a homosexual dying of AIDS, who was a relative of one of our church members. In his home, I shared God's love and grace. I told the dying man, who didn't weigh more than 80 pounds, that God cared about him as a person and wanted to forgive him of his sins. The man repented of his sins and accepted Christ as Lord and Savior. I then baptized him in his bathtub.

My Mother Made House Calls

Growing up I saw my mother bring several of our neighbors to Christ and many fell in the category of the hurting. She would size up her friends' needs and watch for opportunities to serve. For example, Mom would go to the home of our neighbor, Debbie, and fix her hair once a week. I remember as a boy running inside for a drink of water, hearing Mom answer Debbie's questions about Christ, salvation, and the church. Debbie was hurting. She was carrying pain from a bad marriage.

Another neighbor, Lorie, had a prescription drug addiction and went through rehab. Lorie would stay at our home on weekends. Mom would cook, talk, and help Lorie find scriptural solutions to her problems. Lorie came to Christ. Eventually, her oldest son, Steve, went into the ministry.

For fifteen years we had difficulties with a next-door neighbor. As a widowed mother of eleven children, she was overwhelmed by her plight. The children basically reared themselves without supervision. The boys damaged our property and stole from us. On one occasion, they took my dad's battery out of his car. When Dad went to talk to the mother, she called him a liar. Countless times Mom would see opportunities to be kind to this mother. She would take her flowers, talk, and give her food. I remember one Christmas we knocked on her door and gave the family a turkey. Acts of kindness began to melt this family's hearts. Over a period of time, the Smiths became our friends. When the mother died, the children asked Mom to speak at her funeral.

When the Mayhem family's teenager got into trouble, Mom became their friend with encouraging cards and kind acts. Eventually she shared spiritual truths with the family, and they began attending church.

In each instance, leading someone to Christ began with service, some act of kindness, or meeting needs. God loved the hurting through my mother. We all need to do the same with people we know.

The Role of Government and Church

I met with Carrie for weeks before she accepted Christ. Carrie had a secular background with little contact with churchgoing people. As Carrie stood before the church family, before we baptized her into Christ, she announced, "I never realized the church was about helping hurting people. My perception was that the church told people what they could not do, while the government served the people with compassionate social agencies." Social programs that help people are good, but when Christians sit back and assume the government will take care of hurting people, we stifle the church's evangelistic efforts.

In Romans 13, Paul explained that the primary role of government is to execute justice, protect citizen rights, and swiftly punish lawbreakers. The role of the church is to administer the grace and kindness of God to the hurting. History shows how the church cared for the sick and elderly and built hospitals, orphanages, and schools. Caring for the hurting with God's love expanded evangelism around the world.

When the Communists took over Russia in 1917, they opposed the church but did not make Christianity illegal. Their constitution (chapter 5, article 13) guaranteed freedom of religion. However, the Communists did make it illegal for the church to do good works. In his book *The Externally Focused Church*, Rick Rusaw states,

No longer could the church fulfill its historic role of feeding the hungry, educating the young, housing orphans, or caring for the sick. The state would handle those duties. What was the result? After seventy years, the church in Russia was largely irrelevant to the communities in which it dwelt. Take away service and you take away the church's power, influence, and evangelistic effectiveness.[102]

The Vineyard Church in Cincinnati, started by Steve Sjogren, has planted congregations across the country. Every Saturday morning this 10,000-member church sets aside several hours to do "simple acts of service in the community."[103] They are putting into practice what Saint Francis of Assisi pointed out long ago, "Preach Christ at all times and when necessary, use words." The hurting will be reached first by our love and actions and then they will be open to hear God's words of salvation. As we share biblical answers, the Holy Spirit begins to remove barriers much like a cook removes the layers of an onion. The person's heart is convicted by the Holy Spirit, and he or she can respond to Jesus.

Distorted God: The God Who Doesn't Care

The hurting are confused. The mantra of Christians is that God is love, but if that's the case, then why doesn't God intervene? It's obvious that God is all-powerful—just look at creation. The faulty conclusion hurting people make is that he must not care, or that he is punishing them for some sin.

Distorted Belief: God is not Personally Involved

The hurting's distorted belief is that God is not personally involved in their life. They charge that God does not hear their prayers, and is not personally involved in their daily struggles, pain and cares. They charge the proof is, God doesn't hear, nor does he answer their prayers. If God is personally involved with today's world, then why does he allow innocent children to be abused and suffer?

---

102. Rick Rusaw, *The Externally Focused Church* (Loveland, CO: Group Publishing, 2004), 18.
103. Ibid. Pg 11.

HOW TO RESPOND TO THE HURTING

The Old Testament prophet Isaiah identified the characteristics that would mark Jesus' ministry on earth. Jesus, speaking through Isaiah said, "the Lord has...sent me to" (Isaiah 61:1). "Sent" is the key word. God sent Jesus to earth but also sent Jesus into the neighborhoods to meet the needs and hurts of people where they lived. Jesus was sent to proclaim good news to the poor, to bind up the brokenhearted, to proclaim freedom for captives, to release people from darkness, to comfort all who mourn, to provide for those who grieve and to anoint them with the oil of gladness instead of mourning (see Isaiah 61:1-3). As Christians, we have Christ's Spirit within us enabling us to learn to allow Jesus to continue this ministry through us.

LET'S WRAP UP

Christ required his disciples to follow his ministry, going into neighborhoods and our circle of influence to help the hurting.

1. It's good for church groups to take turns feeding the hungry at the community outreach center. As the poor walk through the line to receive their food they are often greeted with warm and generous smiles. It's good to collect coats and have them delivered to various shelters. It's good to have a workday with volunteers to clean a community playground. The element that is often missing though in all these "outreach events" is relationship.

    Service without relationship meets a physical need but misses the opportunity to address emotional and spiritual problems that can only be addressed in a relationship. Serving food or distributing coats becomes the end in itself. Serving one hour in a food line is non-threatening. Christians do not have to interact with broken people.

    To the hurting, the service can become like any other government program. The poor show up to take advantage of the service.

2. Make time to get to know your neighbors. Pray for opportunities to talk. Walk across the street to chat at the mailbox or when your neighbor is working in the yard. Yard sales are great times to greet and

introduce yourself. God will give you more opportunities to connect and have deeper conversations that will lead to God.

CHALLENGE

When God conversations surface, be prepared to answer four questions.

1. **Why is there suffering in the world?**

God never intended for people to suffer. Genesis 2 says God made people in his image, which is how we can know our Creator. God made a perfect world, environment, and resources. He even created satisfying work without failure. God had a perfect relationship with Adam and Eve, but God does not force anyone to love him or be obedient to him. He gave us free will—choice. If at any time a member of Adam's family chose not to love God, or did not want to follow God's plan, all he or she had to do was eat of the tree of the knowledge of good and evil. I always picture in my mind as I read the account in Genesis how Satan was speaking to Eve. Unknown to them, Adam was standing nearby listening. By the time it was over, Satan had convinced them both that God was deceptively withholding status, resources, and wisdom by not allowing them to eat of the tree. When they ate, sin entered the world.

The consequences of sin are listed for us in Genesis 3. Adam and Eve no longer accepted themselves (v. 7) and were alienated from a holy God (v. 8). They were afraid (v. 10) and felt shame and guilt (v. 11). They behaved irresponsibly (v. 12) and began to experience fear and aggression from animals (v. 15). They experienced an increase in pain (v. 16) and the world began to decay and rebel by producing storms, drought, famine, and weeds. Today, the environment is still at odds with people. In essence, Genesis 3:19 says human DNA became corrupt. People began to grow old, experience disease, and die physically as a result of Adam and Eve's sin.

There are consequences for our actions. Some of the patients dying of AIDS contracted the dreaded disease through sexual sin, but what about the millions of HIV babies who have done nothing wrong but still suffer as a result of the choice of the parents? How about people who don't do anything wrong but contract AIDS because of a tainted blood transfusion? What about a loved one who is killed by a drunk driver? Or a family keepsake stolen by a thief who breaks into your home? God did not cause these bad events. Could God have stopped them? Absolutely, but God has given people free will. If God intervenes and takes away the mother's choice to behave in a manner that will have the potential for her to contract HIV, or the choice of the driver to drink, or the choice of the robber to steal, then—to be fair—God would have to take away everyone else's free will in every situation.

2. **Does God care about us?**

Absolutely! The Bible is God's account of his redemptive plan for his people. God sacrificed his Son for us because he loves us. The Psalms are filled with praises for God's loving kindness. For example, Psalm 139 says God knows everything about us. He made us, sustains, cares for, protects, and assists us. There are too many verses in the Bible that tell of God's love to list them all. Here are just a few: Exodus 2:24, 25 says our sufferings burden God and that out of concern for us, God will act on our behalf. The Bible tells us in 1 Peter 5:7 to "Cast all your anxiety on him because he cares for you." Isaiah 40:31 tells us to cast our cares on God and pray, trust, and wait upon the Lord.

In fact, God cares so much about us that he sent Christ to earth to remove the spiritual barrier—sin—by dying for our sins on the cross. Through faith in Christ, we can be spiritually reconciled to God. God lives inside us.

At the second coming of Christ, God will remove the physical curse of sin by destroying the present world system with fire and creating a new heaven and earth (2 Peter 3:7). Those in Christ will receive new bodies that will never be touched by imperfection gain. We will live in a perfect world that will never again work against us (Revelation 21).

The consequences of sin were removed through Jesus, so we can live confidently, overcoming sin as we wait for the day of our redemption (new bodies and new earth). In the meantime, God answers prayer, heals, restores, and intervenes directly in our lives and works through medicine, doctors, hospitals, and caring services. If we are not healed here on earth, we know we will be healed either when we die in Christ or on the day of his return.

3. **Why doesn't God stop injustice in this world?**

God does stop injustice. We have no idea how many times God has intervened in our lives to save and protect us. Psalm 91 says God's angels watch over us. As stated earlier, God does not take away the free will of a person who harms another individual. To be fair, God would have to take away every person's free will, every time. God promises to punish the sinner and bring about perfect justice on Judgment Day. Read 2 Peter 3:10-13 and see God's promises about this.

4. **Can God use bad events for good in our lives?**

A key verse in the New Testament is Romans 8:28. Basically it says God works things together for good if we love him and want to fit into his plan. Therefore, we can view life with optimism. When one door closes, God opens another. God uses our sufferings and disappointments to make this world become less important to us and cause us to place more love and trust in him. At times in the Bible, trials are viewed as fire "purifying our faith" (See 1 Peter 1:6, 7).

A key story in the Old Testament is Joseph's life (Genesis 30—Exodus 1). God used the wicked acts of Joseph's jealous brothers, the greed of merchants, and the lies of a spurned woman to bring Joseph to a place where he could eventually rule the world. Most of us will not have to suffer the trials that Joseph did, but we can still follow his example of faithful, patient obedience.

In our difficult situations, we must ask ourselves, "What is God teaching me? What does God want me to change?" Also, we should watch for a new work of God in our lives. It might be a new direction such as a job or another kind of opportunity that comes as a result of our new-found obedience.

CHAPTER TEN
The Effective Church
SPIRITUAL PROFILING
THE OCCULTIST

Let no one be found among you...who practices divination
or sorcery, interprets omens, engages in witchcraft, or cast spells,
or who is a medium or spiritist or who consults the dead.
Anyone who does these things is detestable to the Lord.
(Deuteronomy 18:10-12)

When someone tells you to consult mediums and spiritists, why consult
the dead on behalf of the living? They will be thrust into utter darkness.
(Isaiah 8:19, 22)

Keep on, then, with your magic spells and with your many sorceries,
which you have labored at since childhood...Let your astrologers
come forward, those stargazers who make predictions month by month,
let them save you from what is coming upon you.
Surely they are like stubble; the fire will burn them up.
(Isaiah 47:12-14)

THE OCCULTIST

History tells us that young men who entered the army of Caesar made a life-changing oath. They forfeited all their former loyalties and committed themselves without reservation to the cause of Caesar and to the advancement of the Roman Empire. Their time and fortunes belonged to the emperor. Caesar's soldiers lived for their emperor. They labored, fought, and died for Caesar. By swearing the oath to serve Caesar, they forfeited their civilian status. The Latin word for this oath is *sacramentum.*

This concept of ownership by the military remains familiar today; the initials "G.I." mean *government issued.* A soldier is government property and can be punished for anything that hinders his or her total, undivided allegiance to the cause. This can include things like neglecting his or her health or physical fitness. Even getting sunburned can earn a sharp reprimand.

The early church said, "We, too, have a King. He is Jesus Christ, the King of kings and Lord of lords. We, too, are pledged to Jesus just as much as any soldier is to Caesar. We give up our rights; we live, we labor, we fight, and we die for our King." The idea of being soldiers in God's army was so integral to the identity of the church that early Christians dubbed those outside the faith *pagan,* a word which originally meant "civilian" or one who was not a soldier.[104] At times, Scripture depicts Jesus as a military general on a mission to free those in captivity and to destroy his enemies at the second coming in the final battle often called Armageddon (Isaiah 61:1, Revelation 19:14-16). For this reason, the church calls baptism a *sacrament,* identifying baptism as the act whereby one takes the oath to become a soldier in the Lord's army. The Christians of the early church met each week to review their call. In this way, the Lord's Supper became a sacrament as well.[105]

The apostle Paul referred to himself as a "soldier of Christ" called to carry out the mission of his commanding officer, Jesus (2 Timothy 2:3, 4). Paul identified other believers as "fellow soldiers" (Philippians 2:25). The weapons with which Christians fight are not the weapons of physical combat. Instead, Christians demolish arguments, presuppositions, and ideologies that are set up against the gospel (2 Corinthians 10:4).

---

104. Adapted from: Joe Ellis, *The Church on Purpose: Keys to Effective Church Leadership* (Cincinnati, Ohio: Standard, 1982), 47-48.
105. Origin of the Eucharist. https://en.wikipedia.org/wiki/Origin_of_the_Eucharist. Accessed September, 2015.

A soldier agonizes, a soldier sweats, a soldier strategizes, and a soldier will even die to complete the mission. Christian soldiers are called to set captives of sin free. Fulfilling that mission is the most important priority to the Christian soldier; nothing else matters. Notice how Paul viewed his spiritual mission: "I don't care about my own life. The most important thing is that I complete my mission, the work the Lord Jesus Christ gave me—to tell people the Good News about God's grace" (Acts 20:24, *NCV*).

Spiritual Profiling of the Occultist

Let me introduce you to my neighbor Carl. He served as a soldier in the Iraq war. He visited our church and eventually joined our ministry team. His background is fascinating. Carl's family was involved in the New Age Movement and the occult. His mother was involved in Wicca, a modern religious cult based on ancient witchcraft traditions. Wicca supposedly manipulates a universal force to help people. Wicca finds its root in pantheism as do most Eastern religions. The occult (magic, astrology, and other so-called spiritual sciences) also promises power to control circumstances supernaturally through spells, chants, incantations, potions, and divination. Carl grew up feeling alone and without a sense of individual importance because of the belief that all things are one with the universal force.

God brought Carl to Christ through the love, godly example, testimony, and sacrifice of another soldier he called "Rev." Rev was Carl's commanding officer. He always led the squad in prayer before missions and talked frequently about how God expressed his love for all people through allowing his Son Jesus Christ to die on the cross. Carl said that Rev was different. He was not a follower but a leader. Rev once told him that before he did anything, he always asked himself the question, "How will this be perceived by others; will it affect, hurt, or help my witness as a Christian?"

Carl described a day at the beginning of February. "I was complaining that I hated Valentine's Day because I didn't have a valentine and felt like no one really loved me." Carl continued, "I always said these things in a joking manner, but Rev would listen as if what I said was of utmost importance to him, and he would listen with a look of genuine care and a kindness in his eyes."

On Valentine's Day 2005, when Carl's squad was on a mission, they were hit by an IED just outside the base. Rev was severely wounded. Carl told me that as he held his commanding officer in his arms, "Rev told me that he left a present in my room on behalf of someone who loved me. Someone who had always loved me. Someone who would always love me and who would always be my valentine. Rev then died in my arms." When Carl finally got back to the base, he said, "I went to my room. There was a Bible with my name in it. Rev had written a note saying Jesus loved me and would always and forever be my valentine."

All through the Bible there are stories about witchcraft and people who use magic trying to manipulate the world around them. God condemns those choices again and again. Let's tag along with Philip and Peter and see how they share Christ with someone involved in that type of belief system.

Philip and Peter's Neighbor

We'll join Philip and Peter in Acts 8:9-25. In this passage, we find our next candidate for salvation, Simon the sorcerer. He amazed people with magic. He boasted of being someone great. Many of the people in the town acknowledged Simon as the *divine power.* In ancient days, dating back to Persia, a magician was someone who had close connections with a deity.[106]

Acts 8:12-19 introduces Philip the evangelist. Apparently, an apostle had laid hands on Philip. The Spirit had *poured out* on Philip the supernatural gift of miracles, the primary gift for the first-century evangelist. Scripture says Philip was casting out demons, "For with shrieks, impure spirits came out of many" (Acts 8:7). It is at this point we meet Simon.

As Philip preached and performed miracles, many came to Christ and were baptized. In verse 13, Simon the sorcerer said that he also believed Philip's message and was baptized. Amazed by authentic miracles, Simon began to follow Philip everywhere. When the apostles in Jerusalem heard a church had been established in Samaria (about 30 miles away), Peter and John traveled to Samaria to lay hands on the new believers so they could receive the outpouring of Holy Spirit. Simon carefully watched the whole thing.

The laying on of the apostles' hands was important because it was how the Holy Spirit passed on supernatural gifts such as prophecy (proclaiming the gospel)

---

106. Dennis Gaertner, *Acts* (2nd ed.; Joplin, MO: College Press, 1995), 144.

to believers. Remember, the New Testament Scripture had not yet been written. These first century prophets would preach the gospel with direct revelation from God. This temporary position enabled the infant church to know God's will and function as Christ's body.

There is a list of all the miraculous gifts in 1 Corinthians 12. Before the apostles died, they wrote much of the New Testament Scripture, along with other inspired men. With the passing of the apostles this ability to pass on miraculous gifts ceased (1 Corinthians 13:8-10). Today we have the completed Word of God and no longer need a supernatural gift to understand God's will. However, in Acts 8, as Simon observed the miraculous gifts transferred through the laying on of the apostles' hands, he wanted that power too. He even offered Peter, John, and Phillip money, so that he could *buy* it.

Distorted God: The Impersonal Force

In the 1970s, the movie *Star Wars* officially introduced God as the impersonal force. "May the Force be with you." Star Wars costumes and lightsabers are common still today. The screen play depicted a good and dark side to the force. Yoda used the force for good and Darth Vader for evil. The occultist also views all the energy around them as a force they can manipulate to make good or bad things happen. They don't recognize one God who is in control of everything, they believe they can use spells, magic, rituals, and their own will to tap into the impersonal "force" found in this world and use it to gain power for themselves to guide their own lives.

Distorted Belief: The Material World can be Manipulated with the Right Power and Knowledge

America and specifically millennials have embraced the occult. Often their greeting is not "Where do you live?" or "What do you do?" but "What's your sign?" Forty two percent of millennials read their horoscopes every day and believe them. Forty one percent believe in psychics. Wicca and witches are also popular.[107]

---

107. Pewforum.org/2018/08/29/the-religious-typology/

Interest in spirituality has been booming in recent years while interest in religion has plummeted, especially among millennials. The majority of Americans now believe it is not necessary to believe in God to have good morals. The percentage of people between the ages of 18 and 29 who "never doubt the existence of God" fell from eighty-one percent in 2007 to sixty-seven percent in 2012.[108] Meanwhile, more than half of young adults in the U.S. believe astrology is a science. compared to less than eight percent of the Chinese public. The psychic services industry, which includes astrology, aura reading, mediumship, tarot-card reading, and palmistry, among other metaphysical services, grew two percent between 2011 and 2016. It is now worth $2 billion annually, according to industry analysis firm IBIS World.[109]

The new age explosion stems from the occult's promise to receive hidden information about the future and the ability to tap into the universal force. As the stars align with the Zodiac, various types of knowledge and power become available to the person who knows how to control it. People become a god utilizing the force to accomplish personal goals.

HOW TO RESPOND TO THE OCCULTIST

In 1 Timothy 4:1, you will find what I believe to be the scriptural definition of the occult: "deceitful spirits and doctrines of demons" (*NASB*). Occultism is a counterfeit because it violates scriptural teaching with its every tenet. Luke tells us Simon believed and was baptized, but it is clear Simon had not repented of his sins or surrendered to Jesus as Lord and Savior. Simon went down into the water a sinner and came up out of the water a *wet* sinner. In Acts 8:20-24, Peter gave one of the strongest rebukes given to any person in the Bible. He identified Simon's heart as being, "full of bitterness and captive to sin." Simon wanted to utilize the power to accomplish his agenda. The word *filled* in the Greek can also mean "controlled." Simon's sinful nature was directing his actions, which opened his life to Satan's schemes and temptations. In fact, the passage suggests Simon was *demon obsessed.*

Obsession is different from possession. With demon possession, a demon takes over a person's body against the individual's will. We see this during the ministries of Jesus (see the gospel of Mark) and the apostles (See Acts 16:16-40). Jesus or

---

108. Ibid
109. Factsandtrends.net/2018/08/31/American-in-god-psychics-and-crystals/

an apostle would "cast the demon out" (see Mark 5:8). Obsession happens when a person willfully and continually gives him or herself over to sin, seeks mystical power to control life, or tries to find truth in the spirit world or occult sciences. The person who does this gives Satan the opportunity to influence their decisions and actions.

In verse 22, Peter said to Simon, "Pray and hope that he (the Lord) may forgive you". Peter was not questioning God's promise to forgive anyone who genuinely repents. Peter was questioning Simon's desire to change. Early church tradition credits Simon as the founder of Gnosticism.[110] Gnosticism teaches that each person can connect with God and receive secret, mystical knowledge. This mystical knowledge is power and salvation. The early church fathers wrote that Simon's quest to connect with the universal force, to obtain secret knowledge, to control people and circumstances, as well as his thirst for admiration, drove Simon's life and he chose never to repent.[111]

Satan worship is on the rise.[112] In Detroit Michigan, the Temple of Satan unveiled a 9-foot-tall statue of Satan. The ultimate goal is to have the statue on display at the Arkansas State Capitol, next to a monument of the Ten Commandments.[113] It's important to understand that Satan worshipers do not believe in Satan. Satanists are hedonists. They abhor any supernatural deity that prohibits their pursuit of pleasure, and worship nothing but themselves.

Why would Jesus and the apostles describe themselves as soldiers? Because they knew they were in battle against an enemy whose mission was to deceive and lead the whole world into captivity (Revelation 12:9). Bringing others to Christ is an act of spiritual warfare and spiritual conquest for Jesus. When a person establishes a right relationship with Christ, Jesus becomes their Lord. Paul told the Corinthians, "We are not unaware of his [Satan's] schemes" (2 Corinthians 2:11). The word *scheme* denotes a well-organized military strategy. Satan knows our personal situations, our weaknesses, our fears, our idols, and our self-centered tendencies. For this reason, Paul wrote, "For our struggle is not against flesh and blood, but against the rulers, against the authorities, against the powers of this dark world and

110. "What's Gnosticism?" http://www.catholic.com/quickquestions/whats-gnosticism. Accessed September, 2015.
111. Irenaeus, *Against Heresies* 1.16
112. The Church Of Satan – Interview. http://wormgearzine.com/2009/01/04/the-church-of-satan-interview/. Accessed September, 2015.
113. Fox News, "Satanic Temple unveils goat-headed statue in Detroit. http://www.foxnews.com/us/2015/07/27/for-one-night-devil-is-in-detroit/. Accessed September, 2015.

against the spiritual forces of evil in the heavenly realms" (Ephesians 6:12). Why do you think Paul repeated the word *against* four times? He did this to separate each of the armed forces of demonic beings.[114] They are organized, strategic, and intentional in their attacks. However, sixty-five percent of American Christians don't believe Satan exists.[115] Satan's greatest weapon is stealth. He "masquerades as an angel of light" (2 Corinthians 11:14). Most people don't realize they have a spiritual enemy. It never dawns on them that they are at war for their very souls. The unsuspecting, including many Christians, are surprised by Satan similar to how the Japanese surprised the Americans on December 7, 1941, at Pearl Harbor. The Japanese were in peace talks with the United States when the strike occurred. As 408 Japanese planes flew to Hawaii, most sailors never suspected an attack. In the same way, not realizing the church has an enemy makes Satan's camouflage, deceptions, and attacks even more effective.

It can also make life confusing for believers. Consider family blowups, breakups, and conflicts. If we do not recognize that Satan is working behind the scenes, we tend to blame ourselves or someone else and never see the real culprit, seeking to "kill, steal and destroy" (John 10:10). Satan simply laughs as we yell at one another. There is no question that we play a part in the drama, but if we look back, we can often see a strategic scheme. Someone working behind the scenes orchestrating ways for us to fall.

In recent years, there has been great advancement in medicine and psychology. There is no question that clinical depression, schizophrenia, nervous system disorders, and other psychological problems exist. These disorders do not necessarily stem from demonic activity. On the other hand, the New Testament shows Christ and the apostles doing real battle with Satan and demons who created all sorts of mental, emotional, and physical problems. Paul told the Thessalonians he and his companions wanted to visit the church, but *Satan stopped them.* We're not sure how, but Scripture says Satan hindered Paul's progress not once or twice but several times (1 Thessalonians 2:18).

The first encounter Jesus had after his baptism was a personal battle with Satan (Matthew 4:1-11). After 40 days of fasting and being tempted, Jesus rebuked Satan, saying, "Away from me, Satan! For it is written: 'Worship the Lord your God and

---

114. John MacArthur, *The Believer's Armor* (Chicago: Moody Press, 1986), 49.
115. "The Barna Group - Faith Revolutionaries Stand Out From the Crowd," n.d., http://www.barna.org/barna-update/article/5-barna-update/160-faith-revolutionaries-stand-out-from-the-crowd.

serve him only.'" Do you see how immediately following his baptism, Jesus had to fight, battle, and conquer temptation through God's power?

After Jesus was thrown out of his hometown for declaring himself to be the Messiah, he went to Capernaum, entered the synagogue, and began to preach a sermon, only to be interrupted by a demon-possessed man (Luke 4:31-37). I cannot read this passage without being reminded of an incident in my own life. My first full-time ministry was at a church in Cincinnati. One Sunday while I was preaching, a person stood up and shouted, "You're a liar!" My sermon that day was entitled "Jesus is the Christ, the Son of the Living God." I was in my twenties and had no idea what to do. Thankfully, a deacon came to my rescue and escorted the person out of the room.

The man in Luke 4 stood up while Jesus was teaching and said, "What do you want with us, Jesus of Nazareth? Have you come to destroy us?" (v. 34). Jesus commanded the demon to be silent, cast out the demon, and (v. 36) "all the people were amazed" at Jesus' power. Isn't it interesting that no one was amazed at a demon-possessed man sitting in church, but people were amazed at Jesus' ability to cast out a demon?

Demon possession was common in Jesus' day. Why did God allow this? It was a temporary phenomenon to demonstrate Jesus' authority over the spirit world, including Satan. The religious leaders hated Jesus. They claimed that Jesus' power to heal and command demons came from Satan. Jesus responded with some basic questions: How can Satan cast himself out? Why would Satan cast out his own demons? Why would Satan fight against himself (Luke 11:15ff)?

Mark 16:15-18 states that the ability to cast out demons was part of the supernatural gifts the apostles later received. Demon possession was temporary and existed only as long as Jesus was on earth and during the lifetimes of the apostles, allowing the demonstration of their authority over Satan.

The death and resurrection of Christ defeated Satan. The penalty for our sin can be paid through the blood of Christ. Through the gospel, people can be set free from the bondage of sin and eternal hell. Paul stated in Colossians 2:13-15,

> When you were dead in your sins and in the uncircumcision of your sinful nature, God made you alive with Christ. He forgave us all our sins, having canceled the written code, with its regulations, that was against us and that stood opposed to us; He took it away,

nailing it to the cross. *And having disarmed the powers and authorities, He made a public spectacle of them, triumphing over them by the cross* (emphasis mine)

Praise God! Satan and his demons are defeated. Revelation 20:2 says Christ has chained Satan and his demons for a thousand years. I believe the amillennial position offers the best interpretation for this verse. The thousand years are symbolic (not literal) of the entire gospel era, which is the time from Jesus' ascension to his second coming. The picture of Satan locked and chained shows a defeated foe. Also note Revelation 20:3: "After that, he must be set free for a short time." Many interpret this verse to mean that right before the second coming of Christ "all hell will break loose." It will be a time of extreme wickedness with counterfeit miracles performed by demons (2 Thessalonians 2:9). This will be the final sifting of God to determine who are truly his. Those who endure this terrible tribulation will be saved (Revelation 7:14). At Judgment Day, Christ will throw Satan and his demons into the fiery lake called hell. He will introduce the new heaven and earth to the faithful (Revelation 21).

Until Judgment Day, Satan is chained but still roams (1 Peter 5:8). His leash prohibits demon possession but does allow demon oppression. Jesus said, "Whosoever will come after me, let him deny himself, and take up his cross, and follow me" (Mark 8:34, *KJV*). God will not take away our free will. People can choose to reject him. Satan deceives the world through counterfeit paths to God (2 Corinthians 11:13-15). He holds people captive to sin through false beliefs and religions. He is the father of lies (John 8:44) and twists the redemptive story of Christ (1 Timothy 4:1-5).

Unrepented sin gives Satan more power and territory in a person's life. Allowing Satan a foothold (Ephesians 4:27) means a person repeatedly acts upon a sinful belief, attitude, or behavior. The individual loses more control and eventually is driven by the twisted belief or habit. The Bible refers to this as a satanic "stronghold" (2 Corinthians 10:4).

LET'S WRAP UP

The main strategy of Satan is to convince people to find truth apart from the Bible. Today, people want to connect with the supernatural. They are driven to find truth, a god, power, and control through astrology, horoscopes, witchcraft, and divination. As a result, spiritism, the New Age, and the occult are becoming very prevalent, especially among teens and young adults. Three out of four teens have engaged in at least one type of psychic or witchcraft-related activity.[116] Nearly seven million teens say they've encountered an angel, demon, or some other supernatural being. More than two million teens say they have communicated with the dead, and nearly two million youth claim they have psychic powers.[117] Who is feeding this occult frenzy? Supernatural beings, stories, and themes have invaded Hollywood and television.[118]

My friend Carl began reading the Bible Rev had left for him. Carl was overwhelmed with God's love story. He said, "I finished reading the entire Bible in about a week." Carl then went to see the chaplain, told him his story and gave his life to Jesus Christ. Carl said, "We prayed together and then I was baptized. My whole company showed up to support me. Five other soldiers came to Christ and were baptized through Rev's witness. I will never forget him. I know Rev is with the Father basking in eternal happiness."

CHALLENGE

As your conversations go deeper with people who dabble in the occult, there are six questions they will ask you. Study these and be ready to give the answer.

1. **Is there harm in horoscopes, divination, or palm reading?**

    The sin is seeking truth and revelation about life, others, and self apart from the Bible. It is seeking guidance from a spiritual, supernatural force that is not God the Creator. It is idolatry in its purest form. First Samuel 15:23 says, "For rebellion is like the sin of divination." A person who dabbles in the occult is, from God's perspective, rebellious. This is also confirmed by Peter's strong rebuke of Simon in Acts 8.

2. **What is the hidden issue with the occult?**

    The hidden issue is how the occult encourages the New Age belief

---

116. "The Barna Group - New Research Explores Teenage Views and Behavior Regarding the Supernatural," n.d., http://www.barna.org/barna-update/article/5-barna-update/164-new-research-explores-teenage-views-and-behavior-regarding-the-supernatural?q=faith+commitment.
117. Ibid.
118. Ibid.

in the divinity of man which is based on the human desire to be (or play) God.[119] The Bible teaches that people are to humble themselves, obey, repent, trust, and follow Jesus Christ. In his book *Under Cover,* John Bevere states,

One of the most interesting principles I learned about occultist practices was this: when initiating an individual into a coven (a group of individuals practicing witchcraft), the leader encouraged him to take drugs, drink, engage in illicit sex, steal, and carry out various other acts that defied the laws of God or our land.... They are taught, the more you rebel, the more power you obtain, and they seek power.... The more they rebel, the more they give access to demonic powers to influence, control, and empower their lives.[120]

The occult says humans are not separated from God by sin because neither exists. The Bible teaches that God made people in his image, not as miniature gods. Before a restored relationship with God the Creator is possible, people who are separated from God by personal sin must find resolution through the blood of Jesus Christ.

The occult relies on the doctrine of reincarnation as taught by Hinduism. The doctrine of karma teaches that a person's actions, both good and bad, will be returned to the person in exact measurement in the next existence. People then atone for their sin through personal suffering from one life to the next until they've paid the full price. They can then enter Nirvana through their good works. However, salvation is not through works but by grace through faith in Christ.

3. **How does the occult view God, heaven and hell?**

The occult position maintains that God is an impersonal force and there is no revealed Scripture. A practitioner communicates with the universal force using occult methods. When New Agers speak of Christ, they mean an energy force that reincarnates a person to the next level of existence.[121] They also believe heaven and hell are a state of mind.[122][123]

119. Ibid., 410
120. John Bevere, *Under Cover* (Nashville, TN: Thomas Nelson, 2001), 68.
121. Martin, *The Kingdom of the Cults*, 413.
122.
123. Ibid., 416

The Bible teaches that God is personal. He loves us deeply and cares for us. God speaks, hears, listens, and is benevolent and kind. He is holy, righteous, and just. God is involved in our lives. He answers prayer. God is working everything toward his ultimate purpose, which is redemption (Ephesians 1:11-14).

Jesus was God in the flesh (Philippians 2:1-5). When, through Scripture, people see and listen to Jesus, they are seeing and listening to God. Satan is a defeated foe and should not be feared, but that doesn't mean his deceptive lies and doctrines can be ignored. Christians need to confront his deceptions and show through godly example and love in action the truth of God's grace and salvation.

4. **Can people talk to the dead? Can spirits visit homes? Are ghosts real?**

Today the ideas of seances and speaking to the dead have become popular. It's understandable to want to stay connected with deceased family members and friends. Another motivation is the desire to acquire secret knowledge for daily decisions and insights about the future.

A good passage to study is the account of the rich man and Lazarus found in Luke 16. Both men die. The rich man is in hell and Lazarus is in paradise. Notice paradise and hell are in view of each other but divided by a chasm (Luke 16:23, 26). Both sides communicate with each other (Luke 16:24). Prior to the cross and resurrection of Christ everyone went to hades. A Christian tradition states that after Christ died on the cross he went down to hades and preached to everyone explaining that he was the Messiah (1 Peter 3:19, 20). Then at his ascension, Christ moved paradise to the throne room of God (Ephesians 4:7). He did this because his death paid for the sins of the faithful in the Old Testament as well as future generations.

The key passage for us in Luke 16 is in verses 27-31. Notice the rich man begged Abraham to send Lazarus to his family, "for I have five brothers. Let him warn them, so that they will not also come to this place of torment." In the next two verses, Abraham stated that the warning of hell comes through Scripture; the spirits of the dead cannot communicate with the living. In verse 31, Jesus made the point that many will not believe his message even after he resurrects from the dead.

5. **What is Gnosticism and how is it impacting our world today?**

Several years ago, Gnostic teaching surfaced through the blockbuster movie, the Da Vinci Code. The term *Gnostic* means knowledge, from the Greek word *gnosis*.[124] An early church father, Epiphanius (ca. 310-403), first coined the phrase "practicing Gnostics." So, they've been around a long time. Many early church fathers labeled this teaching heretical. Today we have as many as 60 different gnostic writings. There are five separate works that are labeled gospels (life of Christ): Truth, Thomas, Philip, Egyptians, and Mary.). They teach Jesus married Mary Magdalene, had children, and that Mary was Christ's successor. They emphasize that Christ and his disciples worshiped the sacred feminist (female goddess) and that Jesus sinned.

Other Gnostic writings include dualism: the physical world is evil and the spirit world good. God could not have created the physical world because of his purity, but a fallen, wicked, arrogant being often called the Demiurge (maker) created the world. He falsely believed himself to be a god.

The implications of Gnosticism today are several: First, some Gnostics suggest the Catholic Church excluded the gnostic gospels because they were not patriarchal (promoting the primacy of men over women). Second, it implies that since the physical world is material, Jesus did not have a physical resurrection. Third, since the physical body means nothing, then Christians are free to indulge in every sort of sinful behavior. Fourth, other Gnostics include asceticism, a denial of the physical body through strict control which includes dieting and sexual abstinence. Fifth, it also implies that revelation from God continues beyond the writings of the apostles (Scripture). People with gnostic abilities can receive messages and revelations from God, spirits, and angels that provide new truths about God, Christ, morality, salvation, as well as heaven and hell. Of course, most of these revelations contradict the Bible.

---

124. Abanes, Richard. *The Truth Behind the Da Vinci Code*, Eugene, OR: Harvest House Publishers, 2004. P. 21

6. **Are Satan and demons real?**

Many people accept good angels but deny the existence of the devil and his demons. Liberal theologians conclude that when the New Testament reads, "Jesus cast out demons" he was healing a mental illness or a physical issue like epilepsy.

Satan is a transliteration of a generic Hebrew word meaning adversary, opponent, one who tries to block your way. There are 52 Old Testament references to Satan and 33 in the New Testament. In the New Testament Satan is often referred to as the devil. The word *devil* means accuser or slanderer. In Revelation 19:11, John referred to Satan as the "destroyer." In Matthew Jesus called Satan the "deceiver" (Matthew 27:63).

Demons are called "evil spirits" (Luke 7:21; 8:2; 11:26) and "unclean" or "impure spirits" (Matthew 10:1; 12:43).

Satan and the demons' main strategy is to move us away from God through false teaching (John 8:44; Revelation 12:9). Satan's primary target is to discredit Scripture and God's character (Genesis 3:4, 5; Luke 8:12). So, it makes sense that Satan works mightily through occult, spiritualist, and Gnostic writers. We also see God's Word under attack by liberal theologians such as Bart Ehrman in his book, *How Jesus Became God: The Exaltation of a Jewish Preacher from Galilee*, and secular atheist writers like Richard Dawkins.

Satan and demons also attack our minds through temptation. Satan wants people to imitate his evil ways instead of following God's righteousness. The protection against temptation is knowing Scripture and choosing to follow God's Word verses our feelings or desires.

CHAPTER ELEVEN
The Effective Church
SPIRITUAL PROFILING
THE SEEKER

The Lord is with you while you are with him.
If you seek him, he will be found by you.
(2 Chronicles 15:2)

I love all who love me. Those who
search for me will surely find me.
(Proverbs 8:17)

If you seek me with all your heart, you will find me.
I will be found by you says the Lord.
(Jeremiah 29:13)

THE SEEKER

To seek and to know God is a desire of every human heart. God placed it there (Ecclesiastes 3:11; Psalm 8; Romans 2:14, 15). Some repress this truth (Romans 1:21), others ignore it (Hebrews 2:3), but many pursue it in search of God. God promises that those who seek him with all their hearts will find him. Let's move on to the next spiritual profile, the SEEKER.

Spiritual Profiling of the Seeker

We join Philip in Acts 8:26-40. God has just sent an angel to tell Philip to go south to the desert road that leads from Jerusalem into Gaza. Philip immediately obeyed God's word. As we travel along the road to Gaza with Philip, we meet an Ethiopian eunuch (providentially—a God encounter). The eunuch is an important, high-ranking official who serves the queen of the Ethiopians.

The Ethiopian is probably a Gentile searching for God. Notice the distance this Ethiopian man is traveling one way to worship—possibly 800 miles. We can surmise that the eunuch was present at the Pentecost experience (Acts 2) and is now traveling home. But what happened in Jerusalem must have shocked him. Being a eunuch, he was not allowed to worship God in the temple (Deuteronomy 23:1). While in Jerusalem, he heard the apostles preaching Christ and using Messianic prophecies from Isaiah 52 and 53 as proof texts that Jesus was the Christ. Perhaps that was when the eunuch purchased the costly scroll of the book of Isaiah, which he was reading when Peter approached him. (By the way, the book of Isaiah is loaded with Messianic prophecies.)

Distorted God: The God Who Hides

To the seekers, God is unknown. He is hiding. Their quests to find God take them to many places, but they cannot find him. They have questions about heaven, hell, spirits, and Judgment Day. They desire to know God's expectations and what they need to do. George Barna states that fifty-four percent of Americans are seeking a relationship with God but don't know where to find him.[125] Fifty-four percent of Americans are seekers.

A seeker is not sure of the identity of Jesus. Seekers in Jesus' day thought he might be a resurrected Elijah, John the Baptist, Jeremiah, or one of the prophets

---

125. "The Barna Group - Americans Have Commitment Issues, New Survey Shows," n.d., http://www.barna.org/barna-update/article/13-culture/155-americans-have-commitment-issues-new-survey-shows.

(Matthew 16:15). Eventually we will need to use the four apologetic arguments of Peter's sermon in Acts 2 when speaking with friends and neighbors who are seekers.

A seeker will listen to arguments about the existence of God and will be open to the study of Scripture, as was the case with the Ethiopian. This is because seekers are looking for answers to life's questions, apparent contradictions, and puzzles. They might also need help with personal problems. The Bible has answers to every quandary humankind encounters.

Seekers are searching for answers to help them deal with today's problems: difficulties with marriages, raising children, money issues, and suffering. Bible solutions to everyday challenges will lead to discussions about God's answer for their sin and his gift of eternal life. They also wonder where a loved one or friend goes after death. Seekers want answers.

Distorted Belief:
Scripture does not Define God's Purpose or Plan for Individuals

Seekers are searching for God's purpose and plan for their individual lives. The truth is God has a universal will (plan) and an individual will (plan) for every individual. The universal plan is that every person be saved through Jesus Christ and take on God's holy lifestyle; a new life that glorifies, praises, and witnesses the gospel (good news) to others.

The individual plan involves discerning one's giftedness and then serving others interdependently within Christ's body and the community at large. This gift should be developed and often time is an area where an individual is employed. Through prayer and godly counsel, Christ will open doors of service. He will provide a place that specifically suits each person.

My personal experience is God often opens more than one door for me to consider at a time. I am given the opportunity to choose from the options what was best for me. The company, church, salary, team and so forth. Colossians 3:17 states, "And whatever you do, whether in word or deed, do it all in the name of the Lord Jesus, giving thanks to God the Father through him."

Mark was a college student at Indiana University while I was attending Raymond Walters College in Cincinnati. We worked together on a golf course during summer breaks. I took the time to get to know him and to be his friend. We talked about sports, college, life, and studies. We golfed together and had great times, but there were many differences between us. When I was in high school, I drifted from the faith. However, I rededicated my life to God and was living a focused life. So, at this point there were major differences between Mark's lifestyle and mine. Mark was a drinker; I was not. He used profanity. I did not. He attended night clubs. I did not. Mark was sexually active. I was not.

My different lifestyle intrigued him. At first, he laughed at me, but when I responded with reasons for my choices and demonstrated confidence in the ways of God, Mark started to get serious. He began to listen. He asked me, "How do you have fun? What do you live for?" I told him about the things I enjoyed. I never missed the opportunity to share quotes or insights from King Solomon's life, because a person without God cannot ultimately be satisfied with his or her life (Ecclesiastes 1:13, 14).

Solomon, the richest man to ever live, wrote the book of Ecclesiastes. The book is a journal of his life in an effort to find lasting happiness. Solomon sought satisfaction in pleasure, wine, great projects, humanitarian works, arts, wealth, sex, and education (see Ecclesiastes 2). His life was not much different from many Americans. Mark agreed that in some ways he could identify with Solomon, "But as I looked at everything I had worked so hard to accomplish, it was all so meaningless—like chasing the wind. There was nothing really worthwhile anywhere" (Ecclesiastes 2:11, *NLT*).

In witnessing to the Thessalonians, Paul wrote about the importance of being different. "You are witnesses, and so is God, of how holy, righteous and blameless we were among you" (1 Thessalonians 2:10). For me to be happy without pursuing the things Mark was pursuing, made a powerful impact on him.

I explained to Mark that Christ was my life (see Colossians 3:4). Christ was the only being who would never leave or disappoint. Jesus gives true meaning to life. Everything in this world is temporary, so why would anyone live for things that pass away? I talked in non-judgmental terms about the negative consequences of sin by sharing national studies and trends. I addressed his lifestyle from Scripture to inform him and to warn him, but not to condemn him. God would judge Mark if he did not repent. I shared Scriptures that showed how his life choices were actually destroying his happiness. We talked about Abraham's choices (Genesis 12-24), David's choices (2 Samuel), and Solomon's choices (1 Kings 11).

Mark agreed that something was missing in his life. We discussed the consequences of abusing alcohol. I talked about how God's plan for sex is within marriage. I cited studies that confirmed multiple partners actually hinder a person's ability to bond emotionally in future relationships.[126] The sexual act makes two people "one flesh" (Ephesians 5:31). God intends for that bond never to be broken (Matthew 19:6). Being sexually active is abusing God's gift. For a Christian, it is connecting God's Spirit to a sinful union (1 Corinthians 6:15-20). We see many harmful consequences from a sex-driven society: trafficking, disease, prostitution, poverty, child exploitation, as well as the inability to enjoy intimacy in marriage. Being out of God's will is the cause of much unhappiness.

Consistency is important. Spending more time with me, Mark began to look for inconsistencies in my life. He wanted to prove that I was no different than he was. When I made mistakes, I would laugh and tell him I was in the process of becoming. I told him I'm forgiven, not perfect (Ephesians 2:10) and that my sins were removed on the cross. Since coming out of the waters of baptism, the Holy Spirit was working, cleaning up my life (a process known as sanctification), preparing me to meet the holy God who saved me through Christ. I am God's workmanship. Some translations say his "masterpiece" (Ephesians 2:10). Actually, the Greek word is God's *poem*. God is writing his character through every Christian as a beautiful expression of his grace and love.

After working three summers with Mark, our last week together was really difficult. We had grown to be good friends. God used my example to change Mark. To be honest, I learned a lot from him too. Several times it appeared he was ready to accept Christ, but then he'd change his mind.

There are several examples in the Bible about people who were seekers. Let's join Philip as he witnesses to the Ethiopian Eunuch.

HOW TO RESPOND TO THE SEEKER

The story of the Ethiopian is found in Acts 8:26-40. In this account the Holy Spirit teaches us some key points for witnessing.

---

126. Wiles, Jeremy, "Charisma News," *Science Proves Premarital Sex Rewires the Brain.* http://www.charismanews.com/opinion/39405-science-proves-premarital-sex-rewires-the-brain. Accessed October, 2015.

- First: The Spirit shows that we must go to the lost. Philip traveled 70 plus miles to find this man. In verse 29, God's Spirit told Philip to "go to that chariot and stay near it."

- Second: Everyone comes to Christ by *hearing* the good news. The book of Romans reads, "Faith comes from hearing the message, and the message is heard through the word about Christ" (Romans 10:17).

- Third: We need to pray for those we wish to reach. It is crucial. God calls us to give support, encouragement, and assistance when needed. We must pray for those opportunities and for God's guidance.

- Fourth: Christians must intentionally position themselves to witness. Notice that Philip placed himself near the eunuch and asked deliberate questions that directed the conversation to salvation. God opens doors, so watch. Remember, God told Philip to go to the chariot and "stay near it."

- Fifth: Think about the work Philip put in to have this conversation. The Ethiopian was riding in his chariot, reading. In order for Philip to "stay near it," he must run alongside the chariot. What an odd thing to do. Philip, in his obedience to God, was willing to do something unusual, something that might have been considered strange. He might have been misunderstood, but his actions gave him the opportunity to share. Engaging a non-Christian in conversation about the Lord sometimes doesn't happen easily. We must watch for an open door and be willing to put ourselves into the situation, however odd it might feel.

- Sixth: Slide the conversation toward God. By this, I mean when a person expresses a need or has a question about life, your move is to subtly shift or slide the conversation to God. This can be done by saying, "I know someone who can help you" or "God made you with a purpose" or "He has revealed your answer in the Bible" or "God loves you and wants you to love him." The person we are talking with will either slide with us, as the conversation shifts, or change the subject. If they slide, God is opening a door, so walk through. Philip approached the Ethiopian with a friendly, non-threatening question,

"Do you understand what you are reading?" The Ethiopian slid with Philip. "How can I unless someone explains it to me?" (Acts 8:31). He was saying, "Give me answers. Help me make sense out of what I read, see, and experience."

- Seventh: The thing to remember is that we must show them that God has the answers they are looking for. "And if someone asks about your hope as a believer, always be ready to explain it" (1 Peter 3:15, *NLT*). There are explanations for everything. A great reason for continuous Bible study with other Christians is to discuss the questions of life and get God's answers. This enables us to be prepared to share them with unchurched people when they ask us questions.

- Eighth: Remember that our seeker friends already know some Scripture, but they are looking for more information. Philip allowed the conversation to happen naturally and worked Jesus into the conversation. Philip didn't assume the man was biblically uneducated but waited to be invited to tell him more about the subject the man was searching. Acts 8:32, 33 records that the Ethiopian was reading a Messianic prophecy written 700 years earlier. The prophecy stated that Jesus was led like a sheep to the slaughter (referring to his crucifixion). He did not defend himself. In an act of injustice, he allowed his life to be taken from him (for our sins). In Acts 8:34, 35, the eunuch asked Philip, "Tell me, was the prophet talking about himself or someone else?" Philip then began with "that very passage of Scripture and told him the good news about Jesus."

You lead a person to Christ by beginning where that person is in his or her point of life and help them find God's answers to their questions. The seeker needs to understand that God is present, providential, and powerful.

God is Present

God is present everywhere. He is omnipresent. God's created universe (including us) is limited to time and location. We can only be in one place at one time, but God is not confined to a single space. He is present everywhere. This is why Christians around the world can worship God at the same time. God does not dwell in any building or location (John 4:20-24).

The seeker thinks God is hiding, but the truth is, God is present. "Am I a God who is only close at hand? Says the Lord. No, I am far away at the same time. Can anyone hide from me in a secret place? Am I not everywhere in all the heavens and the earth? Says the Lord" (Jeremiah 23:22-24). God is communicating through Jeremiah that no one can escape his presence. God is both far off and close at hand. Anywhere we go, God is there. He is ready to help, guide, and provide.

God Works Providentially

God knows everything. He is omniscient. God has all knowledge and all wisdom. Because God is not bound by time or location, he sees the past, present, and future as clearly as you and I see this moment. Therefore, God works all things for our good. He can take both good and bad circumstances and weave them into his perfect plan. "And we know that God causes everything to work together for the good of those who love God and are called according to his purpose for them. For God knew his people in advance, and he chose them to become like his Son, so that his Son would be the firstborn among many brothers" (Romans 8:28, 29). . . . . .

This wonderful promise means there's always hope. All the mistakes made through bad decisions or the injustice from others are opportunities with God. Trust him and let God make you into his masterpiece (Ephesians 2:10).

God is All-Powerful

It follows that if nothing can stop God's plans, he is all-powerful. His power is without limit. One name of God is *The Almighty* (Psalm 91:1). "O Sovereign Lord! You made the heavens and earth by your strong hand and powerful arm. Nothing is too difficult for you! . . . You are the great and powerful God, the Lord of the Heaven's Armies. You have all wisdom and do great and mighty miracles" (Jeremiah 32:17-19). This is why Jesus stated, "With God all things are possible" (Matthew 19:26). Be optimistic.

LET'S WRAP UP

As you study this passage there are two key truths to explain to a seeker.

1. **The NIV Bible places Acts 8:36 at the bottom of the page instead of including it in the text. Is the Bible accurate?**

    It's true that the translators want us to know that not all the ancient New Testament manuscripts include this verse, but the evidence is great enough to include it. We have around 5,800 partial and complete manuscript copies of the New Testament with an accuracy rate of 99%.

2. **What needs to take place before a person is baptized?**

    Before Philip would baptize the Ethiopian, Philip required him to meet a condition. "'If you believe with all your heart, you may [be baptized].' The Eunuch answered, `I believe that Jesus Christ is the Son of God'" (Acts 8:37). This verse shows plainly that a person must be able to recognize and articulate the need for a relationship with Jesus. It also suggests infant baptism was not the intention of the apostles. An infant cannot choose to believe.

    Also, babies have never sinned. It is only when people reach the age where they can make moral decisions (often called the "age of accountability") and then choose to sin, that they need a Savior. Children are born clean and innocent (Matthew 19:14).

CHALLENGE

Here are three questions the seeker will ask you. Study and be ready to give God's answers.

1. **Does God know me?**

    Absolutely. For example, our thoughts are the most private part of the human experience, right? No one else knows our thoughts unless we communicate those thoughts to them. Scripture is clear; God knows our thoughts and everything about us.

    Psalm 139 (*NIV*) declares, "You know when I sit down and when

I rise up; you discern my thoughts from afar." (v. 2). God searches our hearts and is acquainted with everything we do (v. 3). God even knows our words before we speak (v. 4). The psalmist goes further and declares that God formed us in our mother's womb, giving us our personality, skills, and abilities (v. 13). God did this so we might contribute to society and experience joy and success throughout our lifetime (v. 16).

Speaking to Christians, Peter wrote, "Dear friends, God the Father chose you long ago and knew you would become his children" (2 Peter 1:2, *LB*). God created you. He sent Jesus to die for your sins. All these facts communicate that God knows you but also values and loves you. Seek God through Jesus today (Romans 10:13). He wants to have a personal walk with you.

2. **Does God have a plan and purpose for my life?**

Yes. God has both a *universal* and *specific* will for each person. The *universal* will is that every person on earth would come to know Jesus (be saved) and live a holy life (1 Peter 1:3, 4, 13-16).

The *specific* will of God (the way you chose to glorify God in everyday life) involves your choices. Make godly choices. How? Follow God's general principles, guidelines, and boundaries found in Scripture. The Holy Spirit will then guide and bless your decisions. Some examples: There is not one soul mate for you. Your Scriptural boundary is that the person you marry must be a Christian (2 Corinthians 6:14, *NIV*). They must share your love for Christ and live by his values. There is not one job for you. God has given you talents. What do you desire to do? What do others say you do well? How is God opening doors? Whoever you marry and wherever you work, do it all unto the glory of God and he will bless you with happiness and purpose.

What about my sins and mistakes? Does that mess up God's plan for me? Can I miss out on God's plan? We've already mentioned for Christians that God promises to take everything in our past, present and future and work it for our good. The good God will do with all our experiences (good or bad) will conform us into the image of Jesus (Romans 8:28, 29).

3. **How does God talk to me and how do I talk to God?**

Be careful when someone says, "God spoke to me." You might respond with, "Did he speak audibly to you?" They'll probably say, "No, it was an inner feeling that this is what God is wanting me to do." Be careful to attribute inner feelings to God's communication strategy because Satan also speaks to us. It's called temptation. Study Matthew 4 and see how Satan tried to direct Jesus' life. Also read 2 Corinthians 10:13.

God talks to us primarily through Scripture, especially the New Testament (Matthew – Revelation). It defines God's relationship with us through Jesus Christ. Prayer is our way to communicate our praise and requests to God. God answers and gives us our requests if our prayers are in line with God's will (2 John 5:14, *NIV*). God is our loving Father. He can see into the future. He will never give us a gift that will ultimately hurt us down the road. If we hide Scripture in our heart, the Holy Spirit will bring the appropriate Scripture to our minds that will guide us through the maze (Psalm 143:8; Ephesians 6:17).

CHAPTER TWELVE
The Effective Church
SPIRITUAL PROFILING
THE FANATIC

God blesses those who are persecuted for doing right, for the
Kingdom of Heaven is theirs. God blesses you when people
mock you and persecute you and lie about you and say all sorts of
evil things against you because you are my followers. Be happy about it!
Be very glad! And remember, the ancient prophets were
persecuted in the same way.
(Matthew 5:11)

But I say, 'Love your enemies! Pray for those who persecute you!
In that way, you will be acting as true children of your Father in heaven.'
(Matthew 5:44)

When you are persecuted in one town, flee the next.
I tell you the truth, the Son of Man will return before
you have reached all the towns of Israel.
(Matthew 10:23)

THE FANATIC

Every day Americans live with the fear of terrorist attacks. Since 1972, there have been 75 Islamic terror attacks on American soil killing 3,106 Americans.[127] In all fairness, we must note that Christian fanaticism happens as well. *The Order,* a white-supremacist, revolutionary militant group, was convicted of murdering Jewish talk show host Alan Berg in 1984. The *Army of God* is classified as a Christian terrorist group and uses Bible verses to justify bombing abortion clinics, attacking gay and lesbian nightclubs, and the explosion at the 1996 Olympics in Atlanta, Georgia.[128] Larry McQuilliams, who fired over 100 rounds in downtown Austin, Texas, was associated with the *Phinehas Priesthood Yahweh's Elite.* Phinehas priests take their name from the biblical figure Phinehas in the book of Numbers, who thrust a sword through an Israelite man having sex with a Moabite woman. This group opposes interracial intercourse, racial integration, homosexuality, and abortion. Members of the priesthood often resort to violence to achieve their goals.[129]

In our world today, ISIS, other Muslim factions, and many independent radical groups fall into the category labeled fanatics. The most infamous Islamic terrorist group is Al Qaeda. Its leader, Osama bin Laden, issued a *fatwa* (religious ruling) in February 1998 calling for a worldwide Islamic *jihad* (holy war) to kill Christians and Jews. ISIS members believe Allah has not blessed the Islamic countries because Muslims have compromised their allegiance to Allah. Radical Islam is about purging society of this compromise. According to Islamic radicals, God wants them to kill the "unbelievers."

Can people consumed with fanatic zeal change and become good, productive citizens? Gina Fadely, director of Youth With A Mission Frontier Missions, Inc. (YWAM) declares, "God can turn it around." Gina was introduced to a former Islamic State jihadi who confessed to killing Christians and said, "that he actually enjoyed doing so." He shared with Gina that he was about to kill a Christian when the man said, "I know you will kill me, but I give to you, my Bible." The ISIS fighter then killed the man, and he did take the Bible. After reading it, the terrorist

---

127. Islamic Terror Attacks on American Soil. http://www.thereligionofpeace.com/pages/americanattacks. htm. Accessed October, 2015.
128. US Domestic Terrorism, History Commons, Army of God. http://www.historycommons.org/timeline. jsp?timeline=us_domestic_terrorism_tmln&haitian_elite_2021_organizations=haitian_elite_2021_ army_of_god. Accessed October, 2015.
129. The Phinehas Priesthood. http://thinkprogress.org/justice/2014/12/04/3599271/autin-shooter-christian-extremism/. Accessed September, 2015.

began to have dreams at night. A man dressed in white would appear declaring, "You are killing my people." The ISIS terrorist concluded it was Jesus, rejected Islam, and accepted Christ.[130]

Spiritual Profiling of the Fanatic

Meet Luke's neighbor, Saul, a terrorist and religious fanatic. You might be asking, "Are you referring to the author of 13 New Testament books? The apostle who became the most influential Christian to ever live?" He's the one. When you consider Saul, there is no greater demonstration of the transforming power of the gospel. Overnight Saul became a different person. He replaced his Hebrew name Saul with the Roman version Paul. His attitude, his character, and his mission changed as well.

Saul, like all religious fanatics, was shaped by his friendships and family patterns. Saul was a Jew, a Pharisee, the son of a Pharisee (Acts 23:6, *NASV*), a Roman citizen (Acts 22:28), from the city of Tarsus (Acts 9:30), and probably from a wealthy family. We can surmise his financial status from a law enacted at Tarsus in 15 B.C. that declared only wealthy households could hold the rank of citizen of Rome. The poor were relegated to resident status only.

Saul's father was a Pharisee. The Pharisees were political leaders and religious teachers of the Mosaic Law. Over the years, Pharisees had written the "Oral Law," (today called the Mishnah). The Mishnah is a commentary explaining how to keep the Torah (the first five books of the Old Testament). The Mishnah was "The Hedge" to protect Jews from breaking the Mosaic Law. These Rabbis would take a Mosaic Law such as "Keep the Sabbath" and write out hundreds of ways Jews were to obey this command. In Jesus' day the Pharisees elevated their applications of the Law to the same status as God's Word. In the New Testament this "Oral Law" is called the "Traditions of the Elders" which Jesus condemned.[131]

Pharisees were zealous, religious autocrats. They not only taught the law but also served as the spiritual policemen of Judah. They would call people out at any moment

130. Shoebat.come Awareness and Action. http://shoebat.com/2015/06/07/isis-terrorist-takes-christian-man-and-is-about-to-kill-him-the-christian-man-says-i-know-you-will-kill-me-but-i-give-to-you-my-bible-the-muslim-murders-him-and-takes-his-bible-he-then-has-a/. Accessed October, 2015.

131. Bible History Online, "The Pharisees – Jewish Leaders in the First Century AD." http://www.bible-history.com/pharisees/PHARISEESTradition.htm. Accessed October, 2015.

at any location to correct their behaviors. Remember the day Jesus and his disciples were walking through a grain field on the Sabbath? The disciples were hungry, so they broke off some heads of grain in order to eat them. Pharisees were there policing Jesus' progress through the field watching to see if he would do any work. When the Pharisees saw the disciples "working," breaking off some heads of grain to eat, they ran to Jesus in the middle of the field protesting "Look, your disciples are breaking the law by harvesting grain on the Sabbath" (Matthew 12:2, *NLT*).

Saul was raised in this type of legalistic environment. Saul's home would no doubt have had Old Testament Scriptures written on the door frames and gates. Saul's father would have talked to him about the Mosaic Law from dawn to the setting sun. They would have had Old Testament Scripture tied to their hands and arms and would even have written verses on headbands to wear during the day (Deuteronomy 6:6-9).

Saul attended a Jewish school associated with the local synagogue. He memorized Old Testament Scripture from the age of two. Probably around the age of 13, Saul's father sent him to Jerusalem for study under the greatest Jewish Rabbi of his day, Gamaliel. Traditionally a student like Saul would have graduated at the age of 19. He then returned home to learn his father's trade of making tents. A Pharisee had to be self-supporting because he could never take money for teaching lest he be pressured or bribed to compromise Scripture. . . . .

After several years, Saul returned to Jerusalem and began teaching the Torah. He advanced quickly through the political and religious ranks. He demanded the strictest adherence to the Jewish law, obeying the same laws himself without fault (Philippians 3:5, 6).

Let's summarize Saul's background:

1. He was viewed as successful by his peers.

2. He displayed intelligence and skill in applying Jewish tradition.

3. He adopted his father's passion and zeal for God.

4. He believed his role was to teach and police his fellow Jews into obedience.

5. He equated man-made doctrines with the authority of Scripture.

In order to fully understand the events from Acts and Saul's part in them, it will be helpful to give a brief historical summary. Christianity was about three years old. It had exploded on the scene with miracles and signs performed by the apostles (Acts 2, 3). Jews were converting to Christ throughout the city of Jerusalem and across Judea. The Jewish Sanhedrin considered the statement that salvation was found only in Jesus Christ versus obedience to the Mosaic Law, to be a false teaching, a heresy. In an attempt to curb the spread of this new teaching, they arrested the apostles, placed them on trial for violating the Torah (Acts 4), and when found guilty, flogged them according to Jewish law (Deuteronomy 25).

It is also important to understand the political culture that existed when God launched Christianity. There was no freedom of religious expression as we experience it in America. The Roman Empire required all citizens to worship the Emperor. The Jews were the only exception. The Sanhedrin, the Jewish Supreme Court, had the authority to initiate Torah Law throughout Judah, thus giving the Pharisees authority to act as spiritual policemen. Jewish leaders believed God's blessing on their tiny nation was contingent on the people remaining pure to Yahweh and obedient to the Torah. Any idolatry on the part of individual Jews had to be purged before it spread, spiritually corrupting the nation and thereby bringing the judgment of God on Judah.

As we look at Saul, learn his family patterns, see the influence of his father and culture, and understand his spiritual beliefs, we can begin to understand why Saul the Pharisee single-handedly took on the task of cleansing the nation of this Christ heresy. He secured paperwork from the Sanhedrin which gave him authority to arrest Christians. Saul was probably responsible for the first official persecution against Christians. Acts 7 says Stephen was stoned for calling the Jewish leaders rebels for rejecting the prophets and murdering Jesus the Messiah. The crowd laid Stephen's bloody robe at the feet of Saul who "approved of their killing [Stephen]" (Acts 8:1).

On that same day, a "great persecution" broke out against Christians in Jerusalem. Saul "began to destroy the church" (Acts 8:3). The Greek word for destroy indicates a vicious act like a wild animal ripping apart its prey. Saul's method of terrorism was "going from house to house, he dragged off both men and women and put them in prison" (Acts 8:3). Chapter 9 says "Saul was still breathing out murderous threats against the Lord's disciples" (Acts 9:1). Saul was possessed with rage. Everything he said and did was tied to destroying Christianity. Later Paul explained to Timothy that he became the worst of sinners violently and without mercy persecuting Christians (1 Timothy 1:12-17).

Distorted God: The God of Collective Punishment

Collective punishment means the whole receives punishment for the individual's mishap. Collective punishment is popular in some American public schools. An example would be if one child in a class acted up, every classmate would miss out on recess.

Fanatics find their authority in the god of collective punishment. Often fanatics believe that salvation comes and is maintained by their ability to remove what doesn't comply or acknowledge their belief systems. This often leads to the use of violence and force to purge society. Religious fanatics often see cleansing the land of sin as essential to usher in the second coming of their god, Christ, Judgment Day, or a new world.

Distorted Belief: Purge the Sin for National Prosperity

Some isolated Old Testament passages shape this distortion. One is Joshua 7. After God conquered Jericho, Israel was commanded to dedicate the valuable spoils of the battle to the Lord. But an Israelite named Achan secretly kept some of the spoils for himself. As a result, the nation suffered loss at their next encounter with the people of Ai, all because of Achan's sin. Once purged (Achan and the items stolen were destroyed), Israel conquered Ai. A quick explanation is that this was an isolated incident. God told the nation upfront that all the bounty from Jericho was to be used for the temple. The warning was clear; the individual who took or stole anything from Jericho would die and bring trouble on the nation (Joshua 6:18).

Again, Jewish leaders believed God's blessing on their tiny nation was contingent on the people remaining pure to Yahweh and obedient to the Torah. Any idolatry on the part of individual Jews had to be purged before it spread, spiritually corrupting the nation thereby bringing the judgment of God on Judah. Saul believed this "Christ Sect" would bring God's wrath on their nation. It had to be purged. A similar belief is held by Shia Muslims who actually use the text from Joshua 7 as proof too.

Religious fanatics believe in salvation by good works. They justify their violence by claiming the eradication of any opposition is a good work. Others believe that martyrdom is a ticket to heaven and there is nothing more important than the ultimate sacrifice of their own lives. This has been a belief in Christian, Muslim, Islam, and Hindu circles. Most fanatics believe that there is life after death in a better place. They can obtain this by the strictest adherence to their laws or being martyred for the faith. All this brings blessings and eternal life.

HOW TO RESPOND TO THE RELIGIOUS FANATIC

Saul believed it was his God-given duty to eradicate any belief that contradicted his religion. His desire to purge Judah of the heretical movement that claimed Jesus as God moved Saul to arrest and murder Christians. So important was the conversion of Saul, Luke mentioned it three times in Acts (9:1-18; 22:1-21; 26:12-23). Paul also referred to his conversion in several of his letters to New Testament churches. Within his story, there are insights that explain how Saul the fanatic became Paul the preacher. The same zeal that motivated Saul's attempt to destroy Christianity was re-channeled after his conversion to promote Christ and the message of the gospel. Paul is proof that religious fanatics can change and even make the best sort of Christian. It doesn't justify his actions but identifying Saul's family patterns and spiritual background provide insight into his actions and helps us form a strategy for witnessing to a fanatic.

God of the Individual

Through the prophet Ezekiel, God clearly stated,

Does a child pay for the parent's sin? No! For if the child does what is just and right and keeps my decrees, that child will surely live. The person who sins is the one who will die. The child will not be punished for the parent's sins, and the parents will not be punished for the child's sins. Righteous people will be rewarded for their own righteous behavior, and wicked people will be punished for their own wickedness. . . . Do you think that I like to see wicked people die? Says the Sovereign Lord. Of course not! I want them to turn from their wicked ways and live (Ezekiel 18:19, 20, 2).

The New Testament is all about individual versus national salvation. "For God so loved the world that he gave his one and only Son, that whosoever believes in him should not perish but have eternal life" (John 3:16).

Conviction from the Holy Spirit

How is a fanatic converted? In Acts 9, Saul was about 150 miles from Jerusalem, just outside the city of Damascus, and in hot pursuit of Christians who had escaped his tyrannical door-to-door campaign in Jerusalem. Verse 3 states, "Suddenly a light from heaven flashed around him." Saul fell to the ground, and Jesus spoke to him from the light, "Saul, Saul, why do you persecute me?" (Acts 9:4). Notice that when Christians are persecuted, Christ takes it personally. Years later as Paul shared his testimony with King Agrippa, Paul included Jesus also saying, "It is hard for you kick against the goads" (Act 26:14). Jesus was quoting an ancient proverb which referred to a sharp, pointed stick used by farmers to prod cattle or sheep along a path. If the animals resisted the leadership of the farmer, they got jabbed in the side and experienced pain from the prodding. They quickly learned to follow their owner.

Some scholars suggest the goad Jesus was referring to was Saul's wrestling with the Holy Spirit's conviction from Stephen's sermon. In Acts 7, Stephen presented the Old Testament history and made reference to prophesies about the Messiah and how they pointed to the teaching, life, death, and resurrection of Christ. As a member of the Jewish Sanhedrin, Saul may have witnessed the miracles of the apostles. He may have heard Peter explaining the gospel to the Sanhedrin (Acts 4) and heard Peter's statement, "Salvation is found in no one else, for there is no other name under heaven given to mankind by which we must be saved" (4:12).

The Sanhedrin which likely included Saul "saw the courage of Peter and John and realized that they were unschooled, ordinary men" and "they took note that these men had been with Jesus" (Acts 4:13). Was Saul wrestling with his conscience? Was the Holy Spirit convicting Saul of his position and actions? Had Saul heard Stephen's message and seen "that his face was like the face of an angel" (Acts 6:15)? Was Saul struggling with the idea that Stephen had been a messenger of God? It certainly seems Christ had been prodding him, sticking him with the sword of the Spirit, the Word of God, to redirect his life. Saul had been resisting so the prodding got worse. I've had many fanatics tell me, after they came to Christ, that the guilt and conviction of the Holy Spirit they experienced before they surrendered to Jesus was overwhelming.

Scripture teaches the Holy Spirit works on the heart when the gospel is presented through the witness of a Christian's life or testimony. Jesus said the Holy Spirit convicts "the world of its sin, and of God's righteousness, and of the coming judgment" (John 16:8, *NLT*). After Peter pointed out the crowd's sin of rejecting Christ, the people were "cut to the heart" (Acts 2:37). The Spirit of God calls people through the gospel message as proclaimed by Christians, convicting their hearts of sin, showing them their need for righteousness, and reminding them of the coming judgment.

Spiritual Experience

Many Jews and Muslims come to Christ after having some sort of dream or vision that includes a message to them from Christ. The famous Jewish Rabbi Kaduri had a vision. The ISIS terrorist mentioned earlier had a dream with a vision of Christ. The well know Christian apologist Nabeel Qureshi who converted from Islam did so after studying Scripture, but he, too, had several visions of Christ that moved him to become a Christian.

Acts 9:5 reveals that Saul didn't know who the voice he had just heard was. "Who are you Lord?" The Greek word for *Lord* was often used as term of respect. Saul was asking "Who are you, Sir?" Jesus told Saul to get up, go into Damascus, and there he would receive further instruction. Acts 9:7 states the company of men traveling with Saul heard the voice but could make no sense out the conversation.

Pain or Trauma

When Saul opened his eyes, he was blind. The men with Saul now had to lead him by the hand into the city. Totally blind, Saul did not eat or drink anything for three days (9:9). Saul was overwhelmed that his zeal for God was misdirected, that he had harmed God's cause and God's chosen people. It was unbearable for Saul to grasp he had been working against God.

The medical profession tells us a person can live without water for three to five days. Saul was on his third day without any liquid or food. What was he doing? Verse 11 says Saul was praying (I would guess pretty intensely). Saul was seeking God's forgiveness and a new beginning.

In his mercy, God appeared in a vision to a disciple of Christ named Ananias. He commanded him to go to the place where Saul was staying and lay hands on Saul to restore his sight. Ananias knew of Saul. "I have heard many reports about this man and all the harm he has done to your holy people in Jerusalem" (Acts 9:13). Ananias could have been implying, "If something has happened to his sight, then praise God! He's a fanatic." It's hard to have compassion for people who have been violent, cruel, or vicious in their dealings with others. When a child molester is exposed, we think, "Finally!" We immediately feel a sense of justice. We need to remember, as ambassadors of Christ, that God loves the fanatic as much as he loves us. Yes, there will be consequences, but ultimately God wants the person saved. Suffering, trauma, pain, and loss can soften people's hearts. Experiencing pain can create an openness to a new direction for their lives.

Hearing the Gospel

Look how God responded to Ananias, "Go! This man is my *chosen instrument* to proclaim my name to the Gentiles.... I will show him how much he must *suffer* for my name" (Acts 9:15, 16, italics mine). That could be paraphrased as, "I want him saved, but there will be suffering." Ananias went, and when he saw the anguish and pain on Saul's face, the fact Saul had been humbled by blindness, and the shame Saul was experiencing from working against God, then the compassion of God welled up in Ananias. He called Saul "brother" (Acts 9:17) but at this point, Saul was not a Christian. Ananias was being compassionate. Ananias then laid his hands on Saul. Immediately something like scales fell from Saul's eyes. Saul could see. Can you image losing your sight and then being able to see again? Saul must have been overjoyed by God's mercy. We must be willing to do as Ananias did. We must be willing to go to our neighbors and talk with them. We need to reach out in spite of how dangerous they might appear to be to us so we can help them with physical, emotional, and spiritual relief.

After Ananias provided physical relief, he went on and invested time in explaining God's plan to Saul (Acts 22). Ananias explained that Christ had called Saul to be an apostle to carry the message to both Jew and Gentile. Ananias said to Saul, "And now what are you waiting for?" Can't you see God is giving you a second chance? Can't you see God is calling you to proclaim the good news of Christ? What are you waiting for? "Get up, be baptized and wash your sins away, calling on his name" (Acts 22:16). The phrase "wash your sins away" is equivalent to forgiveness (Acts 2:38). Every vile, wicked thought and action in Saul's life was washed away.

LET'S WRAP UP

Saul spent several days with the disciples and "At once he began to preach in the synagogues that Jesus is the Son of God" (Acts 9:20). The persecutor had turned preacher. Saul had become Paul. What a wonderful story of forgiveness and second chances. If Saul could be pardoned to be used by Christ, anyone can. Here are Paul's own words.

Here is a trustworthy saying that deserves full acceptance: Christ Jesus came into the world to save sinners—of whom I am the worst. But for that very reason I was shown mercy so that in me, the worst of sinners, Christ Jesus might display his immense patience as an example for those who would believe in him and receive eternal life. Now to the King eternal, immortal, invisible, the only God, be honor and glory for ever and ever. Amen (1 Timothy 1:15-17).

CHALLENGE

Let's consider several questions and study the biblical answers so we can give people the reason for the hope we have in Christ.

1. **If Christ didn't share the gospel with Saul and if Saul wasn't saved on the Damascus road, then what was the purpose of Jesus appearing to Saul?**

    First, Christ appeared to Saul to call him to be an apostle. In order to be an apostle, Saul had to be called specifically by Christ. Second, Saul had to see the resurrected Christ. Third, Saul spent three years with Jesus as his disciple learning and being prepared for his ministry (See Acts 1:21; Galatians 1:17, 18).

2. **How did Saul/Paul spend three years with Jesus being taught as his disciple? Jesus appeared to Saul/Paul after his ascension.**

    After Saul's baptism, he spent several days with the Christians in Damascus and began to preach publicly that Jesus was the Christ (Acts 9:20-22). Paul then went into the deserts of Arabia and three years later went to Jerusalem. It is possible that it was during this time in the desert that Paul was caught up with the Lord in paradise (2 Corinthians 12). Paul said that he didn't know if his body was taken up into heaven or if it was just his spirit, but he saw and heard things he was not permitted to share. Paul spent three years with Jesus being taught the New Testament plan which fulfilled the second qualification to be an apostle.

3. **Could Saul have been saved when Jesus called him on the road to Damascus?**

    Receiving the Holy Spirit is part of the salvation package (John 7:37-39; Acts 2:38, 39). Ananias was sent to Saul so he could receive his sight and the Holy Spirit. Ananias laid hands on Saul, and he received his sight. The Holy Spirit was given in baptism.

    There are two aorist participles: "rising up" and "calling upon." There are two imperatives: "be baptized" and "wash away." The number and order of the imperatives shows that baptism is a condition for the washing away of sins. The meaning of "wash away your sins" (Acts 22:16) does not refer to moral cleansing of the heart, but rather the washing away of guilt. The only literal agent for washing away the guilt of sin is the blood of Christ (1 John 1:7). Only Christ can apply his blood to us; this is an act of divine power alone. No person can apply Christ's blood to his own or to anyone else's soul. The fact that "wash away" is an imperative means it is the result of something Saul could do.

4. **Why do some Muslims terrorize other Muslims?**
    The original conflict within Islam arose between Sunni and Shi'ite Muslims. Both believe there is one God and Muhammad was the last in a line of prophets from God. Both require the same confession: "I confess that there is no God but Allah, and Muhammad is his prophet." Again, this is the only required faith statement in Islam. Both believe the Qur'an is the final revelation from God. They both practice prayer, rituals, commands, and prohibitions. The differences between the Sunnis and Shi'ites relates to their leadership and how they interpret the Qur'an and use it in legal decisions.

    The Shi'ites or Shia originated in an argument within Islam about who should be the legitimate successor to Muhammad after his death in 632. One group said a leader should be selected who could unite the religious and political leadership of Muslims even if he could not claim "divine succession." This group became the Sunni.

    A minority of Muslims disagreed. They were convinced that God would decide Muhammad's successors and that it must come from Muhammad's family, "divine succession." The Shi'ites believed this leader, a direct decent of Muhammad, is appointed by God and therefore *shares in divine knowledge.* The Sunni then killed all of Muhammad's relatives. Since no divine leader was available, the Shi'ites believe in the Mahdi, the "true guide," the coming Savior. He will come at the end of time. They believe this *might* be Jesus.

    This "guide of truth" leads a group of legal Islamic scholars to "rightly interpret" the Qur'an. They are the *only ones* who can interpret it correctly. They are usually flexible and lenient regarding the "strict laws" and the "harsh" teachings. So, the Qur'an is modified and enhanced as the guide leads them to the correct interpretation in each case. People who say the Qur'an does not speak of beheadings, terrorism, and fighting would come from this side of Islam, the Shi'ite side.

The Sunnis on the other hand take the Qur'an literally. The leader of ISIS is Abu Bakr al Baghdadi. He is said to have a PhD in Islamic studies and holds to the strict interpretation of the Qur'an. There are verses in the Qur'an that speak about killing those who do not convert to Islam, beheadings, and fighting with terror (Surah 47:4). There are also passages that say a Muslim is not to befriend a Jew or Christian (Surah 5:54). So, ISI (Islamic State of Iraq) is a radical Islamic group from the Sunni belief who take a literal interpretation of the Quran. When ISI conquered Syria they changed their name to ISIS (Islamic State of Iraq and Syria).

5. **How important is living out a life of love to Muslims?**

It's everything. Sam Jones is a missionary in Jordan, a 90% Muslim country. He is there on a ministerial visa. Several Christian denominations are sanctioned as legal in Jordan. Sam tells me that hundreds of thousands of Shi'ite Muslims are pouring into Jordan from Syria as refugees. There were middle class people, holding jobs, good citizens, preparing to send their children to college. But ISIS changed all that. Again the Sunnis are persecuting the Shi'ites. Sam says hundreds of Shi'ite Muslims are coming to Christ through gifts of water, food, clothing, and love. Sam says we "go into their neighborhoods. The Arabs are some of the most hospitable people. They offer us crackers and tea. We become their friends and Christ's love through us opens their heart." Sam says in the Christian church he serves each Sunday he unashamedly proclaims the gospel. He boldly declares that the Muslims have been lied to about the Bible. His direct and clear approach, much like Peter's in Acts 2 and 4, is winning many Muslims to Christ.

6. **Why don't Muslims have assurance of eternal salvation?**

Some Muslims believe Jihad guarantees entrance into paradise, thus the Muslim who goes down with a plane or blows himself up in a crowd. But when a Muslim dies, they believe all people must cross the bridge from earth to eternity. Under the bridge is raging fire. No one knows if Allah will allow you to cross or if he will drop you in. You have to simply trust in the fact you did enough "good works" unto Allah, while on earth. At least 51% good works. Other Muslims teach that if one believes in Allah as One and Muhammed as his prophet, Muslims cannot be eternally lost. If one has more sins than good works he or she simply goes to hell and pays off what sins need to be paid, then they are transported to heaven.

How different is Christianity. To live in eternity with a holy, perfect God we must be holy and perfect (Matthew 5:48). There are two ways we can be perfect and holy. The first way is never to sin. But James wrote that even a single sin moves us into the category of "lawbreaker" (James 2:10) and we need a Savior. The penalty for our sins can be paid through the blood of Jesus (Romans 3:21-26). Sin must be punished. Either we will pay for our sin in hell, or we surrender our life to Jesus and allow his blood to clean us from all unrighteousness.

CHAPTER THIRTEEN
The Effective Church
SPIRITUAL PROFILING
THE GOOD PERSON

As the Scriptures say, no one is righteous—not even one.
No one is truly wise; no one is seeking God.
All have turned away; all have become useless.
No one does good, not a single one.
(Romans 3:10-12)

There is not a single man in all the earth who is always
good and never makes a mistake. . . . God has made men upright;
each has turned away to follow his own downward road.
(Ecclesiastes 7:20, 29)

God saved you by his grace when you believed. And you can't
take credit for this; it is a gift from God. Salvation is not a reward
for the good things we have done, so none of us can boast about it.
(Ephesians 2:8, 9)

THE GOOD PERSON

A 2020 study by the Cultural Research Center of Arizona Christian University found only thirty-five percent of Christians surveyed believe they were saved through faith in Jesus Christ only. Sixty-five percent stated in some way they were going to heaven because they were a good person.[132]

Spiritual Profiling of the Good Person

John, a college student who was active in a weekend ministry, heard about Ray through the court system in the town where he preached. Ray sold drugs, spent time in jail, and was known around the town as a troublemaker. John loved a challenge and had a heart for lost people. He became Ray's friend and eventually led him to Christ. Through John, Ray felt valued and accepted for the first time. This brought him to the realization that God loved him. The seed of the gospel transformed his life. Once he had experienced God's amazing love and salvation, it was only natural that Ray wanted to share his experience with others. A year later, excited and longing to be a preacher, Ray came to Bible college where I became his roommate.

The Greek word *dunamis* is a word that means not just power, but power in action. It is our root word for dynamite.[133] It is used 121 times in the New Testament in various ways, 57 times in conjunction with the gospel of Christ.[134] The gospel, shared in a relationship seasoned with unconditional love, is powerful. You and I have seen seeds sprout, break through concrete, and grow into trees. The gospel works in the same way.

Coming to Christ is not a one-time event. Accepting Christ is just the beginning. After Ray enrolled in Bible college, and we got to know each other, we'd pray and study God's Word together as he enjoyed his new life in Christ. My task as his Christian friend included helping Ray see the necessity of weeding the old patterns of thinking from his mind, encouraging him to apply God's Word to life's problems, and helping him create new priorities. Conversations about applying the Bible to his life were frequent. Cultivating the mind requires hard work, similar to maintaining a garden.

132. Thegospelcoalition.org/articles/survey-a-majority-of-American-Christians-don't-believe-the-gospel/
133. Rick Warren, *The Power to Change Your Life* (Wheaton Ill.: Victor Books, 1990), 7-8
134. Francis, Rodney W., *The Gospel Faith Messenger*, "The 'Dunamis' Power of God!" http://www.gospel.org.nz/index.php/articles/faith-messages/311-003-the-dunamis-power-of-god. Accessed October, 2015.

Distorted God: God Saves only the Good Person

After several years, responsibilities took us in different directions. I heard that the church he served did not like his sermons. He also tried to make some changes in the Sunday school program, causing the members to complain. Eventually, the church felt it best for Ray to find a different place to minister. Being a young Christian without a deep spiritual roots, Ray drew several false conclusions.

Rejected by "important" leaders must be a direct message from God. "I'm not good enough. My past has defined me." This was his first distortion of who God was, he interpreted this to mean that God's voice was heard through only the "important" Christians and their words (and judgments). Second, he rejected God. "If this is the way God is, I want no part of him." Ray then walked away from the faith, concluding God saves only the good person, and he did not qualify.

The enemy convinced Ray that God was just like people. The church should have nurtured him. They should have worked to develop their student preacher, considering his long-term potential. But they didn't. The struggle for most growing congregations is shepherding and nurturing. The apostle Paul challenged the elders at Ephesus to "keep watch over yourselves and all the flock of which the Holy Spirit has made you overseers" (Acts 20:28). Congregations must work hard to disciple every believer within their spiritual family and keep them growing and healthy.

Satan's deceptive schemes can include temptation to sin, feelings of rejection, and trials. Satan will do whatever he can to uproot the new believer from God's garden (1 Corinthians 3:5-9).

Distorted Belief: Good Works will Get Me into Heaven

Many good people believe whatever sacred writings they choose to follow are from God. From their "bible" they select a standard to follow in order to be considered good in God's eyes. As you talk to various good people you realize that the standard often varies from on good person to the next, and they are standards they can never keep. All people who believe their good works will get them into heaven believe in God. God is the one they must impress, and they must earn his favor. The good person may or may not believe Jesus exists or that he is God's Son.

The good person who believes Jesus died for their sins might hold a "good works plus grace" concept of salvation. Catholic theology teaches that good works plus Christ's blood saves. Our good deeds earn our way to heaven but if our points fall short of one hundred percent, we can trust Christ to make up the rest. The whole point of being good is to earn one's way to heaven. For the good person Judgment Day doesn't require a yes to the question, "Has your sin be paid through the blood of Christ?" But like the religious, Judgement Day involves the "good works" teeter-totter. If my good deeds outweigh my bad deeds, I'm going to heaven. According to the Catholic Church, Purgatory is the intermediate place for Christians to work off their bad deeds. Once completed, they are transferred to heaven.

The conversion of Cornelius in Acts 10 is a significant conversion in the book of Acts. It offers abundant insights regarding personal evangelism. The key point that makes Cornelius's conversion so special is that Cornelius was the first Gentile to receive salvation. Up to this point, all converts had been Jewish.

If anyone could have gotten into heaven by being good, it would have been Cornelius. He lived in Caesarea, which Rome considered to be the capital city of Judea. Acts 10:1 says Cornelius was a centurion, a commander of more than 100 soldiers in the Roman army. His spiritual qualities were exemplary. Verse 2 tells us he and his family were "devout and God-fearing." Cornelius was extremely generous, helping anyone in need. He was also a man of prayer.

An angel told Cornelius that God had noticed his abundant generosity to the poor and had heard all his prayers. As a result, the angel instructed Cornelius to send for Peter, who happened to be in Joppa (about 30 miles south). Cornelius immediately sent two of his employees and a soldier to contact Peter.

Acts 10:9-13 says the same day, around noon, Peter became hungry. While waiting for his lunch to be prepared, he went up on the roof to pray. Peter fell into a trance. God brought a smorgasbord of foods before Peter on a huge sheet, but the foods did not meet the strict Jewish requirements. Yet, God told Peter to eat and enjoy. Acts 10:14 says Peter responded in shock, saying, "Surely not, Lord.... I have never eaten anything impure or unclean." God commanded Peter a second time to eat and redefined the eating code for Jewish believers. "Do not call anything impure that God has made clean" (Acts 10:15). This same conversation happened three times. Peter came out of the trance and tried to understand what God was saying to him. The three men sent by Cornelius arrived. They told Peter that an angel had appeared to Cornelius and commanded him to have Peter brought to his house.

The next day, when Peter entered the house, "Cornelius. . . fell at his feet in reverence" (Acts 10:25). Notice Peter's response. He commanded Cornelius to stand up saying "I am only a man myself'" (Acts 10:26). Note that Peter refused to accept worship. The New Testament says we come to God directly through Jesus Christ, our high priest (Hebrews 8:1, 2). Christ also speaks directly to us through his written word (Hebrews 4:12) and rules the church directly from heaven (Acts 2:33, 34; Revelation 2, 3).

Jews were prohibited from associating with Gentiles because they were considered unclean. Peter said, "God has shown me that I should not call any man impure or unclean" (Acts 10:28). Peter had learned something, but he still did not understand the full implications of God's message to him when he was on the roof. When Peter heard Cornelius's account of the angel calling for him to come to this Gentile home, he finally understood that God wanted Gentiles in the church. So Peter began explaining Jesus' life and the gospel message to Cornelius.

HOW TO RESPOND TO THE GOOD PERSON

Peter's gospel presentation to Cornelius, the good person, included the same package of information Peter used in Acts 2. Let's summarize Peter's presentation to Cornelius and then give four key truths good people need to hear. Here's the summary: God loves everyone (Acts 10:34). God accepts anyone who respects him (Acts 10:35). God reconciles people through Christ (Acts 10:36). Jesus' power heals (Acts 10:38). Jesus delivers people from Satan (Acts 10:38). Jesus died on the cross (Acts 10:39). Jesus had a bodily resurrection (Acts 10:41). There were many witnesses (Acts 10:41). Jesus fulfills all the Messianic prophesies (Acts 10:43). Believing in Jesus can bring forgiveness (Acts 10:43). Peter baptized Cornelius into Christ (Acts 10:47). Now, let's consider the four key points every good person needs to hear.

Good People Must Understand God's Justice

In verse 36, Peter explained that the good news of salvation involved "peace through Jesus Christ, who is Lord of all." The word peace denotes reconciliation with God through Jesus. Peter explained that our good works cannot make up for bad deeds. The good person thinks that if his or her good deeds outweigh the bad deeds, then God places them in the *good* category. This belief falls short because of God's justice. As we discussed regarding the religious, God is absolutely holy and just. God sets the standard for holiness, righteousness, and justice (fairness). Justice says, "We get what we deserve." If we keep God's law, we stay free. If we break God's law, we pay the penalty. The penalty for one sin is eternal death (Romans 6:23). James says if we break just one of God's laws, we are placed in the category of *law breaker* (James 2:10), guilty before the just God. Either Jesus pays for our sins on the cross or we pay for our sins in hell.

Good People Must Understand Only Jesus is Good

Notice Peter pointed out that "he [Jesus] went around doing good" (verse 38). It's interesting when the rich young ruler asked Jesus, "What good thing must I do to get eternal life?" Jesus responded with, "There is only One who is good." (Matthew 19:17). *Good* in the context of Jesus' conversation refers to moral perfection. Who is morally perfect? Jesus. He never sinned (Hebrews 5:15).

Good People Must Understand Jesus can Pay for Their Sins

Peter called Jesus the "anointed" (Acts 10:38), denoting God's select Savior for the world. Peter went on to explain that Jesus died on the cross but was raised on the third day (10:39). This living, resurrected Christ then ate with the twelve disciples and commissioned them as apostles to share the good news that Jesus had died for people's sins. Jesus can be our substitute, taking on our sins. This resurrected Jesus is Lord. It is he who will judge the world. The basic question on Judgment Day will be, "Are you forgiven of your sins through the name [authority] of Jesus?"

Acts 10:44 is one of the most misinterpreted verses in the entire Bible. It says, "While Peter was still speaking these words, the Holy Spirit came on all who heard the message." The circumcised believers (Jewish Christians) who had traveled with Peter were shocked that the "gift of the Holy Spirit had been *poured out* even on the Gentiles" (Acts 10:45, emphasis mine). Acts 10:46 explains what happened: "For they heard them speaking in tongues and praising God."

This verse is often used to question baptism as the point when the Holy Spirit comes into a believer. Cornelius and his family received the *outpouring of the Spirit* that the apostles received at Pentecost (Acts 2). Cornelius spoke in *foreign languages* just like Peter and the other apostles had at Pentecost (Acts 2). Tongues were a supernatural gift for cross-cultural evangelism. The apostles spent time traveling throughout the known world and the Spirit would enable the apostles to speak the language of any territory they entered.

This outpouring on Gentiles was a one-time event and never happened again. Cornelius was not receiving salvation. This was proof to Jewish believers standing in the room with Peter that God wanted Gentiles to be saved to be a part of Christ's church too. This was the Gentile Pentecost. The ability to speak in various languages was not and is not a sign of salvation. If it were, why wouldn't all who accept Christ speak in tongues at conversion? First Corinthians 14:22 tells us tongues is an apologetic proof used in evangelism (Acts 2), not a sign that one is a believer.

The *indwelling of the Spirit* received in water baptism manifests itself in the fruit of the Spirit (Galatians 5) or character transformation. Refer to chapter 4, for more information on the difference between the outpouring and the indwelling of the Spirit.

Good People Must Confess Their Sins and be Baptized into Christ

Peter said, "Surely, no one can stand in the way of their being baptized with water. They have received the Holy Spirit just as we have" (Acts 10:47). Peter was referring to the twelve apostles at Pentecost (outpouring = miracles). Their Jewish background caused them to oppose worshiping with a Gentile, let alone allowing a Gentile to become one of *God's chosen.* Peter had Cornelius and his family baptized in Acts 10:48. They received the indwelling of the Holy Spirit.

LET'S WRAP UP

Isn't being a *good person* enough to get to heaven? Cornelius was a fine, sincere, generous individual. He practiced his religion as best he knew how. But remember, to go to heaven one must be right with God (never breaking one of God's laws, according to James 2:10). Jesus said, "No one is good—except God alone" (Luke 18:19). There is no way on earth for any person to be good enough to get to heaven by his own merits. Every one of us needs the forgiveness offered by Jesus, our Lord.

CHALLENGE

Talking to the good person will often lead to the following questions. Study them and be prepared to give the right answers.

1. **Do good people need the blood of Christ to be saved?**

   In order to be saved, one must be sinless, because God is holy. In the presence of sin, the holiness of God turns to wrath. God provides a second way for us to be holy—faith in Christ's redemptive work on the cross which washes our sins away. Judgment Day is not a balance scale with good deeds weighed on one side and bad deeds on the other. Often, we think that if our good deeds outweigh our bad, we go to heaven. The truth is that *one sin* separates us from God, but the gift of God is righteousness through faith in Christ (Romans 3:22-24).

2. **Is salvation for all people?**

   Peter's Jewish background negatively impacted his openness to Gentiles' receiving salvation. It didn't click in his mind until he was standing in the home of Cornelius. Often, the Christian church in America lacks cultural diversity. The congregations believe supporting foreign missions is important, but they are not as aggressive in bringing the different cultures that exist within their cities into their fellowships.

   A congregation should reflect the demographics of its surrounding communities. For example, if five percent of the community is Hispanic, then the church family should reflect a five percent Hispanic population too. A church could start Hispanic churches in the area, but the better strategy is to bring Hispanics into the existing church family through a Spanish ministry. This strategy is a powerful witness that

Jesus Christ breaks down all barriers (Ephesians 2:14-18). If we truly believe God when he commands us to go into all the world and save people, we have other types of prejudices to overcome as well. It is not just ethnic difference we must embrace, but we must also embrace cultural and lifestyle differences. The apostle Paul wrote:

> Don't be deceived: Neither the sexually immoral nor idolaters nor adulterers nor male prostitutes nor homosexual offenders nor thieves nor the greedy nor drunkards nor slanderers nor swindlers will inherit the kingdom of God. And that is what some of you were. But you were washed, you were sanctified, you were justified in the name of the Lord Jesus Christ and by the Spirit of our God (1 Corinthians 6:9-11).

Notice getting drunk is in the same list as greed, slandering, prostitution, and homosexual sin. Don't churches need to begin to consider outreach ministries to homosexuals comparable to those they already have for alcohol and drug abusers? In the early church, people from many different backgrounds and various sins were being saved and it should be the same today.

3. **Do conversions happen through relationships?**

Peter indicated that no one could stand in the way of Cornelius and his family being baptized with water (Acts 10:47). Apparently, Cornelius had invited his friends and family to his house to hear what Peter had to say (Acts 10:24). House evangelism is a major strategy in New Testament times. Church growth experts call it "oikos evangelism."[135] *Oikos* is the Greek word for *house*.

Dr. Thom Wolf has done extensive studies in this area and promotes house evangelism as *the* New Testament model. It is a major strategy being used around the world. Usually trust, camaraderie, influence, and commitment already exist in the family or in friendships. These connections go a long way in allowing a person to hear the gospel with an open heart and mind. In New Testament times, "the household"

---

135. J. Hampton Keathley, III, "The Stewardship of God's Truth Through Evangelism." n.d., http://bible.org/seriespage/stewardship-god%E2%80%99s-truth-through-evangelism-part-2.

included servants, friends, family members, and even business associates.[136] It was the social network of an individual.

Consider some passages that suggest this strategy of evangelism:

a. "Go home (*oikos*) to your own people and tell them" (Mark 5:19).

b. "Today salvation has come to this house (*oikos*)" (Luke 19:9).

c. "So he and all his household (*oikos*) believed" (John 4:53).

d. Cornelius's friends and family were baptized (Acts 10:48).

e. Lydia and the members of her household [*oikos*] were baptized (Acts 16:15).

f. The jailor and all his family [*oikos*] were baptized" (Acts 16:33).

Research conducted by the Institute for American Church Growth shows that 97 out of every 100 decisions for Christ that take place at an isolated event or that happen independently from the new believer's social network are never incorporated into a church.[137] Seventy-five to 90 percent of people who join a local church say that a friend or relative influenced their decision.[138] Consider your network of friends. Make a list of people you know who are not Christians or who do not go to church. Then consider ways your church group might befriend your non-believing friends.

4. **Aren't there hypocrites in the church who only want people like them in the church?**

Christians are people in a saving relationship with God through Jesus Christ. It's sometimes hard to feel comfortable with people from different cultures or backgrounds. What do we say or talk about with them?

This *homogeneous factor* in church growth involves shaping ministry to reach a particular people group. Congregations use a traditional, blended, contemporary, or mosaic service. As Christians

---

136. Colin Brown, *The New International Dictionary of New Testament Theology* (Rev. ed. Carliste: Paternoster, 1986), p 253.

137. Ibid., p 152.

138. Ibid., p 153.

grow and mature in their faith, they begin to remove barriers and seek to allow Christ to create unity (see Ephesians 2:11-22.).

5. **As long as people are sincere, does it really matter what they believe about God?**

Cornelius was a good person, yet he was lost. His understanding of salvation needed correcting, so God set in motion an encounter with Peter. His sincerity and good deeds were not enough. God demanded more. It was only after Peter came and shared the gospel story that Cornelius found salvation.

Suppose you have a good neighbor who is a Mormon. This person does good works and has the greatest attitude in the world. However, according to the doctrine established by Joseph Smith, the founder of Mormonism, this neighbor, even though he or she is a good person, is trusting in a mere man (Jesus) who became one of many gods. This Mormon is trusting in this man/god to forgive him of his sins. The Jesus of the Mormon faith doesn't exist. Or suppose you have a Muslim friend who is trusting in Allah for salvation. The god described in the Qur'an does not exist.[139] The only way to salvation is through Jesus and the acceptance of the gospel of salvation.

---

139. Charlie Campbell, *One-Minute Answers to Skeptics* (Eugene, OR: Harvest House Publishers, 2010), p 93.

CHAPTER FOURTEEN
The Effective Church
SPIRITUAL PROFILING
THE SUCCESSFUL

Keep your lives free from the love from the love of money
and be content with what you have, because God has said,
"Never will I leave you; never will I forsake you."
So, we say with confidence, The Lord is my helper;
I will not be afraid. What can mortals do to me?
(Hebrews 13:5, 6)

Honor the Lord with your wealth, with the first fruits
of all your crops; then your barns will be filled to
overflowing, and your vats will brim over with new wine.
(Proverbs 3:9, 10)

You say you are rich; I have acquired wealth and do not need a thing.
But you do not realize that you are wretched, pitiful, poor,
blind and naked. I counsel you to buy from me gold refined in the fire,
so you can become rich; and white clothes to wear, so you can cover your
shameful nakedness; and salve to put on your eyes, so you can see.
(Revelation 3:17, 18)

THE SUCCESSFUL

According to a Pew Research study, the major goal of nearly seventy percent of Americans is to have enough money "to do whatever they want."[140] Nearly sixty percent believe the key is to become wealthy.[141] One out of four Americans believes they will be rich.[142]

Spiritual Profiling of the Successful

We all know godly successful Christians who are wealthy. The kingdom of God is blessed by their charity that provides clothing, housing, special needs, and facilities for Christians to gather. Jesus was buried in the tomb of a rich man (Isaiah 53:9; Matthew 27:57-60). Wealthy women financially supported Jesus and the disciples' ministry (Luke 8:1-3). Scripture tells us God is the giver of every good and perfect gift, including wealth (James 1:17; Ecclesiastes 5:19). Success comes from God too. He promised Joshua that if he would meditate day and night on God's Word and follow his instructions, Joshua would "be successful wherever" he would go (Joshua 1:8).

Jesus himself had unlimited resources (Matthew 26:53; Luke 4:40-42), yet he used his power and position to bring the good news to the poor and bind up the brokenhearted (Isaiah 61:1). He also succeeded in his redemptive mission on the cross. Jesus declared, "It is finished" (John 19:30).

The apostle Paul is one of the most successful people who ever lived. After Paul's conversion, he spent time with Peter, James, and John in Jerusalem. They reminded Paul to "remember the poor" (Galatians 2:10). Paul did. On his second missionary journey, he collected money for Christians in the Judean region who were experiencing a famine. Regarding wealth, Paul wrote to Timothy,

> Command those who are rich in this present world not to be
> arrogant nor to put their hope in wealth, which is so uncertain, but
> to put their hope in God, who richly provides us with everything
> for our enjoyment. Command them to do good, to be rich in good

---

140. Pewsocialtrends.org/2008/04/30/who-wants-to-be-rich/.
141. Ibid.
142. Gobankingrates.com/money/wealth/americans-confident-they'll-be-rich/.

deeds, and to be generous and willing to share. In this way they will lay up treasure for themselves as a firm foundation for the coming age, so that they may take hold of the life that is truly life (1 Timothy 6:17-19).

In Acts 16, Luke introduces us to Lydia, the successful, a God-fearing Jewish woman who owned a lucrative clothing business in Thyatira. The city was known for expensive purple dye extracted from shellfish. It was used to color clothing. In today's world, Lydia might own Macey's. She had traveled to Philippi to potentially open up a new store. She had already purchased a large home and had some family and workers with her.

In Acts 16:13, the apostle Paul searched along the river, "where we expected to find a place of prayer. We sat down and began speaking to the women who had gathered there." Philippi was a Roman colony, meaning that it followed the strict Roman values, laws, customs, and religion. The city answered directly to Caesar. This might explain why this small band of Jews was meeting outside the city by the river. Judaism would be banned for condemning Roman polytheism.

Scripture states that the Lord opened Lydia's heart to respond to Paul's message. "When she and her household (*oikos*) were baptized, she invited us to her home. 'If you consider me a believer in the Lord, come and stay at my house.' And she persuaded us" (Acts 16:14-16). Lydia's home became the gathering place for the church at Philippi and no doubt she financially supported Paul's missionary team to evangelize the area.

Distorted God: God is Santa Claus

God has used and continues to use many successful and wealthy believers to bless and advance Christ's kingdom. However, a large number of the successful believe their wealth, positions of power, and influence are tied to a righteous, favored status with God, who is like Santa Claus and is there to provide everything on their wish lists because they've been good. Those who are poor, or experience hardships, trials, or sickness are sinners temporarily or permanently outside of God's favor. This was probably the case with the Laodicean believers in Asia Minor. Consider Jesus' words.

I know your deeds, that you are neither cold nor hot. I wish you were either one or the other! So, because you are lukewarm—neither hot nor cold—I am about to spit you out of my mouth. You say, "I am rich; I have acquired wealth and I don't need a thing." But you do not realize that you are wretched, pitiful, poor, blind and naked. I counsel you to buy from me gold refined in the fire, so you can become rich; and white clothes to wear, so you can cover your shameful nakedness; and salve to put on your eyes, so you can see. Those whom I love I rebuke and discipline. So be earnest and repent (Revelation 3:15-19).

Laodicea was the banking capital of Asia Minor, with a clothing industry and medical center second to none. The Greek god of medicine, Aesculapius, was worshiped there.[143] His symbol, a serpent wrapped around a pole, is still used in the medical profession. As you carefully read Jesus' revelation describing the believers' true spiritual conditions, it is obvious they were deceived in believing their wealth stemmed from a righteous, favored status with God. Those who were not successful fell outside the anointing of the Lord.

Distorted Belief: God Wants Me Healthy and Wealthy

A popular religious belief known as the "word of faith," or the "faith formula," or the "health and wealth gospel" states that success, wealth, and health are always the will of God for his people. Some of the proponents of this belief are John Hagee, Joel Osteen, Benny Hinn, and Kenneth Copeland. This erroneous belief can depict faith as the "force" through which a person can create their own reality. Joel Osteen explains that what determines the quality of your life are the words you speak.

Our words have creative power. When we speak something out, we give it the right to come to pass. It's one thing to believe you're healed, but when you say, "I am healed," that releases the healing. The Scripture says the spirit of faith is our words. When you say, "I have favor and I'm coming out of debt," good breaks will find

---

143. En.wikipedia.org/wiki/Aesculapius

say to this mountain, 'Move from here to there,' and it will move. Nothing will be impossible for you" (Matthew 17:19-21).

Jesus explained the disciples were too busy questioning if God would drive the demon out on their request instead of exercising the faith that God would drive the demon out in Jesus' name. If they had focused on faith, they would have been successful because all it takes is the smallest faith, even as tiny as the mustard seed, for God to move mountains for believers. It's not the size of faith but the size of our God.

Not receiving the desired results of prayer can also be attributed to God's sovereign plan for the believer. God's purpose is to bake Christ's character into every Christian (Romans 8:29). The injustice and difficulties of life are often tools used to change us (Romans 5:4). John stated it this way, "This is the confidence we have in approaching God: that if we ask anything according to his will, he hears us. And if we know that he hears us—whatever we ask—we know that we have what we asked of him" (1 John 5:14, 15). Notice God the Father answers prayer based on what is best for his children. God is more interested in our character development then our happiness.

4. **It is an erroneous belief**

According to Pew Research, eighty-four percent of the world lives on less than twenty dollars a day.[145] The majority of the world is poor. Many Christians are born into poverty and experience sickness from contaminated drinking water, malnourishment, and limited access to medicine. It is arrogant, offensive, and erroneous to declare that the majority of believers around the world who live in poverty are second class Christians because they do not have access to wealth and adequate healthcare.

5. **It is in direct contrast to the lives of Jesus and Paul**

As Jesus walked along a road a man joined Jesus and declared, "I will follow you wherever you go" (Luke 9:58). Jesus wanted the man to understand the hardships before he made his decision. "Foxes

---

145. Wsws.org/on/articles/2015/07/11/poor-jll.html

have dens and birds have nests, but the Son of Man has no place to lay his head" (Luke 9:59). Many nights Jesus had to sleep under the stars. Jesus' ministry was supported by women (Luke 8:3). He was a man acquainted with much suffering, pain, and held in low esteem (Isaiah 53:3).

Paul was often sick. Because of the grand revelations Paul was privy too, God gave him a "thorn in his flesh" to keep him humble (2 Corinthians 12:10). This might have been a chronic eye problem. Paul mentions to the Galatians, "I can testify that, if you could have done so, you would have torn out your eyes and given them to me" (Galatians 4:15). Paul explained to the Philippians that he had learned how to be content in every situation, "whether well feed or hungry, whether living in plenty or want" (Philippians 4:12). Clearly the health and wealth theology contradicts the lives of Jesus and Paul.

LET'S WRAP UP

God is not like Santa Claus and his job is not to deliver everything on our request list. On the other hand, we must remember:

1. **God is able to heal us**

    One name of God is Jehovah-Rapha, the God who heals. "I will not bring on you any of the diseases I brought on the Egyptians, for I am the Lord, who heals you" (Exodus 15:26). Jesus and the apostles healed people (Luke 4:40, 41; Mark 16:17, 18). When believers are sick, the apostle James states the sick should call the elders for prayer and anointing with oil for healing (James 5:14, 15).

2. **God's plan was not for people to suffer, live in poverty, and experience brokenness**

    Suffering, poverty, and brokenness entered the world when Adam and Eve sinned. Guilt, shame, death, sickness, pain, irresponsibility, fruitless labor, famines, droughts, windstorms, are all consequences of sin (Genesis 3). The world and everything in it is now dying and subject to frustration. Christ's people, as well as the world, wait for the redemption of the universe at Christ's return (Romans 8:18-25).

In the meantime, the church is the physical body of Christ, sent out to reach broken people. As his arms, feet, voice, and ears, Christians apply the love of Christ and the gospel to the brokenness. Christ heals and restores people. But the consequence of sin will remain until Christ returns, when he will make all things new (Revelation 21:5).

CHALLENGE

1. **Understand God's Foreknowledge**

    God's foreknowledge is a wonderful truth we can live with daily. The apostle Peter said the cross and resurrection stemmed from "God's deliberate plan and foreknowledge" (Acts 2:23). Foreknowledge means God sees what will happen in the future. This is how God can work all things together for our good (Romans 8:28).

    Understanding God's foreknowledge will embolden you to ask God to bring people into your path daily to hear or see the good news. God wants to speak to every person. When you share Scripture, or Scriptural truths, you become God's voice.

2. **Understand the fallacies of the health and wealth theology**

    Be able to engage the successful with the truth. God will do the rest.

CHAPTER FIFTEEN
The Effective Church
SPIRITUAL PROFILING
THE ABUSER

Your path took me through the sea. Your way through
the mighty waters, a pathway no one knew was there!
(Psalm 77:19)

But you, God, see the trouble of the afflicted; you consider
their grief and take it in hand. The victims commit themselves
to you; you are the helper of the fatherless. Break the arm of the
wicked man; call the evildoer to account for his wickedness
that would not otherwise be found out.
(Psalm 10:14, 15)

There is no fear in love. But perfect love drives out fear
because fear has to do with punishment. The one who fears
is not made perfect in love. We love because he first loved us.
(I John 4:18, 19)

THE ABUSER

We all have family portraits hanging on the walls of our house. When we visit another person's home, often we're introduced to the family through a photo or painting. We stop in front of a portrait and hear a funny story about a brother and then an explanation of where he's been and what he's doing with his life. We might say, "He looks just like his dad," and they respond, "He's got his dad's personality, too."

Family Patterns

Families pass down physical traits through their gene pool. They also pass down spiritual legacies through their beliefs and actions. We pass on attitudes, coping mechanisms, habits, traditions, values, communication patterns, and decision-making processes.

Because there are no perfect people, there are no perfect families. Values modeled to the next generation may include healthy attitudes but also dysfunction, sin, and self-destructive behavior. For example, the family may teach that problems are solved with violence. Some children learn they must tear others down to build themselves up. The Hatfield and McCoy feud continued for almost thirty years because family honor was believed to be achieved through retaliation.

The Jukes and Edward Study

In 1874 Richard Dugdale, a prison counselor, noticed six brothers all incarcerated at the same time. The New York prison board wanted to find out why, so they traced the family line back to a man and his wife living in 1720 whom they fictitiously labeled, "the Jukes."[146] This couple had low moral character and were lazy and chemically dependent. Here's what the report revealed about 1,200 descendants of the couple: 300 were homeless; 160 were prostitutes; 180 suffered from chemical dependency; 150 were criminals. In 1916, more research was done on the new descendants of the Jukes and then again in 2001. The good news was some descendants broke the "Juke" cycle, but the bad news was the family pattern had continued for hundreds of years.

The same research group then studied another man and his family who lived around the same time in the 1720s, Jonathan Edwards.[147] He and his wife were

146. Thinkgospel.wordpress.com/2014/10/28/the-juke-edwards-story-a-contrast-in-family-legacy/.
147. Ibid.

deeply religious with strong moral values and a good work ethic. Together Jonathan and Sarah Edwards had 11 children. The researchers studied 1,400 descendants of this couple. They found 13 were college presidents; 65 were college professors; 100 were attorneys; 32 were state judges; 85 authored books; 80 held political office; one became vice-president of the United States, and 100s more served as leaders in their communities.

For years, these studies promoted the idea of legalizing sterilization to stop certain people from having children because behavior was tabbed genetic. Years later, science confirmed what the Bible has always taught: that physical traits and personality tendencies are passed down genetically, but attitude and behavior are learned.

<u>Family Cycles</u>

It's called family patterns, which usually turn into family cycles. God declared in Exodus 20 that destructive patterns may be passed down to the third and fourth generations. Families tend to reproduce their own cultures that includes both positive and dysfunctional behaviors. An alcoholic parent is more likely to produce an alcoholic child. Surveys show that seventy percent of people incarcerated have a parent or relative who was incarcerated and on and on we can go.[148] You may be thinking of people you know who broke their family patterns and are now living productive lives.

It's hard to have compassion for people who have been violent, cruel, or vicious in their dealings with others. When a child molester is exposed, we think, "Finally." We immediately feel a sense of justice. "They got what they deserved!" We need to remember, as ambassadors of Christ, that God loves the abuser as much as he loves us. Yes, there will be consequences, but ultimately God wants the person saved.

Spiritual Profiling of the Abuser

Abusers are not born, they are made. Sometimes those who have been abused take on the mindset of their abusers, the family member or the influential person in their lives. Family patterns turn into family cycles. People who hurt others have

---

148. Tdcj.texas.gov/gokids/gokids_articles_children_impacted.html#:~text=Nationally%2C%207.3%20
million%20children@20have,some%20points%20in%20their20lives

been hurt themselves. I'm sure you can look back and recall an abuser in your life. Maybe it was a parent or ex-spouse, a family member or a peer at school. Abuse is common in the workplace. Sixty-five million Americans are affected annually by bullying at work with 60 percent of those being women.[149] Kamal Saleem, former Islamic terrorist and now a convert to Christianity, says that he was taught at the age of four that the sword is the entrance to heaven. The only way to please Allah was through hard work or the giving of blood through jihad. In his book, *The Blood of the Lambs,* Saleem writes of being taken to terrorist training camps at seven years of age. Kamal says, "That is all I knew."[150]

Acts 16 records how Paul ventured into a Philippian neighborhood. There Paul and his friends, Silas, Luke, and Timothy, encountered a diviner who had made a great deal of money through his demon possessed slave girl. The demon supposedly predicted the future. The neighbors had become dependent on her supernatural guidance and usually consulted her before they made major decisions.

Interestingly, the demon moved the slave girl to follow Paul throughout the neighborhood (Acts 16:17). Using the girl as his megaphone, the demon identified Paul and Silas as "servants of the Most High God, who are telling you the way to be saved" (16:17). It was a true statement, but it came but from the wrong spokesperson. The demon possessed girl was getting more attention than Paul. And her endorsement created suspicion of Paul's gospel. Paul observed the abuse this girl was receiving and the negative effect on his evangelistic encounters, and he miraculously cast the demon out of her.

But the diviner, who was a classic abuser, realized his source of income was gone and reported the exorcism to his neighborhood. The neighbors seized Paul and took him to the authorities. Paul and Silas were charged with violating *religio illicita* (approved religion status) and thus violating the *Pax Romana* (Roman Peace).[151] Why were Timothy and Luke not included in the charge? They were Gentiles. Jews were frowned upon in the Empire. Racial prejudice was playing a major role, too.

Also, understand the Roman world was very much influenced by magic and divination. Most people consulted diviners before any major decision.[152] That's why

149. workplacebullying.org/multi/pdf/WBI/-2014-US-Survey.pdf
150. Truthandliberty.net/bio/kamal-saleem/
151. Gaebelein, Frank. *The Expositor's Bible Commentary,* Vol. 9. Zondervan Publishing House. Grand Rapids, MI. 1981. P. 463.
152. Gaertner, Dennis. *Acts.* College Press Publishing House. Joplin, MO. 1993. P. 255.

the city authorities immediately had Paul stripped and beaten with rods.[153] Verse 23 says that Paul was "severely" flogged. In other words, Paul and Silas were beaten countless times, then placed in maximum security (the inner cell). If the Jailer was the *lictorae*, the one who administered the beating with rods, he continued his abuse by placing Paul's feet in the stocks.[154] The Roman stocks had a variety of holes that allow the Jailer to put Paul's legs into painful twisted positions.

Distorted God: God the Punisher

Abusers often believe the people they abuse deserve to be punished. They do it to control and squelch any independent rebellious spirit they perceive as a threat to their power or to the norms of the community.

Distorted Belief: Emotional and Physical Abuse

Paula grew up with an alcoholic father. Her dad, Jordan, and her mother, Eunice, met through Eunice's father who worked with Jordan on the railroad. Both Jordan and Eunice were musically talented. Their songs were played on the radio. It was through playing in bars and receiving free drinks that Jordan discovered his "confidence" through alcohol, a self-assurance that he never had. Coming home drunk and terrorizing his wife and children became the norm. The power and respect he felt by terrorizing his family became an addiction that grew with each episode. The abuse went on for fourteen years. Paula discovered at the age of nine that if she met her dad at the door each night, offered him a cooked meal, ran his bathwater, and "fixed" anything in the home that was "out of place," she could appease her father's anger. Sometimes it worked and other times it didn't. As a result of her father's inability to hold a job, Paula attended thirteen different schools, was often malnourished, and lived in poverty. After fourteen years Eunice divorced Jordan, took Paula and moved away.

---

153. Ibid.
154. *The Expositor's Bible Commentary,* Vol. 9. P. 465.

HOW TO RESPOND TO THE ABUSER

Let's work through key points Paul and Silas used to witness to their abuser.

1. **Believe Romans 8:28.**

   The apostle Paul wrote to the Christians at Rome, "And we know that in all things God works for the good of those who love him, who have been called according to his purpose" (Romans 8:28). The context of the passage is about character transformation into Christ's image. God uses both good and bad, the just and the unjust in our lives, to make us new in Christian character. Never waste a pain. Learn key lessons about yourself. Sometimes God reveals weakness in our characters so that we can make changes and produce growth. We learn more about others, life, and ourselves through adversity.

   "We can rejoice, too, when we run into problems and trials, for we know that they help us develop endurance. And endurance develops strength of character, and character strengthens our confident hope of salvation" (Romans 5:3, 4, *NLT*).

   Throughout Scripture, the providential hand of God can be seen using abusive situations to bring the abuser to salvation, or to accomplish a greater purpose of God. Consider Joseph and David in the Old Testament. Joseph had several abusers: his brothers, Potiphar's wife, and even the cupbearer (Genesis 37-50). David's brothers were abusive to him, and Saul's abuse lasted more than seventeen years (1 Samuel 17-30). David protected himself by leaving Saul's presence. He also allowed God to bring justice and vindication.

   God used Paul and Silas to reveal Christ to their abuser, the jailer. Again, if you are in an abusive situation, protect yourself. Jesus instructed his disciples about persecution when sharing the good news. "When you are persecuted in one place, flee to another" (Matthew 10:23). But realize that God will use your witness to speak truth into the abuser's life and potentially bring salvation. It will take time but allow the Holy Spirit to convict and reveal Christ through you.

   It's interesting that Paul could have stopped his beating by declaring his Roman citizenship. But he did not, until after God "broke" Paul out of jail through an earthquake. That's when the jailer talked with Paul and came to Christ.

2. **Give your pain to God.**

Paul wrote often of suffering for Christ and the gospel (2 Timothy 1:8; Romans 8:17; 2 Corinthians 1:5; Philippians 3:10). Suffering came to Paul because he was living right and sharing the gospel, not because he had done anything wrong. Many Christians are afraid to suffer for Christ, or they misinterpret the trial as God's punishment. That is simply not true. Persecution comes because there is an enemy who wants to intimidate Christians to be silent. Silence regarding the gospel can hinder people from coming to Christ.

Paul and Silas had been flayed by Roman scourging. Their feet were twisted painfully in stocks yet verse 25 says, "About midnight Paul and Silas were praying and singing hymns to God." How could they rise above their abuse? What was the content of their prayers? It's only speculation, but could they praise God for the privilege of suffering for Christ's name? Another possibility is that they were praying for their abuser. Stephen prayed as he was being stoned, asking God to forgive his abuser. Remember that one of Stephen's abusers was Paul (Acts 8:1). Both Stephen and Paul imitated our Lord who on the cross prayed, "Father forgive them for they do not know what they're doing" (Luke 23:34).

3. **Forgive the abuser.**

For your benefit, forgive the abuser. Our Lord commanded us to do the same. In the Sermon on the Mount Jesus spoke of loving our enemy (Matthew 5:43). The word is *agape* and denotes a willful desire for the enemy to see, know, and be changed by God. The word does not necessarily denote a friendship or even the necessity of liking the enemy. But to pray for God to change them for the better and avoid hell is an act of love.

Forgiveness is at the core of Christianity. Jesus continued to address the necessity of forgiving our enemies in the Sermon on the Mount: "For if you forgive men when they sin against you, your heavenly

Father will also forgive you. But if you do not forgive men their sins, your Father will not forgive your sins" (Matthew 6:14, 15).

It's also important to realize that forgiveness doesn't mean we minimize the offense or forget what happened. Paul later told the Corinthians about this beating and his suffering for the gospel (2 Corinthians 11:23-25).

Forgiveness does not mean we must continue the relationship. Forgiveness and trust are two different actions. Forgiveness is instantaneous, but trust must be earned over time by continued change and growth. Biblical forgiveness means we relinquish the right to get even and that we respond to evil with good (Romans 12: 17-21).

4. **Expect God to work things for good.**

Acts 16:25 tells us that Paul and Silas were singing hymns to God. They didn't praise God for a few minutes, they praised him for as long as it took. It was "about midnight." They did not stop praising at 9:00p.m. or 11:00p.m. They praised God until their attitudes changed and they could see God's plan.

Again, their physical pain must have been dreadful. They had been publicly humiliated. They were in jail for doing a kind act to a little girl. All good reasons to be depressed, angry, protesting, and despondent. Yet they believed God is always present and ready to help. When God saw that the two evangelists had risen above the abuse by forgiving the jailer and were expecting God to bring something good from their terrible situation, he acted. "Suddenly there was such a violent earthquake that the foundations of the prison were shaken. At once all the prison doors flew open, and everybody's chains came loose" (16:36).

The jailer saw the prison doors open, drew his sword, and was about to kill himself. A Roman guard who lost a prisoner would be executed. The jailer didn't want to face public humiliation, so he planned to commit suicide. But Paul shouted, "Don't harm yourself! We are all here!" (16:28). Why would Paul and the other prisoners stay?

5. **Share the gospel.**

The jailer no doubt heard Paul and Silas praying and singing hymns. The strength, courage, and optimism of the two believers were something beyond the ordinary. Normal people would not stay in jail with the doors wide open so their abuser could avoid getting into trouble, but Paul and Silas knew that leaving would be a death sentence for their abuser and even though he deserved it, they chose to forgive and stay in the hope of saving him. The Holy Spirit convicted the jailer's heart through the kindness, forbearance, and forgiveness of Paul and Silas.

The jailer now ran to Paul and wanted to know how to be saved. "Believe in the Lord Jesus, and you will be saved you and your household" (16:31). Paul then explained the gospel consistent with Peter's explanation in Acts 2. The jailer and his whole family, as well as close friends, came to Christ and were baptized. But notice what the jailer did *before* he was baptized. "At that hour of the night the jailer took them and washed their wounds" (16:33). Paul and Silas's love and forgiveness moved the jailer to love them. God can do this with your abuser, too.

LET'S WRAP UP

Paula's Story Continued

Paula became a Christian and continued to "love her father." Paul wrote, "Forgive just as Christ forgave us" (Colossians 3:13). Both Paula and her husband were kind to her father, Jordan. They even provided a place for him to live when he was old and without resources. Many times, they shared God's love in word and action by simply taking care of his needs.

When Jordan was diagnosed with cancer, Paula and her husband brought him into their home for his final days. During that time, he was able to be reconciled to his daughter and apologized. Jordan's eyes were opened to God's truth and grace through their Christlike love. Jordan repented and was baptized. The love of God expressed through believers can melt a heart of stone. Throughout the Old Testament Scripture, God promises to cleanse us from all our impurities and give us a new heart. "I will remove from you your heart of stone" (Ezekiel 36:26).

CHALLENGE

Here are two key questions abusers need answered. Study and share.

1. **Family patterns and cycles are almost impossible to break. Yet the story of Paula's abuser and the jailer demonstrate that through the power of Christ, it can be done. Does Christ instantaneously remove the dysfunctional patterns of our abuser, or does something else have to happen for a family pattern to be broken?**

   Two key words are important to understand when it comes to living a changed life. One is justification, and the second is sanctification. Scripture says that God "justifies the ungodly" not by works of the law but by the blood of Christ (Romans 3:20, 24, 28). Justification has to do with righteousness and justice. When God justifies us by his grace, through our faith and in our baptism, God declares us righteous. God counts us right with his law. Justification does not change our inner condition, nor does justification transform our fleshly nature. God no longer condemns us for our sins. We are forgiven.

   Sanctification occurs the moment we are saved. The term means to make holy. Being justified, we are made holy through the blood of Christ. This is also called initial sanctification. It occurs the same time as justification in our baptism.

   Progressive sanctification begins the moment "we arise to live a new life" (Romans 6:4) out of the waters of baptism. Progressive sanctification is the process of growing in the grace and knowledge of God, overcoming sin, and developing a holy character (Ephesians 4:22-24). Paul wrote,

   > Therefore, my dear friends, as you have always obeyed—not only in my presence, but now much more in my absence— continue to work out your salvation with fear and trembling, for it is God who works in you to will and to act in order to fulfill his good purpose (Philippians 2: 12, 13).

Our role is to study Scripture and to learn Christ's way. Paul said we are to daily put off the old man and put on the new person; the character, mission, and life of Christ (Ephesians 4:17-24). We get into the script of Christ, then act it out on our stage of life (Ephesians 5:1). It's a daily renewing of the mind, then acting out the new pattern through obedience. We cannot live this new way without power. The Holy Spirit regenerates our spirit and gives us a new heart (Ezekiel 36: 26, 27), but he also gives us the power to obey (Galatians 5:25).

Our motives also change. We no longer try to perform or impress God to earn our salvation by works of the law. We are grateful for God's mercy and Christ's sacrifice. We are overwhelmed that everything we have and hope to be is found in Christ. We truly are thankful and love God because he first loved us. Our faith works out Christ's character through our lives, but our motives are gratitude and love for what Christ has done for us (Galatians 5:6).

Christian fellowship models the new life in Christ. We find support, prayer, accountability, and love living in Christian community (See Acts 2:42ff). We will never be perfect, but we will be transformed by the Holy Spirit with ever increasing character to reflect our Lord (see 2 Corinthians 3:18).

2. **How can one get past the abuse and objectively pray for an abuser? How can the victim of abuse then do "good" unto them (Romans 12:17-21)?**

First, seek to understand where your abuser came from. What factors turned him or her into an abusive person? Solomon counsels, "Wisdom is supreme; therefore, get wisdom. Though it cost you all you have, get understanding.... For wisdom is more precious than rubies, and nothing you desire can compare with her" (Proverbs 4:5, 7; 11:8).

People are not born abusers. Abusers are often made by the abuse they experience as a child or adult. At one time in their lives, they were innocent, pure, and emotionally healthy. Something or someone shaped their perspectives and thinking. Hurt people usually hurt people.

Second, pity your abuser. God pitied us in our sin. Paul says in

Ephesians 2:3-5,

> All of us lived among them at one time, gratifying the cravings of our sinful nature and following its desires and thoughts. Like the rest, we were by nature objects of God's wrath. But because of his great love for us, God, who is rich in mercy, made us alive with Christ even when we were dead in transgressions-it is by grace you have been saved (Ephesians 2:3-5).

God doesn't want anyone to perish but everyone to have eternal life. What a privilege we have to apply the truth and grace we've received from God to our abusers.

Third, forgive your abuser and help them to see that God loves them, that he desires to forgive them and give them a brand-new life.

Fourth, praise God continuously for his grace and truth. Praise him for working pain into something good in the future. While in prison, Paul wrote, "Rejoice in the Lord always. I will say it again: Rejoice" (Philippians 4:4). Paul challenged the Christians sixteen times to rejoice in the Lord through their ordeals. Why? God is always good and promises to work situations out for good and to advance his kingdom. "I will praise you as long as I live, and in your name I will lift up my hands" (Psalm 63:4).

CHAPTER SIXTEEN
The Effective Church
SPIRITUAL PROFILING
THE SKEPTIC

I see that in every way you are very religious... I even found
an altar with this inscription: TO AN UNKNOWN GOD.
So, you are ignorant of the very thing you worship-
and this is what I am going to proclaim to you.
(Acts 17:22, 23)

When they heard about the resurrection of the dead,
some of them sneered, but others said, `We want
to hear you again on this subject.
(Acts 17:32)

It was Mary Magdalene, Joanna, Mary the mother of James,
and the others with them who told this to the apostles.
But they did not believe the women, because
their words seemed to them as nonsense.
(Luke 24:10, 11)

THE SKEPTIC

I grew up in a Christian home with parents who modeled Christ and kingdom values. I was taught right from wrong, how to pray, study the Bible, share my faith, and how to live a godly life. Upon graduation from high school, I attended a local University. That was the day I entered uncharted territory. For the first time, I met friends and neighbors called skeptics. Have you met them in your neighborhood?

Whenever the conversation turned to God, I'd quote scripture to prove my point. My skeptic friend would reply, "But how do you know the Bible is true?" At other times, I'd speak of God coming to earth in the person of Jesus to die for my sins. My agnostic neighbor would respond, "What empirical data do you have to prove such a claim?"

I'll never forget the day the professor in my biology class asked, "How many of you believe God made the world?" I noticed just a few raised hands. Next he asked, "How many of you believe the world was not created by God but came to exist through an evolutionary process?" Hands shot up all over the room. I thought to myself, "How do I defend my position that God is creator? How can I respond to the theory of evolution from a biblical perspective?"

I realized if I wanted to lead any of my skeptic neighbors to Christ there were several intellectual questions that had to be addressed before they were ready to hear the good news of Jesus. I wasn't prepared to give those answers. That's when I began to learn basic apologetics. The Greek word *apologia* means to *give a defense*. That is the goal of this chapter. When we meet the skeptics in our neighborhoods, we want to have the ability to give a basic defense of God's existence and answer other questions related to Christianity or salvation.

Distorted God: The Unknown God

Many years later, I met John at a Bible study in a restaurant. He came as a favor to a friend. After the study, John told me he was not sure there was a God. He was comfortable with this belief as an agnostic. The death of his wife and personal sickness had moved John to question God's existence. I told John I'd love to learn how an agnostic thinks. With no strings attached, I asked him to write down ten questions he had about life and God and could I discuss possible answers to his questions? Here is John's list:

1. How can you prove God exists?
2. How did the world come to exist?
3. Why are there war, pain and loss in life?
4. The church is full of hypocrites, why?
5. How do you know the Bible is true?
6. If there are miracles in the Bible, why not today?
7. Was Jesus really God in the flesh?
8. Why didn't Jesus write His own book?
9. Why did Jesus die on the cross?
10. How can I know God?

John's questions are common among skeptics. In order to better understand how to share the good news with our skeptic friends, let's spend some time with Paul on one of his trips to Athens.

Distorted Belief:
All They do is Talk and Listen to the Latest Ideas about God

In Acts 17:16-33, Paul was alone in Athens waiting for Silas and Timothy to arrive. To pass the time, he began to walk the streets. He looked in shops, talked to venders, visited landmarks and historical sites. As Paul toured the neighborhoods, he became distressed by the abundance of idols. Statues, engravings and other religious artwork were everywhere. Each one represented an object of worship. Paul found temples on every corner. Each temple was dedicated to a god and contained altars. The worshippers were coming and going, presenting their gifts and offerings.[155]

Acts 17:16 tells us that Paul became "greatly distressed." The Greek term implies the idea of being "infuriated."[156] As Paul continued walking, he connected with a group of skeptics in the marketplace (Acts 17:17).

---

155. Dennis Gaertner, *Acts* (2nd ed. Joplin, MO: College Press, 1995), 271.
156. Ibid.

The Epicureans and Stoics

Paul ran into Epicurean and Stoic professors (Acts 17:18). *Epicureans* are polytheistic (believing in many gods), but they believe the gods are largely uninvolved in the lives and the affairs of people. The greatest good, from their perspective, is happiness, so they try to avoid pain and *silly* ideas of judgment and the idea of an afterlife.[157] The *Stoics* believe in an impersonal divine force that holds the universe together. They are pantheistic, believing the divine spark lives in everything. They teach fate and self-sufficiency.[158]

These professors accused Paul of "babbling." Actually, they called Paul a "bird picker."[159] A bird picks up seeds here and there. The accusation was that Paul was picking up an idea here and an idea there then creating his own religion. As we have seen in previous chapters, this accusation was wrong. Paul had historical evidence, fulfilled prophesies, and miraculous events to support the Gospel.

Spiritual Profiling of the Skeptic

Skeptics hold to human reason, critical thinking, and the scientific method. The scientific method arrives at answers using empirical or measurable evidence that meets specific guidelines and principles. Skeptics fall within one of three categories: First *agnostics*. An agnostic is one who is not sure if God exists. Second *atheists*, who reject the idea of God based on the perception that there is a lack of scientific evidence to support his existence. Third, *deists* believe a god or gods exist, but they are not involved with the affairs of people. Human reason alone is sufficient for understanding the universe.

Most skeptics acknowledge Jesus as a humanitarian and philosopher whose ethics impacted western civilization. Few skeptics question Jesus' existence because extra-biblical evidence validates Jesus as a historical character. (Jesus is mentioned in the writings of ancient non-Christian historians such as Tacitus, Pliny the Younger, and Josephus.)

Skeptics will tell you that skepticism is a method not a position. It is the application

---

157. Ibid.
158. Ibid.
159. Ibid, 272.

of reason and the scientific method to any and all ideas.[160] The Skeptics Society is a nonprofit scientific and educational organization whose mission is to engage leading experts in investigating the paranormal, fringe science, pseudoscience, and extraordinary claims of all kinds, promote critical thinking, and serve as an educational tool for those seeking a sound scientific viewpoint.[161] The Society has rejected creationism and the Bible as the revealed word of God. The Society has created its own manifesto in which they identify what they see as contradictions between biblical statements and scientific fact. Skeptics place a strong emphasis on science and nature. This means having discussions about *general revelation* are a great way to connect with a skeptic.

The idea of general revelation originated with Francis Bacon in the early 1600s. It is the concept that the natural world with all of its beauty, intricacies, and complexity shows humankind that there is a creator. Creation doesn't tell us who God is. Creation tells us *there is a God* who does the creating. We can construe from what is seen that God is powerful, wise, creative, and caring (provides air, food, water, medicine).[162] In fact, the Psalmist wrote, "The heavens declare the glory of God…" (Psalm 19:1).

Skeptics often share a basic tenet of secular humanism. In *The Humanist Manifesto*, Paul Kurtz states, "We believe…that traditional dogmatic or authoritarian religions that place revelation [salvation], God, ritual, or creed above human experience do a disservice to the human species…We find insufficient evidence for belief in the existence of a supernatural; it is either meaningless or irrelevant to the question of the survival and fulfillment of the human race."[163] In other words, skeptics want empirical proof of the existence of God.

Skeptics are open to the idea of afterlife. For example, the skeptic Michael Shermer has written extensively on scientific evidence for the afterlife. He has friendly debates on college campuses with another skeptic, Deepak Chopra, who attempts to disprove the theory of life after death in his book, *Life after Death: The Burden of Proof.*

Now we've seen what skeptics believe, let's see what some good basic

160. "Shermer, Michael. "Skeptic. A Brief Introduction," http://www.skeptic.com/about_us/. Accessed August, 2015.
161. Ibid.
162. Lutzer, Dr. Erwin W., *The Difference between General and Special Revelations,* Moody Church Media. http://www.moodymedia.org/articles/difference-between-general-and-special-revelations. Accessed 7/2015.
163. Brodd, Jeffery, *World Religions: A Voyage of Discovery.* (Winona, MN: Saint Mary's Press), 272.

responses for our skeptic neighbors might be as we venture with the apostle Paul into his neighborhood full of skeptics in Athens, Greece.

HOW TO RESPOND TO THE SKEPTIC

There are *five basic arguments* for God's existence: the cosmological argument, the teleological argument, the ontological argument, the moral argument, and the argument from the existence of pain.

As you read the next section, you will notice that Paul presentes three of the five arguments to his skeptic neighbors: the cosmological, teleological and ontological arguments. We will consider the other two proofs of God, the moral argument and the argument from the existence of pain, when we learn how to respond to the hedonist.

Show the Probability of God

It's important to realize no one can empirically prove or disprove God's existence. Our goal with skeptics is to help them see the possibility or the probability of God based on the five arguments. If they acknowledge God as a possibility or probability, the next step is to say, "If God exists, if God created everything we see, it must also be true that God is *capable* of revealing himself to us and wanting a relationship." At that point, we tell the story of Jesus.

God is Almighty and Personal

Paul jumped into the religious conversation and eventually shared the "good news about Jesus and the resurrection" (17:18). The idea that God came to earth and died for our sins was completely foreign to the Greeks, so they asked Paul to give further explanation.

Paul argued from the general to the specific. He began with the fact God is the creator of all things, and he ended with, "For in him we live and move and have our being" (17:28). The creator of the universe knows, watches, supports and cares for each individual in everything he or she does. This all-powerful God is very personal and wants to know us. That's when Paul introduced Jesus. Paul presented him as the creator of the universe who came down to visit with, talk to, and redeem us from our sins.

God is the First Cause

In Acts 17:24, Paul presented God as the first cause: God created everything we see and experience. This is called the cosmological argument. Think about it, can something come from nothing? It is impossible for nothing to create matter. Nothing plus nothing does not equal something. Where did the material to make the world come from? Matter must have a creator.[164]

God is Transcendent

Paul described who the creator was, "The God who made the world and everything in it is the Lord of heaven and earth and does not live in temples built by hands" (Acts 17:24). God exists independently from his creation. He is transcendent. You and I are dependent on our environment. God is independent from his creation. He needs nothing: "And he is not served by human hands, as if he needed anything…" (Acts 17:25a). Pagan gods were fed by the worshiper. The pagan priest put a portion of the burnt offering (i.e., meat of the animal sacrificed) in the mouth of the god and ate the other portion himself, thus having communion with the god. Paul said the universal God needed no food or human care.

God the Creator

I remember talking to my biology professor after his lecture that claimed the universe came into existence via evolution and not God. He spoke of the Russian scientist Alexander Oparin, who theorized that in the beginning there was a soupy substance that contained hydrogen, methane, oxygen, and carbon. Lightning struck the soup creating a chemical reaction that generated amino acids, peptide bonds, and the conditions for the formation of life. This became known as Oparin's Primordial Soup Theory.[165] I asked my professor, "Where did the hydrogen, methane, oxygen and carbon come from?" He said, "We must take that by faith." I asked, "Who created the energy, the lightning?" He responded again, "We must take that by faith too." I thought after our conversation that it took more faith to be an atheist than a Christian because Christians believe there is a first cause. "In the beginning God…" (Genesis 1:1). God is our starting point, our presupposition. The atheist starts with nothing. Nothing plus nothing equals hydrogen, methane, oxygen and carbon?

---

164. Iron Chariots. org. *Cosmological argument*, http://www.wiki.ironchariots.org/index php?title=cosomogical_argument. Accessed 7/2015.
165. *The Physics of the Universe: Difficult Topics Made Understandable.* "Important Scientists: Alexander Oparin. www.physicsoftheuniverse.come/scientists_oparin.html, accessed August 6, 2014.

That's just not possible.

God the Designer

The second argument Paul uses is the *teleological argument* which states that the design of the universe demands a designer. To put the teleological argument into modern terms, we can say that the laws of physics, chemistry, biology, astronomy, medicine and mathematics, prove that unchanging, absolute universal laws do exist. Some of these universal laws are the Law of Gravity, the Laws of Motion, and the Law of Thermodynamics. Everything in the universe has a purpose and design, thus, it all fits together. When *design* exists, there must then be *designer*![166]

William Paley (1820s) made this argument well known. To illustrate his point, Paley took apart his watch and placed the parts in a box. Paley shook the box before his audience and said, "I can shake the box for one hundred years, but the parts will not go together by themselves. They were designed by a watchmaker. Every part was created with a purpose. The universe has design because there is an Almighty Architect." Paley's argument was so convincing that a man named Charles Darwin set out to prove it wrong. Darwin rejected Christianity. He created an *origins system* that has design but no designer.[167]

The Reason for Pain, Injustice and War

Yet, if God cares about his creation, then why are there pain, conflict and death? Paul stated that humankind has rebelled against God and must repent (17:30). Every person's actions will be judged with justice and each person will receive his or her due (17:31).

The Consequences of Sin

In the beginning, God created a perfect world and placed Adam and Eve in this paradise called the Garden of Eden (Genesis 2:8). Genesis 3 explains that God walked with Adam and Eve in the cool of the evening. Our first parents had a perfect environment and a faultless relationship with one another, with the animals, and

---

166. Philosophy of Religion, *The Teleological Argument*. http://www.philopsophyofreligion.info/theisitic-proofs/the-teleological-argument. Accessed 7/2015.
167. Schlossberg, Herbert. *Conflict and Crisis in the Religious Life of Late Victorian England.* 2009, Transaction Publishers, New Brunswick, New Jersey. pg 38.

with God. God did not make people as robots. He gave us the ability to choose so we could either to love or reject God. Imagine God willing to experience rejection in the hopes of true love relationships with his children.

God explained to Adam and Eve that if they wanted a relationship with him they could not eat of the tree of knowledge of good and evil (Genesis 2:15, 16). If they wanted to walk away, that was their choice, just eat of the tree. Deceived by Satan, they ate. The consequence of their sin was devastating. Immediately they experience shame (Genesis 3:7), fear (Genesis 3:8), guilt (Genesis 3:10), and they began acting irresponsibly (Genesis 3:11). The long-term effects were enmity with the animal world (Genesis 3:14), pain in childbearing (Genesis 3:16), tension in the marriage relationship (Genesis 3:16), and conflict with the environment—weeds, storms and droughts (Genesis 3:18). Physical and spiritual death also entered the world (Genesis 3:19).

In Romans 8, Paul explained that when Adam rebelled against God, creation became subject to frustration, bondage and decay (Romans 8:20, 21). Creation now works against humankind and not for us. This struggle will continue until Christ returns and creates a new heaven and earth never touched by sin! At that time, Christ will also give us new bodies.

It is Human Tendency to Resist God

Scripture also teaches that Adam's nature became corrupt through sin. This tendency to rebel against God's word is passed down to the next generation (see Romans 5:12-20). No one has to sin, but we are born with this tendency. Without regeneration and transformation by the Holy Spirit, human beings are capable of the worst kinds of atrocities (See Romans 1:18-32). Just a few chapters after creation, humankind became so depraved that God had to destroy the world with a flood (Genesis 6-8).

It is this tendency to sin that causes mankind to live in a constant state of tension. Humans strive to overcome nature, physical weakness, emotional trauma and other humans. Done outside of God's will and plan, it creates pain, war and ultimately death.

God the Redeemer

Paul says to his skeptic neighbors that we are "God's offspring, we should not think that the divine being is like gold or silver or stone—an image made by human design and skill. In the past God overlooked such ignorance, but now he commands all people everywhere to repent..." (17:29, 30). By stating we are God's offspring, Paul is declaring that people are made in God's image and that God is our heavenly Father. Of course, anthropology declares that *gods* are created by people and cultures. In a sense, it's true. Instead of knowing the true God, men "exchanged the glory of the immortal God for images made to look like a mortal human being and birds and animals and reptiles" (Romans 1:22, 23). In his speech recorded in Acts, Paul continues, "God has overlooked such ignorance in the past..." but something so colossal has occurred, that today, God demands all people to repent (17:30).

Humankind is Created with the Ability to Know God

Before the Athenian skeptics could learn what the monumental event was, Paul affirmed what they had already heard, that God desired all people to "seek him and perhaps reach out for him and find him, though he is not far from any one of us" (17:27). God made humans with the capability of knowing him and having a relationship with their creator. St. Anselm identified this as the *ontological argument*.[168] The very fact we can comprehend God and seek to know our creator is proof that God created us. God gave us the capacity to know him. Solomon said, "He has also set eternity in the human heart..." (Ecclesiastes 3:11). No animal has this skill, only people made in God's image (Genesis 1:27). So again, what is this gigantic event that now requires all people everywhere to repent and turn to the living God?

Jesus is God in the flesh

Paul introduced Jesus in verse 31. God will judge the world through Jesus. God came to earth in the person of Christ and Jesus Christ is Lord of all. Jesus will judge the living and the dead. His resurrection proves that he is God!

Verse 18 states Paul had been teaching the good news about Jesus and the resurrection. What good news? The gospel is the good news. I Corinthians 15:3,

---

168. "Anselm's Ontological Argument," Princeton Univerisity. www.princeton.edu/~grosen/puc/phi203/ontological.html, accessed July, 2015.

4 explains that the gospel is the death, burial and resurrection of Jesus. Through Christ's death and resurrection, God makes atonement for sins and gives the world the opportunity for reconciliation. This is the reason God now demands everyone to change and turn back to God. Reconciliation is now possible through Jesus.

Notice in Acts 17:32, "When they heard about the resurrection of the dead..." Paul was interrupted by sneering and people were mocking him. However, Paul persevered, and God brought fruit. A few people became *Paul's followers.*

No doubt Paul spoke to these new followers of Jesus being the perfect mediator—both God and man. In their studies, Paul might have shared the virgin birth, the miracles Jesus did, the resurrection and its proof, and no doubt the substitutionary work on the cross. Jesus' cross opens the door of reconciliation to God that had been previously shut by sin. Paul further explained the meaning of the gospel and the ramifications of being a Christ follower.

LET'S WRAP UP

There is a progression from *general to specific* in Paul's personal evangelism strategy to the skeptics. First, Paul shows the probability of God as creator by pointing to creation itself with simple logic: Is there a creator? Yes, creation demands a creator. More specifically, there are design, purpose, and universal unchangeable laws throughout creation. The cosmos demands a designer.

John's Response

John and I worked through each question once a week at a breakfast over a two-year period. Each question gave me the opportunity to grow with John as I did my homework and interacted with my friend. When his questions were resolved, he gave his life to Christ. It was a grand day when John stood before the church family, gave the good confession and was baptized.

As you use these arguments, your skeptic friend might inject, "You can't prove God exists." It's true, but he can't prove God doesn't exist, either. *The goal is to show the probability of God.* If your friend admits God is probable, you've opened the door and your friend is ready for salvation!

"Slide" the Conversation to Spiritual Topics

In Acts 17:22, Paul began by saying, "I see that in every way you are very religious." Was Paul complimenting their religiosity or was he calling the Athenians superstitious? The Greek word Paul used has a meaning that is ambivalent. I think Paul was complimenting the group for searching and being willing to discuss the possibility of God. It's important we communicate respect and humility as we share Christ.

Paul said, "For as I walked around and looked carefully at your objects of worship, I even found an altar with this inscription: TO AN UNKNOWN GOD." The phrase is literally *Agnosto theo.*[169] You can see our English word *agnostic* is derived from the Greek.

Can you see how Paul was *sliding* the conversation to Christ? He is using their altar; dedicated to Agnosto theo to explain about the God they're not sure exists. In your conversations with friends, watch for *slides* to move the conversation to spiritual topics. Sliding the conversation to Christ made Paul appear less polemic and more caring and natural in his conversation.

Exalt God and Stay Positive

Paul started off with the greatness of God. Read Acts 17:24-28. "He made the world and everything in it and is the Lord of heaven and earth... (17:24). Paul wasn't correcting his skeptic neighbors right out of the gate, rather he was revealing God's wonderful attributes, such as omnipresence (God is everywhere), omniscience (God is all-wise), transcendence (God is above his creation needing no one to support him), sovereignty (God is in control of the nations), and omnibenevolence (God provides and cares for us). He was also stating God was their creator, their heavenly Father. Paul was stating God was personally involved in their lives and loved them. "God did this so that they would reach out for him and find him, though he is not far from any one of us" (17:27). Once Paul identified God and his love for every person, Paul pointed out the skeptics flawed and incorrect beliefs about God.

---

169. Ibid., 275.

CHALLENGE

There are seven challenges that will appear as you work with the Skeptic. Study these seven and share!

1. **How could a person be an atheist?**

   James S. Spiegel in his book, *The Making of an Atheist,* gives the two top explanations. The first is the presence of war, disease, death and corruption in the world. As George Carlin said, "If this is the best God can do, I am not impressed."[170]

   A second explanation why people may become atheists is that they had an absent or abusive father. Atheists like David Hume, Friedrich Nietzsche, H. G. Wells, Hitler and many others, project their images of bad dads onto God and therefore don't want anything to do with a heavenly father.[171]

   Understanding these two causes can give you great insight as you talk to an atheist. You first can explain the consequence of sin. Pain is not God's idea. God provides the solution and will end all pain at the second coming. Also, you can show Jesus' interactions with people, and reveal what the personality of our heavenly Father really is (see Luke 15).

2. **How can we respond when skeptics object that Jesus can't be the only way to God?**

   Scripture says our sins have offended, angered and separated us from our creator God. If you offend a friend, would you be able to go to other people and apologize? No. The same is true of our broken relationships with God. We must go back to God through Jesus Christ—not through Buddha, Mohammad, Krishna or any human priest. On the Day of Judgment, people who have put faith in another savior will be disappointed and in terror for their gods do not exist (Isaiah 43:11; 45:5).

---

170. James Spiegel, *The Making of an Atheist: How Immorality Leads to Unbelief* (Chicago, IL: Moody Publishers, 2010), 62.
171. Ibid., 64-65.

3. **How do we respond to proponents of Darwin and his theory of evolution?**

Darwin believed in God, but not the God of Christianity. He believed God existed because of the ontological and teleological arguments. Darwin writes:

> To suppose that the eye, with all its contrivances for adjusting the focus to different distances, for admitting different amounts of light, and for the correction of spherical and chromatic aberration, could have been formed by natural selection seems, I freely confess, absurd in the highest possible degree.[172]

Darwin describes himself as a theist:

> [Reason tells me of the] extreme difficulty or rather impossibility of conceiving this immense and wonderful universe, including man with his capability of looking far backwards and far into futurity, as the result of blind chance or necessity. When thus reflecting I feel compelled to look at a First Cause having an intelligent mind in some degree analogous to that of man; and I deserve to be called a Theist.[173]

4. **What major argument can we use against evolution?**

There are several, but the evidence that convinced Anthony Flew was the teleological argument and DNA. Flew at one time was a leading atheistic philosopher and debater. In 2004, he abandoned atheism because of the code found in DNA. Flew states honestly that the informational code in DNA could not just happen but shows "that intelligence must have been involved." [174]

5. **How do we respond when skeptics ask, "Why is the church full of hypocrites?"**

According to Thom Rainer seventy-two percent of Americans who

---

172. Charlie Campbell, *One-Minute Answers to Skeptics* (Eugene, OR: Harvest House Publishers, 2010), 58.
173. Ibid., 60.
174. Ibid., 58.

do not attend church say the reason is the church is full of hypocrites, yet seventy-eight percent state they would love to talk to a Christian face-to-face about Christianity and how it impacts the believer's life.[175] The neighbors around us who don't have a relationship with Christ, believe the church is all about religion, organization and programs. They've never personally experienced God's love through a believer. They've never seen the transformation of a person into Christ's likeness. Hypocrisy is not as widespread as these non-church goers assume. The problem is that Christians are not going into their neighborhoods and getting to know their neighbors. Christians are to be God's miracle of transformation, testifying to God's power to change and restore any person. Until we let our neighbors know us and see our transformation firsthand, they will continue to believe hypocrites are what church is about.

6. **What do we tell our skeptic friends when he or she says the Bible isn't true?**

You can study these proofs found in chapter seven (7). Be ready to share them with your skeptic neighbors.

7. **How can we respond when the skeptics ask, "Why don't miracles still take place today like they did in the Bible?"**

God launched the church in Acts 2 with a display of miracles. The Holy Spirit came down upon the apostles. The outpouring of God's Spirit manifested himself through miraculous signs. These signs were to confirm the apostles' message about Jesus was true and Jesus was alive. These miraculous gifts were also used to give us the New Testament as the Holy Spirit revealed the word of God to the apostles so they could write it down and share it with the world. Christianity is rooted in history. We can confirm scripture to be true through historical facts. God's Spirit today dwells in believers. The indwelling of the Holy Spirit manifests himself by producing "fruit" (Galatians 5:22). Character transformation is the miracle today that confirms the gospel message is true. You are the miracle that proves Jesus is alive.

---

175. Jones, Sarah Bruyn, *Tuscaloosanews.com*, "72% say church is full of huypocrites." www.tuscaloosanews.com/article/20080119/news/345220246?p=1&tc=pg. accessed August, 2015.

CHAPTER SEVENTEEN
The Effective Church
SPIRITUAL PROFILING
THE MISINFORMED

But as for you, continue in what you have learned and have become
convinced of, because you know those from whom you learned it,
and how from infancy you have known the Holy Scriptures, which
are able to make you wise for salvation through faith in Christ Jesus.
(II Timothy 3:14, 15)

We have much to say about this, but it is hard to make it clear
to you because you no longer try to understand. In fact,
though by this time you ought to be teachers, you need
someone to teach you the elementary truths
all over again. You need milk not solid food!
(Hebrews 5:11, 12)

Like newborn babes, crave pure spiritual milk,
so that by it you may grow up in your salvation,
now that you have tasted that the Lord is good.
(I Peter 2:2)

THE MISINFORMED

The New Testament declares that sharing Christ is the *stewardship* of every Christian. According to Webster's Dictionary, "stewardship" comes from two Greek words which are translated as "keeper" and "house." Thus, a steward manages or oversees the resources of an enterprise, house, or ranch. A steward is responsible to be faithful and creative, always advancing the cause of the owner within the boundaries of the law.[176] Stewards are rewarded based on job performance and are required to give account of how the owner's affairs have been managed (Luke 16:2).

Perhaps you remember the incident involving the steward from JetBlue Airways Flight 1052 in August 2010. After the plane landed, a steward named Steven Slater announced on the intercom that he was quitting his job after twenty years. Slater said a passenger had uttered profanities and attacked him with a luggage bag, so he was through. Slater then pulled the emergency evacuation system and exited triumphantly down the slide. He was arrested later that day by the FDA, charged with "criminal mischief, reckless endangerment of the passengers, and criminal trespass."[177] He was fired and underwent mental illness testing in an effort to avoid jail time.[178]

In several parables, Jesus called his follower's *stewards*, responsible for managing and advancing God's enterprise, the church. In the parable of the shrewd manager (Luke 16), we learn that it's essential to follow Christ's doctrines. We can be pragmatic regarding *strategies* to reach lost people, but we cannot compromise *doctrine*. How we, as stewards, manage the *product* (doctrine) and *process* (evangelism and discipleship) can reflect whether or not we have authentic faith in Christ. "Whoever can be trusted with very little can also be trusted with much, and whoever is dishonest with very little will also be dishonest with much. . . . And if you have not been trustworthy with someone else's property, who will give you property of your own?" (Luke 16:10, 12).

The implication is that if we misuse, misguide or misappropriate Christ's *doctrine* and *process,* we have not been faithful as stewards. In the parable of the talents, an added ingredient of genuine faith is *productivity*. The steward who buried

---

176. Colin Brown, *The New International Dictionary of New Testament Theology* (Rev. ed. Carliste: Paternoster, 1986), 244-245.

177. "JetBlue Flight Attendant Incident", n.d., http://en.wikipedia.org/wiki/Steven_Slater.

178. William J. Gorta, "Ex-JetBlue Flight Attendant Steven Slater Trying to Broker Plea Deal in Air-Rage Case", n.d., http://www.nypost.com/p/news/local/ex_jetblue_attendant_steven_slater_FAUzEbhlBpL2mPKrXhh2ON.

his talent was called wicked, lazy, and worthless (Matthew 25:26, 30). The apostle Paul repeated the necessity of correct *doctrine* and the *disciple-making process* when he said, "So, look at Apollos and me as mere servants of Christ who have been put in charge of explaining God's mysteries [revelation]. Now, a person who is put in charge as a manager must be faithful" (1 Corinthians 4:1, 2).

Spiritual Profiling of the Misinformed

Acts 19 introduces Luke's next neighbor, the misinformed. I define the misinformed believer as one having incomplete information about key New Testament doctrine. For example, according to George Barna surveys:[179]

1. Forty-one percent of Christians believe the Bible is accurate. Think about that. If the Bible is filled with errors, then how do we know what is true or incorrect?

2. Sixty-eight percent of Christians do not believe they have any responsibility to share their faith. How is the world to know salvation if Christians have no knowledge of Christ's command for every believer to evangelize? What then is the Great Commission all about (Matthew 28:19, 20)?

3. Seventy-three percent of American Christians do not believe Satan is a real being who can influence people. No wonder the majority of believers in America live like unbelievers.

4. Sixty percent of Christians believe Jesus sinned while on earth. If Jesus sinned, then his redemptive act on the cross is in vain, Jesus needs a Savior.

5. Thirty percent of Christians do not believe Jesus arose from the grave. If Jesus did not raise on the third day, then how can Christians believe in any bodily resurrection at Judgment Day (I Corinthians 15:12-19)?

So, according to Barna's research most American Christians are misinformed!

---

179. Barna, George. The Barna Group. "Religious Beliefs Vary Widely By Denomination," https://www.barna.org/barna-update/5-barna-update/53-religious-beliefs-vary-widely-by denominations#.VjOmLtKrSUk. Accessed November 2015.

Distorted God: The God without Absolute Truth

There is another type of misinformed religious group that is growing by the day. My neighbor Jim embodies their beliefs. We have had some interesting conversations. He loves to share his views of God, Christianity, and global religion. He is always reading the latest books on the Bible, other sacred books, articles on the afterlife, and more. He is very confident in his beliefs and will engage in conversation with anyone. Jim thinks the global neighborhood needs a *global religion* to unite nations, peoples, and cultures as one. I have asked him, "Jim what does global religion teach?" The following section is what he answered. He also made reference to the United Nations' work in this area.

Distorted Belief: Religious Pluralism

According to Jim, this is a rough sketch of what global religion teaches. I will also use some of the United Religious Initiative (URI) / Global Religious Initiative material too.[180] The *Global Religious Initiative* was created by Bishop William Swing of the Episcopal Church in 1993 by invitation of the United Nations. It was officially launched in San Francisco in the year 2,000.

Religious pluralism is the foundational truth. It teaches that all religions have spiritual truth. Each religion's truth may contradict another religion's belief, but that's okay within the frame of religious pluralism. Spiritual truth is whatever a person sees it to be. Truth in the spiritual realm is relative not absolute. Truth in the spiritual world is different from scientific evidence that can be confirm or disproved by empirical testing. My neighbor Jim claimed to be a Christian but believed in reincarnation.

I shared that reincarnation is taught as a Hindu doctrine. Jim wasn't overly concerned. I explained, Hinduism teaches that karma is about suffering for your own sins. If one responds with submission, he or she is reincarnated into another person of a *higher cast* in the next life. Eventually, through reincarnation people can reach god status. I explained Jesus Christ pays for our sin on the cross. According to Scripture, without Christ each person can only pay for their sins in hell (See II Peter 2:4-22). So, Hinduism and Christianity have two completely different

---

180. Uri.org/who-we-are/cooperation-circle/united-religions-initiative-united-nations

solutions regarding payment for sin. Jim wasn't concerned about the contradiction. His answer was, "I believe both can be right."

According to the charter of the *United Religious Initiative* a doctrine of God is not discussed. Whatever you deem God to be is right by you. For Christians to believe in Jesus as Lord and Savior is fine, but Christians must allow other religions to have their own Lord and Savior too.

The *United Religious Initiative (URI)* is now in eighty-four countries. Not once does their charter refer to eternal life or any concept of heaven. The goal is heaven on earth. This world religion is to build cultures of peace and justice, to heal and protect the earth. According to the URI, all religions share a common heritage and interdependence. They respect the sacred wisdom of each religion.

Universalism is what many believe today, including Christians. Universalism says everyone eventually goes to heaven. Universalism translates into people claiming to be Christian but without any compulsion to live out the faith or grow in the knowledge of Scripture.

HOW TO RESPOND TO THE MISINFORMED

Apollos was a native of Alexandria in Egypt, a city known for its scholarship, world-famous library, and Jewish community. We don't know why he traveled to Corinth. During the Pax Romana (a period of relative peace throughout the Roman Empire A.D. 27- A.D. 180 established by Caesar Augustus) Rome built a system of roads that allowed for world travel, opening the door for global commerce and evangelism for the church.[181] Apollos was a "learned man, with a thorough knowledge of the scriptures" (Acts 18:24).

From Acts 18:25, we learn Apollos had accepted Christ as Lord and Savior. Someone explained to Apollos that Jesus' life fulfilled the Old Testament prophesies regarding the coming Messiah. This verse also tells us that Apollos was a very intense and energetic speaker. He spoke with "great fervor." The Greek word is *zeo,* which can mean "zeal, bubble, hot," or "overflow."[182] He also taught about Jesus "accurately," which means Apollos defined the Messiah, his role, and his function correctly. However, Apollos *was misinformed* because he only "knew the baptism of John."

---

181. "Pax Romana", n.d., http://en.wikipedia.org/wiki/Pax_Romana.
182. Spiros Zodhiates, *The Complete Word Study Dictionary: New Testament* (Chattanooga, TN: AMG Publishers, 1992), 34.

Baptism Misunderstood

John's baptism was prior to the death, burial, and resurrection of Christ. No forgiveness of sin or indwelling of the Holy Spirit were available until Pentecost (Acts 2; John 7:39). John's baptism was a preparation for Christ's kingdom. John taught that acceptance of Jesus as Lord and Savior and repentance were essential before one could experience cleansing of sin and entrance into God's kingdom (see Matthew 3).

In Acts 18:26, Apollos met Aquila and Priscilla who were solid New Testament Christians. They appreciated Apollos' proclamation of Christ, but his message was incomplete. He excluded Christian baptism, the Holy Spirit, and sanctification from his teaching. So, this wonderful couple invited Apollos to their home and privately "explained to him the way of God more adequately." Notice Aquila and Priscilla's spirit of love and grace. They did not call Apollos a heretic or false teacher. They did not slander Apollos to other Christians. They realized the truth about all of us: we are all in the process of learning, becoming, and clarifying the gospel.

Lay Aside Denominational Creeds and Embrace New Testament Christianity

Many people who join your church family come from Christian denominations. One statement I hear over and again about the non-denominational, New Testament church is how refreshing it is to simply follow the Bible rather than creeds and dogmas. None of us agree on every point of scripture, but we make the commitment to accept one another as fellow believers with the goal of coming together by restoring, as best we can, the New Testament pattern.

My religious genealogy includes Methodist, Nazarene, Baptist, and the Christian church. You can say I am a Heinz 57 Christian. My great grandfather built the altar in his Methodist church and even preached fairly often. My father attended the Church of Christ when he was a child, but he was never baptized. My mother began to read scripture and was captured by the simple Christianity presented in the New Testament. She no longer wanted to be called a Baptist or Methodist or Nazarene but simply Christian, a follower of Christ. Her background regarding baptism was sprinkling. She was convinced that the New Testament method was immersion. She had taken communion quarterly, but the New Testament church met weekly for the Lord's Supper. She decided to lay aside her denominational creeds and become simply Christian. Becoming a New Testament Christian did not mean she condemned her friends and relatives but was motivated to help family and friends to find their assurance in the New Testament Scripture versus denominational tradition.

Our spiritual life is a journey. We continuously learn, clarify, and grow into New Testament Christianity. Mom still appreciated the religious teaching she received from her Methodist Sunday school teacher. Each congregation helped her grow in some unique way. It was all a part of her journey to wholeness in Christ. We should be willing to evaluate our traditions in light of the New Testament pattern and make adjustments along the way. As Jesus told a crowd one day, we must allow God's pattern in scripture to shape us instead of clinging to our human traditions (Mark 7:8).

Be Gracious in Non-Salvation Issues: Work Toward Biblical Unity in Essential Doctrines

Apparently, in Acts 19, the doctrine in this new church at Ephesus was off target. When Paul was given the opportunity to speak, his first words were, "Did you receive the Holy Spirit when you believed" (Acts 19:2)? Can't you see the apostle squirming as he sat through the misinformed presentation of salvation and the Christian walk as the teacher delivered the lesson?

Discipleship is essential. Healthy churches involve Bible study and mentoring relationships. We need to be liberal regarding non-salvation issues and never judge one another, but when it comes to salvation issues, we need to work toward doctrinal unity.

In the church, mentoring relationships may not be a premium, because church has been relegated to the Sunday morning event. It requires a lot of effort and meetings to manage the church as an institution. The key is to work toward balance and not make discipleship/mentoring ministries a second-class priority.

In Acts 19:2, we see these disciples of Christ were not even aware of the Holy Spirit. They had only heard of John's baptism. Does this sound familiar? Some believe *Apollos* established this congregation.[183] Both good and bad doctrine spread like "yeast" (Matthew 13:33).

LET'S WRAP UP

Consider Joseph Smith in the early 1800s. Smith was originally a part of the Christian Church/Churches of Christ. He began with the intention of restoring New Testament Christianity. Smith said an angel appeared to him and explained that the Bible was corrupt. The Church of Jesus Christ of the Latter-Day Saints was created as they introduced a "corrected" version of the Bible. This group has over fourteen million Mormons knocking on doors to spread the Mormon faith. In Utah, 62.4 percent of the population is Mormon.[184]

Paul explained with great success the difference between John's baptism and Christian baptism. As we read in Acts 19:5, "On hearing this, they were baptized into the name of the Lord Jesus." In Acts 19:6, we see that Paul, as an apostle, laid his hands on believers giving them the outpouring of the Spirit displayed by the miraculous gifts. Without the written New Testament, the first century church would receive New Testament teaching directly from the Holy Spirit. The church could now function according to Christ's teaching and leadership. Today we have the completed written Word of God. We are commanded to study the word and be able to give the correct meaning to everyone we meet (II Timothy 2:15).

CHALLENGE

The Misinformed will ask you four questions. Study the answers and be ready to share.

1. **Why are there so many different Christian denominations?**
    In his *World Christian Encyclopedia,* David Barrett identifies 33,820 different Christian denominations.[185] Actually he includes para-

183. Dennis Gaertner, *Acts* (2nd ed. Joplin, MO: College Press, 1995), 297.
184. "Utah Local News - Salt Lake City News, Sports, Entertainment, Business - The Salt Lake Tribune", n.d., http://www.sltrib.com/.
185. David Barrett, *World Christian Encyclopedia: A Comparative Study of the Churches and Religions in the Modern World* (2nd ed. Oxford: University Press, 2001), 1:16-18.

denominations in his count, however, that is a lot. Such splintering is a bad witness to the world. One of the most common questions I get from non-believers is, "Why are there so many different Christian denominations? If Christians can't agree on God's teaching, how am I supposed to know what God wants me to do?" About the only thing I can say in defense of these groups is that most Christian denominations agree on the key fact that salvation is found in the death, burial, and resurrection of Jesus Christ versus the good works of individuals.

Denominations disagree on God's role in saving people, how a person accepts salvation, and hundreds of non-salvation issues such as how often to take the Lord's Supper, views of interpreting the book of Revelation, church polity (governance) and cultural issues such as music, worship styles, appropriate dress, and views on dancing, drinking and so forth.

The beauty of the Christian churches and Churches of Christ is that our goal is to restore the New Testament pattern of Christianity in hopes of re-uniting Christian denominations as one church. Our effort is labeled the *Restoration Movement*. We ask all denominations to lay aside creeds and dogmas to embrace the simple pattern and teaching of the New Testament. United, the church of Jesus Christ will be a powerful force of positive change in the world. This was Jesus' goal. He prayed in John 17:20, 21, "I pray … that all of them may be one, Father, just as you are in me and I am in you."

2. **What are the differences between the Catholic and Protestant faith traditions?**

There are four main differences between these two traditions:

The authority of scripture

Protestants have long championed the belief that the Bible alone gives us the necessary information regarding sin and salvation (see 2 Timothy 3:16). For Catholics, the traditions and/or teachings of the church are equally binding upon Christians.

The office and authority of the Pope

While Protestants hold that Christ alone is the head of the church

(Ephesians 5:23) and that fallible man could never be a proper substitute for him, the Catholic church holds that the Pope is the visible head of the church. Thus, he has the authority to speak "ex cathedra" (literally: "from the chair") to issue edicts regarding faith and practice that are considered both infallible and authoritative for all Christians.

Salvation

Catholicism teaches that one does receive grace by faith in Christ, but this grace must be supplemented with "meritorious works," namely the seven sacraments: baptism, confirmation, Eucharist, Penance, anointing of the sick, Holy Orders and matrimony. Protestants believe that man is saved by grace alone, which comes through Jesus.

Doctrine of the afterlife

Although both parties believe that unbelievers are damned to Hell, Catholics believe that Christians who still cling to sin and have not fully received the punishment due their transgressions, will spend time in Purgatory (a place of temporal punishment for sin) before going to Heaven. On the other hand, Protestants believe that Christians are saved fully through the grace of Christ and depart this life to be with the Lord (Philippians 1:23).[186]

3. **Are the Mormon Church, Christian Science, and Jehovah's Witness Christian denominations?**

No, they are categorized as Christian cults because they claim, "extra biblical revelation." Anytime a religious leader states an angel appeared to him or her and then changes any core New Testament doctrine, such as salvation by grace through faith in Christ alone, that teaching is labeled cultish.

Joseph Smith (1830s), the founder of Mormonism, stated there are three sacred books in addition to the Bible: *The Book of Mormon, Doctrine and Covenants* and *The Pearl of Great Price.* He taught that salvation is a resurrection that also includes exaltation to a god status in the celestial Heaven. This salvation must be earned through "self-

---

186. This question and its answer were an adaptation of "What is the difference between Catholics and Protestants?", n.d., http://www.gotquestions.org/difference-Catholic-Protestant.html.

meriting works."[187] The Mormons teach that God begot all humans by having sex with many wives in Heaven and then sent us all to earth for potential exaltation to godhood.[188]

Charles Russell (1870s), the founder of the Jehovah's Witness, claims he had a revelation from an angel who told him Jesus was not Jehovah God. Jesus was the first and only direct creation of God. Jesus then made the universe. Russell rejected the Trinity of God the Father, God the Son, and God the Holy Spirit. A simple way to understand the Trinity is to think of three distinct personalities all made of the same God stuff. They have always existed. Genesis 1 and Colossians 1 state that in creating the universe God the Father spoke matter into existence. God the Spirit shaped matter. Jesus Christ sustains the universe. Regarding spiritual salvation, God the Father creates redemption by grace, God the Son becomes the sacrifice for sin, and God the Spirit reveals the plan and regenerates the heart. Charles Russell the founder of the Jehovah Witness religion stated Jesus did not have a physical resurrection but rose as a mighty spirit creature.[189] The dead exist only in God's memory. The wicked will not be punished but extinguished forever.[190]

Mary Baker Eddie (1870s), the founder of Christian Science, was influenced by a Dr. Quimby of Portland, Maine, who created mental healing.[191] Eddie taught that disease is created in the mind and thus can be cured through the mind. God is a divine principle not a person. Jesus is not God. The incarnation and resurrection of Jesus never happened. Scripture has many mistakes in it. Sin, death, and evil do not exist.[192]

4. Is the Bible God's Word?

Yes, Scripture answers the basic questions about life on earth and after death. Genesis for example reveals the origins of the universe, earth, animals, plants, humankind, sin, death, languages, a global flood

---

187. Walter Martin, *The Kingdom of the Cults* (Rev., updated, and expanded ed. Minneapolis, MN: Bethany House, 2003), 192.
188. Ibid.
189. Ibid., 48.
190. Ibid.
191. Ibid., 151.
192. Ibid., 147.

and God's plan to redeem the world through the Messiah (Genesis 3:15; 12:2, 3). Other passages define God's design for family, marriage, parenting, relationships, money, identity, purpose in life and much more. The Bible is our *script* for life and eternal life.

Scripture defines two covenants, the Old and New Covenant. The term "covenant" is of Latin origin (con venire), meaning a coming together. It presupposes two or more parties who come together to make a contract, agreeing on promises, stipulations, privileges, and responsibilities. God's covenant with humankind is by God's grace and God's truth. The two parties, God and Humankind are not equal! We cannot negotiate and change His covenant! The Old Covenant was specifically for Israel. The conditions include loving the Lord with all their hearts by keeping the Mosaic Law. No one could perfectly keep God's Law, therefore the need to for the New Covenant that offers forgiveness of sin and God's indwelling of the Holy Spirit through Jesus' redemptive work on the cross and his resurrection. God clearly *defines* for us what we must do to be saved and to maintain a vibrant relationship with our creator. We cannot change this covenant. It is by God's mercy and grace we have this opportunity.

Jesus said Scripture is completely true (John 17:17). All Scripture is God-breathed (II Timothy 3:16), which means God himself is its origin and source. Scripture is called "the word of God" (Matthew 15:6). Our call is to learn Scripture then step out in faith obeying God's plan for our life, with a motive of gratitude and thanksgiving for the salvation Jesus offers.

CHAPTER EIGHTEEN
The Effective Church
SPIRITUAL PROFILING
THE HEDONIST

So, I tell you this, and insist on it in the Lord, that you must no
longer live as the Gentiles do, in the futility of their thinking.
They are darkened in their understanding and separated from
the life of God because of the ignorance that is in them due
to the hardening of their hearts. Having lost all sensitivity,
they have given themselves over to sensuality so as to
indulge in every kind of impurity, and they are full of greed.
(Ephesians 4:17-19)

You were taught, with regard to your former way of life, to put off your old self,
which is being corrupted by its deceitful desires; to be made new in the attitude of
your minds; and to put on the new self, created to be like God
in true righteousness and holiness.
(Ephesians 4:22-24)

Put to death, therefore, whatever belongs to your earthly nature; sexual
immorality, impurity, lust, evil desires and greed, which is idolatry.
Because of these the wrath of God is coming.
(Colossians 3:5)

THE HEDONIST

A hedonist is a pleasure seeker. According to Lawrence R. Samuel Ph.D. there is a Happiness Movement throughout the world. People are pursing pleasure, and whatever else they think will make them happy, with little restraint. Studies show that one's social, economic, education, income, and intelligence have little to do with happiness."[193] Sounds a bit like Solomon's pursuit, "I denied myself nothing my eyes desired; I refused my heart no pleasure... Yet when I surveyed all that my hands had done and what I had toiled to achieve, everything was meaningless; a chasing after the wind" (Ecclesiastes 2:10, 11).

Spiritual Profiling of the Hedonist

I first met Mike at a car dealership when I was looking for a great deal on a car. He was outgoing, friendly, easy to talk to, just a great guy. I visited Mike several times. We'd take ten or fifteen minutes to browse the newest arrivals; then, we would sit on the front porch of the showroom and talk about any and everything. During a conversation about college football I said, "As you know, I'm a preacher and I'd just like you to know, I think you'd make a great Christian." He laughed and said, "That's not for me!" I responded, "Why not? The Christian life is the greatest life in and out of this world! How can you argue with forgiveness, the power to be a new person, answered prayer, avoidance of eternal fire, and eternal life in paradise?" I then smiled and said, "Sorry, I didn't mean to get so preachy!"

He laughed and said, "That's OK, but I've *got* the greatest life now! I do anything that makes me happy. I'm not bound to one woman, one place, or one thing. I have no rules that bind me. Why would I want a different life?"

Distorted God: God wants Me to be Happy

In Acts 24, the Jewish leaders had falsely accused Paul of violating Jewish temple laws. Paul was arrested in Jerusalem; he then demanded to have a hearing before Caesar to prove his innocence. As a Roman citizen, Paul had the right to stand before the emperor. On the way to Rome, Paul and his guard went through Caesarea.

---

193. Psychologytoday.com/us/blog/psychology-yesterday/201811/the-american-pursuit-happiness

Felix, a governor of a Roman province stationed in Caesarea, heard his case.

Felix was an interesting character. Actually, nothing good can be said about him. He was a slave set free and given political power by his brother Pallas.[194] Tacitus, the Roman historian, said of him, "He exercised the prerogatives of a king with the spirit of a slave."[195] He married and divorced quickly for political advantage or desire. Acts 24:24 says his current wife was Drusilla, a beautiful young woman with Jewish roots. Her story today would make the *National Enquirer*. She was the youngest daughter of Agrippa (the Herod of Acts 12).[196] At the age of fourteen, she married a king in Syria. Felix saw her beauty and wanted her to be his wife. Through the trickery of a magician, Felix convinced Drusilla to leave her husband. Felix promised her true happiness.[197] Barclay says Felix was "completely unscrupulous."[198] So, with desire as his moral compass, Felix was driven by pleasure and selfish ambition. Barclay says he was "capable of hiring thugs to murder his closest supporters."[199]

Pleasure seekers throughout the centuries have worshipped a goddess called Aphrodite. We see her name appear throughout the Old Testament as Ashtoreth, Astarte, and Ishtar (Babylon). After the Philistines killed Saul, the king of Israel, they placed Saul's armor in her temple as a trophy (1 Samuel 31:10). Aphrodite was popular in New Testament times as well. She had a temple in Corinth. She was the goddess of sexual love and pleasure. The Romans knew her as Eros (erotic pleasure). Her followers could engage in erotic sex with temple prostitutes in her house of worship. The Canaanites were destroyed for worshipping the goddess of pleasure and so was Judah by Babylon in B.C. 587 (Jeremiah 17:12).

Pleasure seekers may or may not believe in God. If they do, their theology includes God wanting them to be happy. The argument goes God made humans with the capacity to enjoy pleasure so one should engage in pleasure to its fullest extent. The term "hedonist" comes from the Greek word meaning pleasure seeker.[200]

Joseph Fletcher (1905-1991) is responsible for developing the philosophy known as Situational Ethics during his tenure at Harvard University (1944-1970). Fletcher taught that Bible mandates were no longer absolute and should give way to the best expression of love for each situation. The problem with Fletcher's ethics

---

194. Dennis Gaertner, *Acts* (2nd ed. Joplin, MO: College Press, 1995), 364.
195. William Barclay, *The Acts of the Apostles* (Philadelphia: Westminster Press, 1976), 168.
196. Gaertner, *Acts*, 375.
197. Ibid.
198. Ibid.
199. Ibid.
200. "Hedonist", n.d., http://www.merriam-webster.com/dictionary/hedonist.

was that he elevated human reason above biblical revelation. Interestingly, Fletcher became the leading academic who shaped America's perspective on abortion, infanticide, euthanasia, eugenics, and cloning.[201] Later, his true colors surfaced when Fletcher proclaimed himself an atheist. The American Humanist Association then named Fletcher "Humanist of the Year" in 1974.[202]

The premise for Fletcher's decision-making process is the end justifies the means. Each person decides what is right or wrong for him or her, and, if the person can show that the action brings happiness or love, then it is acceptable. Today, when people justify any action from homosexuality, to cheating, to divorce, to promiscuity, to murder; they are using Fletcher's system. Elevating human reason above God's revelation is the reason a large portion of America is drifting into hedonism.

Both my friend Mike and King Felix were living for pleasure. They used situational ethics to make their decisions. Both of them made moral decisions based on what would bring them the most pleasure or which course of action would best minimize the amount of interpersonal conflict at the moment. Mike, Felix, and hedonists live for the moment. They give little thought to the physical, emotional, or spiritual consequences of their actions and avoid thinking about death and Judgment Day.

This makes it very easy for them to hurt, use, and even abuse people to achieve their goals. Mike was willing to deal drugs and destroy countless lives to support his luxurious lifestyle. Felix was willing to destroy a marriage in order to have what he wanted—Drusilla as his wife. Mike and Felix both lived as if there was no life after death, no judgment, and no eternal consequences for their actions.

HOW TO RESPOND TO THE HEDONIST

The apostle Paul was always looking for open doors to share the gospel (Colossians 4:2-6). In Acts 24:11-13, Paul stated that the charges against him were completely false and could not be proven. In the next verses, 14-21, Paul moved on to defend his innocence, and also laid the foundation to bring Felix and Drusilla to salvation. Here's the classic way to witness to the pleasure seekers, the hedonists, in your neighborhood.

201. "Joseph Fletcher", n.d., http://en.wikipedia.org/wiki/Joseph_Fletcher.
202. Ibid.

Identify Yourself as a Follower of Jesus

Paul said to Felix, "I admit that I worship the God of our fathers as a follower of the Way…" (Acts 24:14). In his defense, Paul made sure he brought up Jesus and casually declared that Jesus is the ultimate fulfillment of Judaism—the Messiah.

Identify Jesus as God Who Came to Earth as the Savior of the World

Early Christians identified themselves as "followers of the Way," a term that declared not only direction, invitation, answers, and salvation but also exclusion— "Followers of _the_ Way." Jesus referred to himself as "the Way,"[203] meaning his substitutionary work on the cross is the way to have sin removed and be right before God. Jesus said, "No one comes to the Father except through Me" (John 14:6). This exclusive gospel brought persecution from Jews who saw Paul discarding the Mosaic Law as the means of salvation. What other incredible claims does Jesus make about himself that will further prove Jesus is the way to salvation?

"Jehovah" or more specifically, "Yahweh" is the name God gives himself in the Old Testament. To Jews, the name is so holy they will not pronounce it. When writing God's name in the Old Testament, they removed the vowels and wrote YHWH. God introduced himself to Moses as "I AM WHO I AM" (Exodus 3:14). The name has to do with "God's self-existence."[204] This was a major reason the Jewish leaders wanted to kill Jesus. This doctrine of incarnation is a major reason Muslims oppose Christianity. Jesus claims to be Yahweh. Norman Geisler gives examples:

> In light of this, it is no wonder that Jews picked up stones and accused Jesus of blasphemy when He claimed to be Jehovah. Jesus said, "I am the Good Shepherd" (John 10:11), but the Old Testament said, "[Yahweh] is my shepherd" (Psalm 23:1). Jesus claimed to be the judge of all men (Matthew 25:31ff; John 5:27ff), but the Prophet Joel quoted Yahweh as saying, "For there I will sit to judge all the surrounding nations" (Joel 3:12). Jesus prayed, "Father glorify Thou Me with Thine own Self with the glory which I had with Thee before the world was" (John 17:5 KJV).

203. See Matthew 7:13 and John 14:6
204. Norman Geisler, _When Skeptics Ask: A Handbook on Christian Evidences_ (Grand Rapids: Baker Books, 2008), 106.

But Yahweh of the Old Testament said, "I will not give My glory to another" (Isaiah 62:5; Hosea 2:16). The risen Christ says, "I am the first and last" (Revelation 1:17)-precisely the words used by Yahweh in Isaiah 42:8. While the Psalmist declares [Yahweh] is my light" (Psalm 27:1), Jesus said, "I am the light of the world" (John 8:12). Perhaps the strongest claim Jesus made to be Yahweh is in verse 58, where he says, "Before Abraham was born, I AM." This statement claims not only existence before Abraham, but equality with the "I AM" of Exodus 3:14.[205]

Identify Jesus as Judge: Judgement Day is Coming

I tell you the truth, a time is coming and has now come when the dead will hear the voice of the Son of God and those who hear will live. For as the Father has life in himself, so he has granted the Son to have life in himself. And he has given him authority to judge because he is the Son of Man (John 5:25-27).

Paul also emphasized to the pleasure seeker a general resurrection that leads to Judgment Day. "…I have the same hope in God as these men, that there will be a resurrection of both the righteous and the wicked. So, I strive to keep my conscience clear before God and man" (Acts 24:15, 16). The resurrected Christ will raise the dead and judge all people and determine their eternal destiny. A universal judgment was an integral part of Paul's message throughout his ministry. Paul was saying to Felix something like, "The realization of Judgment Day influences my thoughts, my words, and my actions every day. I do and say certain things. I don't do and don't say other things because I know I will stand before God and give an account." If Paul was concerned about being judged, how much more should Felix have been concerned?

Other scriptures that state a universal judgment are Romans 14:10 and 2 Corinthians 5:10. Solomon said that God will "deal with each man according to all he does" (2 Chronicles 6:30). Through the prophet Jeremiah, God says "I, the Lord,

---

205. Ibid.

search the heart, and examine the mind, to reward a man according to his conduct, according to what his deeds deserve" (Jeremiah 17:10). Jesus said he "will reward each person according to what he has done" (Matthew 16:27).

Every believer agrees that on Judgment Day, Christians will receive their rewards, but will our sins as Christians also be revealed? Some scriptures seem to say yes and others no. Here are a few that say yes: "God will bring every deed into judgment, including every hidden thing, whether it is good or evil" (Ecclesiastes 12:14). Private acts of kindness done for God's people will be revealed and rewarded (Matthew 6:4, 6, 18). Secret sins will be exposed (Luke 12:2). Paul said, "God will judge men's secrets" (Romans 2:16). He also states the Lord "will bring to light what is hidden in darkness and will expose the motives of men's hearts" (1 Corinthians 4:5).

Here are two passages that suggest God will not reveal the sins of believers on Judgment Day. Psalm 103:12, "As far as the east is from the west, so far has He removed our transgressions from us." Another favorite is "For I will forgive their wickedness and will remember their sins no more" (Jeremiah 31:34).

Which scriptures are right? Jack Cottrell, a Christian church theologian, referring to Psalm 103 and Jeremiah 31 states:

> These texts do not mean, though, that the omniscient God literally forgets about our sins and never mentions them at judgment; they mean that, thanks to the blood of the New Covenant, He will *never hold them against us again.* They will not condemn us, not even on the Day of Judgment. But they *will* be displayed. But why is this necessary? The issue is the vindication of the righteousness of God. By judging us according to our own works, God's impartiality again is demonstrated; and the degrees of reward and punishment assigned to all are shown to be utterly fair.[206]

Having both good and bad deeds brought before us on Judgment Day was probably Paul's motive for saying to Felix, "So I strive always to keep my conscience clear before God and man."

---

206. Jack Cottrell, *The Faith Once for All: Bible Doctrine for Today* (Joplin, MO: College Press, 2002), 557.

Identify the Need for Repentance and Faith in Christ to Achieve Salvation

In Acts 24:24, Felix brought his wife Drusilla to hear Paul teach. Paul spoke about the necessity of faith in Jesus Christ and began a discourse "on righteousness, self-control and the judgment to come...." The Greek word for discourse is *dialeipo*, which means "to say thoroughly." The definition also includes "dialogue, arguing, disputing, reasoning and exhortation."[207]There comes a time when we need to sit with a friend and be honest. State the fact that the direction his or her life is headed is toward Hell. Your friend might come back with arguments like, "Nobody's perfect, I've never killed anyone, God knows my heart, I still believe in Jesus, I do good things for others," and "I don't hurt people." If you talk about judgment, you will hear these common excuses from people.

Identify God's Expectation of Righteous Behavior

Paul said righteousness and self-control were demanded by the eternal Judge. A self-controlled life directed by God's righteous decrees is what Christ expects. Paul "discoursed on...the judgment to come" (Acts 24:24). He goes into great detail, delivering a lengthy argument on the specifics of judgment. He is very direct and states the facts clearly. Why shouldn't Paul? Why shouldn't we? Are we afraid to offend our friends? Do we not believe what the Bible says about Hell? The reality of eternal Hell should move us to warn and plead with people to come to Christ (Acts 2:40). Review what the scripture says about Hell in chapter three of this book and share it.

The reality of Judgment Day struck *terror* in the heart of Felix, who then interrupted Paul saying, "That's enough for now!" (Acts 24:25). The verse also says, "Felix was afraid." The Holy Spirit used Paul's description of eternal damnation to convict Felix and move him toward a decision to repent and accept Christ. However, Felix resisted the Spirit's call by ordering Paul to leave.

Identify When God Needs Time to Work but Stay Connected

To continue my story from earlier about my friend Mike, I hesitated before giving Mike my answer to make sure that I came across as sincere and kind. With a

---

207. Spiros Zodhiates, *The Complete Word Study Dictionary: New Testament* (Chattanooga, TN: AMG Publishers, 1992), 433.

smile I said, "Mike, living as a Christian is the greatest life in the world! There are consequences to every action. We all die. As a matter of fact, our lives can end at any moment. Scripture says that at death you will face Christ as your judge. To be quite honest, some of the events that you've described in our conversations are what the Bible calls sin. They will land you in Hell. I'm not trying to be rude. That's just what the Bible says, and you *did* ask me, 'Why should I change?' Right?"

He smiled and said, "You're right, I did ask." Then he changed the subject and we landed back on football, closing out with a fun argument over who was the best team in the NCAA. Several months passed and I had no contact with Mike. Primarily because I decided to buy a car from a different dealership. A friend of Mike's named Tom started attending our church. He informed me Mike had overdosed on drugs and asked if I would give Mike a call.

When I got to the hospital, Mike shared with me that a girlfriend had left him. He felt he didn't have anything to live for and decided to take his life. I told Mike that God had spared him for a new life, a new purpose and a new future. I communicated, "God has intervened and given you a second chance!"

He explained that he'd been using drugs since Viet Nam. We continued to talk for several more months, and then he dropped the second bomb shell: Mike was a drug dealer and in trouble with some really rough characters.

Identify the Gospel and Find Time to Share

We studied the Bible together for about six months, trying to get the complete picture of the human condition that sin puts us in; the struggle between the flesh and our spirit, salvation by grace and, of course, judgment that leads to Heaven or Hell. During that time, Mike also relapsed several times; each time we would go through the whole process of starting over and seeking to discover God's direction and will.

I'll never forget the day I baptized Mike. He wanted a private baptism, so it was just the two of us in the auditorium. As he came up out of the water he began shouting, "I'm forgiven!" His first question was, "Am I really forgiven of every bad thing I've ever done?" I said, "Absolutely! That's the power of the blood of Christ!" Mike then ran around the auditorium shouting, "I'm forgiven! I'm forgiven! I'm forgiven!" I'll never forget that picture of a full-grown man who truly understood what it meant to be saved from eternal Hell.

Mike saturated himself with scripture after his baptism. I can honestly say I've never seen such a dramatic transformation so quickly in any other person. He memorized verses on a daily basis, and the Holy Spirit filled Mike with such power and joy that he bubbled over with God (Acts 18:25). He began to witness and lead people to Christ. He went to Bible College, then into ministry and used his story as a powerful witness of God's grace and power. Heaven drove Mike each day. Problems, temptations, and temporary pleasures were laid aside for his eternal home.

LET'S WRAP UP

Recently, Mike had a sudden heart attack and passed away. Mike is enjoying true pleasure and happiness today with his eternal family in Heaven. I look forward to seeing my friend again someday. He left me a gift. Apparently, Mike had a business on the side called "Michael's Knives." He created and crafted some beautiful, unique knives and placed them in glass cases. On the front of his card, Mike stated that 50 percent of all the profits would go to help the poor. On the back of his card, Mike had Hebrews 4:12, 13 with this note: *Just as a sharp knife can draw blood from the flesh. God's Word is even sharper, for the Bible says:*

> For the word of God is living and active. Sharper than any double-edged sword, it penetrates even to dividing soul and spirit, joints and marrow; it judges the thoughts and attitudes of the heart. Nothing in all creation is hidden from God's sight. Everything is uncovered and laid bare before the eyes of Him to whom we must give account.

Remember, as we lead others to Jesus, the Holy Spirit convicts and judges their hearts, but each person must make his or her own choice. Working through a decision takes time, because attachments to the world are not always easy to release. Felix said, "When I find it convenient, I will send for you" (Acts 24:25). Felix listened to Paul "frequently" for two years. Felix flirted with Christ's invitation, but (as far as we know) never accepted.

CHALLENGE

There are five questions that are tied to Hedonists. Learn the answers and be ready to share.

1. **Does the pleasure seeker ever get tired of seeking pleasure? Do they reach a point when they become frustrated and empty?**

   Absolutely, Solomon reached this point in his pursuits of pleasure. Read Ecclesiastes 2.

2. **Why is Judgment Day such an important topic to discuss with pleasure seekers?**

   Because people must know they are lost in their sins and will face Christ on Judgement Day. Without salvation they will spend eternity in Hell (Revelation 20:11-15). Here's a timeline I often use:

   - Christ returns with saints from heaven (Matthew 26:54; I Thessalonians 4:14)

   - Wicked are taken into the air (Matthew 13:30)

   - The Dead in Christ rise (1 Thessalonians 4:16)

   - Believers who are alive on earth will be caught up into the air (1 Thessalonians 4:17)

   - Believers receive their glorified bodies (1 Corinthians 15:42-57)

   - Both wicked and believers go into the Throne Room of God for Judgement (Revelation 20:11-15; Matthew 25:31-46)

   - During Judgment Day the earth as we know it is being purified with fire (2 Peter 3:10)

   - Wicked are cast into the Lake of Fire (Revelation 20:15)

   - Christ reveals the new heaven and earth (Revelation 21)

   - Believers live with God forever (Revelation 22).

3. **Why can't I have my fun now and repent later?**

   - The answer is consequences. Sin brings consequences: waste, pain, brokenness, regrets and shame. Mike's body incurred physical and emotional scars that stayed with him the rest of his life. At times, the apostle Paul struggled to forget the past and press on toward the prize. Read Philippians 3:12-16.

- Sin gives Satan another hook by which to tempt you. A smoker told me that after seventeen years of not smoking, if he smelled his old brand of cigarettes in a restaurant after a meal, the desire/ temptation to smoke would still come back. (This was back when people could still smoke in restaurants.) The same is true for those who have been caught up in pornography, sexual sin, lying, cheating, and so forth.

- We don't know when Christ will come or the day we will die. Read 2 Corinthians 5:10 and Hebrews 9:27. Jesus frequently warns us to be ready. Read Matthew 25:1-13.

4. **How can you say certain behavior is evil?**

Good and evil are defined by the Creator of the universe in Scripture, not by people. God is good, and evil is defined as rebelling against whatever God defines as good. God has a right to tell us how to live because He made us. Just as the creator of a car, a watch, or any product creates the product for a specific purpose, so God has created us for one purpose and that is to give Him glory through obedience (Deuteronomy 6:1-3; John 14:23).

5. **If evil is bad, why does God allow it or punish me?**

To stop all evil, means God would have to stop every person from all sin thereby removing all free will. The Bible says that a day is coming when God will stop evil (2 Peter 3:7-13); however, for now, God allows it so that every person can have the choice to love and follow God or to follow the path of evil. Make no mistake, however, God will judge all people and put those outside of Christ away forever. God is gracious today and gives us many opportunities to choose him and to change (Hebrews 3:7-11, 15).

Conclusion

As long as the definition of church remains vague in the minds of church members, they will not embrace God's purpose for their lives—to *be* the church; taking on Christ's character and doing Christ's mission (which is to make disciples). A shared biblical identity among the members will enable the Holy Spirit to mobilize Christ's body to storm the gates of hell! This is the picture of the first believers in Acts. The word that marked their lives was *devoted* (Acts 2:42). Knowing their true identity, they "devoted" themselves to be trained to live out their new calling. Their three-year training paid off. Acts 8:4 states, "Now those who were scattered went about preaching the word." Think about this. These everyday, ordinary, three-year-old believers started churches in Judea, Samaria, Cyprus, Antioch, and beyond!

The gospel, the Holy Spirit, and Christ's purpose for his church have never changed in 2020 years. Christ declared that he would build his *ekklesia* to advance his kingdom family. That promise includes us today. God can use you to bring your friends and family to the Lord.

Sharing the gospel message can be a little complicated. There's more to it than just telling somebody what the gospel is and how to respond. Each person has his or her own baggage—cultural, intellectual, and emotional barriers—that need to be removed before the simple gospel can take root in the heart. We categorized these distortions of God through *spiritual profiling*. Luke revealed his neighborhood in the book of Acts. Each neighbor had a unique *spiritual profile*: The religious (Acts 2), the hurting (Acts 3), the occultist (Acts 8), the seeker (Acts 8), the fanatic (Acts 9), the good person (Acts 10), the successful (Acts 16), the skeptic (Acts 17), the misinformed (Acts 19), and the hedonist (Acts 24). Interestingly, Luke's neighbors are also found in our neighborhoods. Every spiritual profile has a certain distortion of God that needs to be corrected before a person becomes ready to embrace the gospel. Together we've learned all the distortions with biblical responses. Remember, no one can be released from spiritual bondage until there is an accurate understanding of the God revealed in Scripture. The task of every Christian is to present God as seen in Jesus and us (transformation).

When someone gains a clearer understanding of the God of Scripture, the Holy Spirit will convict them of sin and create a longing to know their heavenly Father. That's when we present the Acts 2 gospel message. Our friend's sins are washed away through faith, in their baptism (Acts 2:38). But our job doesn't stop there. We then equip, train, and disciple them to make more disciples. It is their call too, their purpose and reward in heaven. **Turning members into disciple makers** is the process we follow till Jesus comes. My prayer is that the Holy Spirit will use this book as a resource in your training process.

Resources with this Book

To secure the video training KIT that compliments the book, go to www.CCLNetwork.com. Call or email the CCLNetwork to receive your free code. Email: tim.wallingford@myccl.org. Call: 423-956-5700.

About the Author

TIM WALLINGFORD

Executive Director

CENTER FOR
CHURCH
LEADERSHIP

Person: Dr. Tim Wallingford is presently serving as the Executive Director of The Christian Church Leadership Network. He's been married to Patty 43 years, has two boys and three grandchildren.

Education: Tim's education includes a B.S. from Cincinnati Christian University, M.A. in Apologetics, M.M. Church Growth and M.Div. from the Cincinnati Bible Seminary. Tim did doctorate studies at Southern Baptist Seminary and received his D. Min from Emmanuel School of Religion.

Ministry: Tim has served in the local ministry 40 years. His experience includes being the lead minister of four congregations ranging from small to emerging mega churches.

Author: Tim has authored *Transforming Neighborhoods One Life at a Time*, *100 Answers for the Neighborhood*, and co-authored, *The Character of Christ*, and *RePOSITION*.

Professor: Tim has served on the faculty of the Louisville Bible College and the Cincinnati Bible Seminary.